Frederick C. Crews is Associate Professor of English, University of California, Berkeley. He is the author of *The Tragedy of Manners: Moral Drama in the Later Novels of Henry James, E. M. Forster: The Perils of Humanism,* and *The Pooh Perplex.*

THE SINS OF THE FATHERS

The Sins of the Fathers

HAWTHORNE'S PSYCHOLOGICAL THEMES

✳ ✳ ✳

FREDERICK C. CREWS

New York
OXFORD UNIVERSITY PRESS
1966

FOR BETTY

CONTENTS

ACKNOWLEDGMENTS

My main debt is to Elizabeth Crews, who spent countless disagreeable hours challenging my ideas and red-pencilling my prose. The reader is indebted to her, too; the book is shorter by half because of her criticism. I extend sympathy and thanks to the two groups of Berkeley seniors who provided a captive but by no means submissive audience for my views; they too have influenced this book. I am grateful to my research assistant, Marcia Jacobson; to my typist, Mrs. Henry Lynn, Jr.; and to Whitney Blake, Leona Capeless, and others at the Oxford University Press who have given me help. I also wish to thank the University of California for departmental funds and for a Humanities Research Fellowship in the spring of 1964.

The editors of *PMLA*, *American Quarterly*, *New England Quarterly*, and *American Literature* are thanked for permission to reprint the essays that appear here, in altered form, as Chapters V, VII, VIII, and XI; and I also thank the Harvard University Press for permission to quote from Edward H. Davidson's edition of Hawthorne's *Doctor Grimshawe's Secret*.

F.C.C.

A NOTE ON EDITIONS CITED

References to Hawthorne's works, when cited only by volume and page, will imply the so-called Riverside edition, *The Complete Works of Nathaniel Hawthorne*, ed. George Parsons Lathrop, 13 vols. (Boston and New York, 1882-83). Wherever possible, however, I have preferred to use the emerging volumes of the authoritative Ohio State University Press *Centenary Edition*, eds. William Charvat *et al.* Volume and page references to these texts will be preceded by the letter *C*.

THE SINS OF THE FATHERS

"Modern psychology, it may be, will endeavor to reduce these alleged necromancies within a system, instead of rejecting them as altogether fabulous."

—HAWTHORNE, *The House of the Seven Gables*

I

Psychological Romance

"Hawthorne appalls—entices."
—EMILY DICKINSON

Two curious and seemingly unconnected things have been happening to our image of Nathaniel Hawthorne over the past fifteen years. Hawthorne is now regarded as "better adjusted and more in tune with fellow human beings and the life of his period" [1] than was previously thought. It is no longer fashionable to say, as Van Wyck Brooks once did, that the real Hawthorne was a "phantom" who "had lived too long in this border-region, these polar solitudes where the spirit shivered, so that the substance of the world about him hung before his eyes like a thing of vapour." [2] Such impressionism elicits only a condescending smile from the biographer of today, whose respect for circumstantial facts prevents him from mistaking Hawthorne's literary manner for the tone of his life. The Hawthorne whom Brooks dismissed as misleading and irrelevant—the work-aday Hawthorne of the Liverpool consulship, for example—is now given priority over the less easily witnessed Haw-

1. Walter Blair, "Hawthorne," *Eight American Authors: A Review of Research and Criticism*, ed. Floyd Stovall (New York, 1963), p. 108.

2. *The Flowering of New England, 1815-1865* (New York, 1936), pp. 225, 224. See also Herbert Gorman, *Hawthorne: A Study in Solitude* (New York, 1927); Lloyd Morris, *The Rebellious Puritan: Portrait of Mr. Hawthorne* (New York, 1927); and Newton Arvin, *Hawthorne* (Boston, 1929).

thorne of the "haunted" years after his graduation from Bowdoin. Indeed, it is the presumption of recent biographers that there is nothing haunted about Hawthorne at all. His very essence, we are told, is repose.[3]

The other main development is one of literary criticism. Unlike the critics of an earlier generation, who strove to recapture Hawthorne's gentle melancholy and antiquarian charm, critics since the 1950's have insisted upon his *symbolism* and his *didacticism*. They have credited Hawthorne with the complexity of image-patterns and the steadiness of moral purpose that characterize a great allegorical poet. His works, we now learn, came directly out of his "philosophy," which is said to be "a broadly Christian scheme which contains heaven, earth, and hell." His true subject is Man's Fall and subsequent growth toward redemption —a redemption occurring "in a series of communions in which the bread and wine of the past vitalizes the present." And Hawthorne himself, far from being guilt-ridden, is said to have dealt with sin and perversion only in order to demonstrate his magnanimity. "Hawthorne never sought to demean man, but to love him as Christ loved man— especially the outcast and the sinner." [4]

3. Hubert H. Hoeltje, *Inward Sky: The Mind and Heart of Nathaniel Hawthorne* (Durham, North Carolina, 1962), Preface, p. [xii]. See also Randall Stewart, *Nathaniel Hawthorne: A Biography* (New Haven, 1948); and Edward Wagenknecht, *Nathaniel Hawthorne: Man and Writer* (New York, 1961).

4. The three quotations are from Richard Harter Fogle, *Hawthorne's Fiction: The Light and the Dark* (Norman, Oklahoma, 1952, revised ed., 1964), p. 5; Roy R. Male, *Hawthorne's Tragic Vision* (Austin, Texas, 1957), p. 54; and Henry G. Fairbanks, "Sin, Free Will, and 'Pessimism' in Hawthorne," *PMLA*, LXXI (December 1956), 987. See also Hyatt H. Waggoner, *Hawthorne: A Critical Study* (Cambridge, Mass., 1955; revised ed., 1963); and Leonard J. Fick, *The Light Beyond: A Study of Hawthorne's Theology* (Westminster, Maryland, 1955).

I would like to suggest that these two developments are not only unfortunate and misleading but also closely related; they are expressions of the same cultural phenomenon. For in different ways both the biographers and the critics have been anxious to depart from the emotional texture of Hawthorne's imagination. The religious-didactic Hawthorne of the symbolic critics is already implicit in the biographies, which—having disposed of psychological speculation by declaring it unscientific—deftly skip from a sober and debunking rehearsal of evidence to awe at Hawthorne's inspirational value.[5] Hawthorne is important because he offers us "an admonition and a gift which are timeless"[6]—meaning that he enables us to see how our technological society falls short of the Christian ideal. Naturally, then, the positivistic-theological biographers feel themselves to be in harmony with their sometime foes, the analysts of symbols. As Hawthorne's "definitive" biographer has explained, our "Golden Age of Hawthorne Criticism" coincides with the Christian revival of the 1950's. "The new symbolical approach to the reading of Hawthorne, as well as Melville, James, and Faulkner, has after a fashion allied itself with this same neo-orthodoxy, so that we have been witnessing a revolution not only in criticism but in religious thought."[7] It is my hope that this timid little revolution has now run its course.

Although I am writing a book of criticism, it will be hard to refrain from chiding Hawthorne's biographers from time to time. Their normalization of Hawthorne springs not from "evidence which can be checked by other investigators"[8] but from a failure of intuition. Their belief

5. See especially Wagenknecht's and Hoeltje's final chapters, significantly titled "God's Child" and "To Gladden the World."

6. Stewart, p. 265.

7. Randall Stewart, quoted on dust jacket of Male, *Hawthorne's Tragic Vision*.

8. Wagenknecht, Preface, p. viii.

that the "man and writer were one" [9]—healthy, pedestrian, moral—is the sign of a simplistic psychology that looks only at surfaces—an especially drastic weakness in approaching Hawthorne. When Julian Hawthorne, after his father's death, finally read the famous tales and romances, he found himself "constantly unable to comprehend how a man such as I knew my father to be could have written such books." For Julian "the man and the writer were, in Hawthorne's case, as different as a mountain from a cloud." [10] There was evidently a side to his father that was never turned toward the family, much less toward the public—a Hawthorne who can be obscurely glimpsed behind the atmosphere of his fiction. Of this Hawthorne our recent authorities say nothing; or worse, they deny his existence.

The traces of this elusive Hawthorne, however, are much more abundant than the "evidence" that turns him into an odd combination of plodding democrat and religious tutor to posterity. How plausible is it to make a saintly allegorist of a man who almost never went to church, who described his masterpiece as a "hell fired story," and who confessed to his journal, "We certainly do need a new revelation—a new system—for there seems to be no life in the old one"? [11] Such passages can, it is true, be overmatched by others that express what might be called a rudimentary Christianity; but the biographer is responsible for his subject's contradictions as well as his uplifting statements. Was Hawthorne's temperament that of a dogmatic moralist? Everything we hear about him suggests the opposite: he was peculiarly diffident, and rarely held to the same opinion

9. Hoeltje, p. 555. For an identical principle see Wagenknecht, Preface, p. vii; and the same assumption is implied throughout Stewart's book.

10. Julian Hawthorne, "The Salem of Hawthorne," *The Century Magazine*, XXVIII (May 1884), 6.

11. See Horatio Bridge, *Personal Recollections of Nathaniel Hawthorne* (New York, 1893), p. 112; and *Nathaniel Hawthorne, the American Notebooks*, ed. Randall Stewart (New Haven, 1932), p. 165.

for very long. Presumably, then, the doubting habit itself might be given prominence in a fair account of Hawthorne's mind. And indeed, once we have ceased trying to make him into a source of oracular wisdom, we perceive that Hawthorne's keynote was neither piety nor impiety, but ambivalence. There is in his writings, as Philip Rahv observed long ago, "a submerged intensity and passion— a tangled imagery of unrest and longing for experience and regret at its loss . . . He was haunted not only by the guilt of his desires but also by the guilt of his denial of them." [12] In short, Hawthorne was emotionally engaged in his fiction, and the emotions he displays are those of a self-divided, self-tormented man.

When his "submerged intensity and passion" are ignored Hawthorne becomes, I fear, a very boring writer. The moralistic element prized by his recent critics is the least original thing about his work; it is what he shared with nearly all his lesser contemporaries in the sentimental vein. Nor is this fact much mitigated by our insisting that Hawthorne was more ingenious in symbolism and more orthodox in doctrine than his fellow purveyors of ladies' fiction. Image-patterns that are assumed to originate in a consciously instructive balancing of "light" and "dark" elements end by implying a coldly smug creator; and this in fact is the impression of Hawthorne that prevails in academe. As for his orthodoxy, it can be upheld only at the price of refusing to examine the psychological implications of his plots. In the typical Hawthorne tale there is a jarring dissonance between the "sweet moral blossom" that is served up with an obliging flourish and the "human frailty and sorrow" that compose the story.[13] Hawthorne's ambiguity—to which every critic pays lip-service before going

12. "The Dark Lady of Salem," *Image and Idea: Fourteen Essays on Literary Themes* (Norfolk, Connecticut, 1949), p.23.

13. These words are from the last sentence of Chapter 1, *The Scarlet Letter, C,* I, 48.

on to build a tower of allegory—is not a didactic strategy but a sign of powerful tension between his attraction to and his fear of his deepest themes. For behind his moralism, and often directly contradicting it, lies a sure insight into everything that is terrible, uncontrollable, and therefore *demoralizing* in human nature. Hawthorne himself, like his latest admirers, wanted to be spared this insight, but beneath layers of rationalization and euphemism it asserts its right to expression.

Far from being a novelty, this view of Hawthorne was taken in one of the earliest essays about him, Melville's response to *Mosses from an Old Manse:*

> Still more: this black conceit [of human depravity] pervades him through and through. You may be witched by his sunlight,—transported by the bright gildings in the skies he builds over you; but there is the blackness of darkness beyond; and even his bright gildings but fringe and play upon the edges of thunder-clouds. In one word, the world is mistaken in this Nathaniel Hawthorne. He himself must often have smiled at its absurd misconception of him. He is immeasurably deeper than the plummet of the mere critic.[14]

It is customary to say that Melville was here talking about himself. Yes; but he was also faithfully describing Hawthorne's sense of reality. Yet very few critics since Melville have seen fit to repeat his distinction between the initial appearance and the ultimate nature of Hawthorne's fictional world. In the 'twenties there was D. H. Lawrence; in our own time, Leslie Fiedler and the authors of miscellaneous perceptive articles; but on the whole we have been witnessing a process of canonization, and like all saints Hawthorne has ascended to dullness.[15]

14. "Hawthorne and His Mosses," *The Literary World,* VII (August 17, 1850), 126.

15. See D. H. Lawrence, *Studies in Classic American Literature* (New York, 1923), and Leslie A. Fiedler, *Love and Death in the*

If Hawthorne criticism has become a sterile academic pastime, and Hawthorne himself an object of tiresome study and faint praise, the blame cannot be laid entirely upon neo-Christianity. The theological critics share with many others a search for some overriding thematic idea which, once abstracted from the texture of Hawthorne's ambivalent plots, can be treated as an independent controlling principle. One critic is looking only for mythic patterns that will put Hawthorne in the mainstream of American culture. Another tells us that "five major arcs of Faustian definition" suffice to describe Hawthorne's entire literary achievement. Another, concluding regretfully that Hawthorne considers Oneness inscrutable, claims that the concept of "multiplicity" governs the tales and romances. And still another, in a book whose title *The Power of Blackness* might suggest a Melvillian approach, turns out to be primarily interested in "the possibility of a literary iconology." He claims to have "respected the integrity of the symbols," meaning that he has "not attempted to reduce them to the literal plane." Thus the immediate emotional force of Hawthorne's symbols must give way before the iconologist's consistent theorem. These are, one and all, subtle and intelligent men; it is their very ingenuity of method that leads them to smooth out Hawthorne's contradictions, slight his characteristic air of anxious brooding, and—occasionally—misrepresent the literal course of his plots.[16]

American Novel (New York, 1960). Both these books may be said to err by exaggerating Hawthorne's "inner diabolism" (Lawrence, p. 122) at the expense of his sincere wish to be conventional. In the tradition of Hawthorne criticism, however, such exaggeration has been highly salutary.

16. The allusions in this paragraph are, consecutively, to Daniel G. Hoffman, *Form and Fable in American Fiction* (New York, 1961); William Bysshe Stein, *Hawthorne's Faust: A Study of the Devil Archetype* (Gainesville, Florida, 1953), p. 142; James K. Folsom,

Hawthorne's ambivalence, whatever its emotional sources, is most strikingly discernible in his stated views about the nature and quality of his art. Certain passages can be used to show that he thought of himself as a genteel trifler, wistfully aware that his works "afford no solid basis for a literary reputation" (II, 45). He assures us that they are not intended to be profound, and still less are they "the talk of a secluded man with his own mind and heart" (I, 17). Again and again Hawthorne announces that his fiction has neither outward reality nor inward depth. Where it is allegorical, the allegory is merely a vice of temperament; where it attempts some picture of society, the picture is said to be faded and blurred. Judging only from such statements we might well conclude that Hawthorne's art resulted from an unhappy compromise between harmless, irresponsible fantasy and an effort to please readers accustomed to plain sense and moralism.

Certainly it would be wrong to dismiss this self-estimate as sheer false modesty; anyone who reads completely through Hawthorne's tales and sketches must be struck by the superficiality and imperfection of many pieces.[17] Still, it is clear from many rival passages that Hawthorne had some understanding of his special province as a writer. Perhaps most notably, in his Preface to *The Snow-Image* he described himself as a man "who has been burrowing, to his utmost ability, into the depths of our common

---

Man's Accidents and God's Purposes: Multiplicity in Hawthorne's Fiction (New Haven, 1963); and Harry Levin, *The Power of Blackness: Hawthorne, Poe, Melville* (New York, 1958), pp. xf.

17. See, as representative samples, "Little Annie's Ramble," "Snowflakes," and "The Lily's Quest," from *Twice-Told Tales;* "Fire Worship" and "Buds and Bird Voices," from *Mosses from an Old Manse;* and "A Bell's Biography" and "Little Daffydowndilly," from *The Snow-Image.* I feel justified in leaving such trivia out of account, for they show us a Hawthorne who is scarcely distinguishable from his fellow gift-book contributors.

nature, for the purposes of psychological romance" (III, 386). Unlike some of his biographers, Hawthorne does not suppose that this buried "common nature" is either very accessible or very dignified. "In the depths of every heart," he says in "The Haunted Mind," "there is a tomb and a dungeon, though the lights, the music, and revelry above may cause us to forget their existence, and the buried ones, or prisoners, whom they hide" (I, 345). The business of psychological romance is not to make fanciful efforts at picturesqueness but to penetrate the deceptive, congenial surface and reach the terrible core of man's being.

Yet this exaggerates the forthrightness of Hawthorne's purpose. As we shall discover, his penetration into secret guilt is compromised not only by his celebrated ambiguities of technique but by reluctance and distaste. He was aware that in exposing our common nature he was drawing largely upon his own nature, and he was disturbed by what he found. Many of his self-deprecatory passages have the function of protesting overmuch that the author's deepest self has been kept inviolate. Thus, for example, he presents us with an equivocal rebuff in "The Old Manse":

> Has the reader gone wandering, hand in hand with me, through the inner passages of my being? and have we groped together into all its chambers and examined their treasures or their rubbish? Not so. We have been standing on the greensward, but just within the cavern's mouth, where the common sunshine is free to penetrate, and where every footstep is therefore free to come. I have appealed to no sentiment or sensibilities save such as are diffused among us all. So far as I am a man of really individual attributes I veil my face; nor am I, nor have I ever been, one of those supremely hospitable people who serve up their own hearts, delicately fried, with brain sauce, as a tidbit for their beloved public. (II, 43f.)

Here we see an ill-concealed animosity toward those who would presume to know the author through his works; yet the very expression of immunity begs us to guess at what we have not been told. If we are standing just within a cavern, and if the author's face is veiled (both images recur insistently in Hawthorne's fiction), then surely he has something worth hiding from us. Elsewhere he indicates that a writer's deeper self *can* be known, though not by his external habits or casual associates. "These things hide the man, instead of displaying him. You must make quite another kind of inquest, and look through the whole range of his fictitious characters, good and evil, in order to detect any of his essential traits" (III, 386). With one arm Hawthorne strikes a pose of cold dignity and holds us at bay, but with the other he beckons us forward into the cavern of his deepest soul. And the more he speaks of his intention to "keep the inmost Me behind its veil" (C, I, 4), the more certain we may be that he is uneasy with the self-revelatory aspect of his work.

Hawthorne's balance between confession and evasion is reflected in his style, whose distance and abstraction are often confused with Augustan serenity. The meditative poise, the polite irony, the antitheses, the formal diction, and the continual appeal to sentiments that are generally shared, all serve to neutralize the dangerous knowledge that lies at the bottom of his plots. For Hawthorne regards language as a fearful thing. "Words," he reminds himself in his notebook, "—so innocent and powerless as they are, standing in a dictionary, how potent for good and evil they become, in the hands of one who knows how to combine them!" (*American Notebooks*, p. 122). Hawthorne is by no means certain that he can exercise this potency without falling victim to it.

To Hawthorne's own uneasiness we must add that of his "belovedest" Sophia, whose taste he did not care to offend. Mrs. Hawthorne, with her neurasthenic headaches, her vaporous Transcendentalism combined with churchgoing piety, her taste for moral rhetoric, and above all her easily shocked sensibility, had much to do with domesticating Hawthorne's interests after 1838. The Hawthorne who wrote to Sophia about his recently forsworn habit of smoking in the house, "Thou wast very sweet not to scold me fiercely, for allowing myself to be so impregnated," [18] was rather different from the one who called man's heart a "foul cavern" (II, 455) and sneered at the prospect of its ever being purified.[19] His Phoebe, as he named her, held out to him a blissful release from his years of brooding,[20] but the price was high. Though the ending to *The Scarlet Letter* gave Sophia a bad headache, when she finished *The House of the Seven Gables* she knew that her husband had reached the summit of art. "There is unspeakable grace and beauty in the conclusion," she observed, "throwing back upon the sterner tragedy of the commence-

18. *Love Letters of Nathaniel Hawthorne,* 2 vols. (Chicago [1907]), II, 93.

19. On the other hand, note Hawthorne's image of impregnation —a fine example of the charged language discussed in the next paragraph.

20. That Hawthorne declared himself ideally happy in marriage and was relieved to move from private phantasms to a common, solidly "real" tranquility with Sophia is a fact that has been much sentimentalized by his biographers. His extraordinary dependence on Sophia and his tendency to immerse himself in recording the trivia of their family life show that Hawthorne approached marriage almost as a therapeutic program, a means of getting a firm hold on reality at last. Even Randall Stewart suggests that this meant a betrayal of his deepest interests as a writer: "It is significant that during the courtship of nearly four years his productivity fell off sharply. There were other reasons to be sure, . . . but the free play of personal emotion seems to have been incompatible with artistic creation" (*Nathaniel Hawthorne,* p. 49). To a less indulgent biographer this might indicate that Hawthorne's prior emotional life had found an outlet, however unsatisfactory, in his fiction; but of this Professor Stewart gives no further hint.

ment an ethereal light, and a dear home-loveliness and satisfaction." [21]

Randall Stewart's study of Mrs. Hawthorne's tampering with the notebooks after Hawthorne's death provides an invaluable guide to the nature of her moral influence. Wherever Hawthorne had expressed skepticism about marriage, womanhood, America, or Christianity, Sophia improved the text by deletion or revision. References to smoking and drinking were generally suppressed, as were, of course, all passages of sexual interest. She could not admit the comparison of some pond lilies to "virgins of tainted fame," and still less could she allow posterity to learn of her forty-six-year-old husband's fancy, which had struck him while he was peering into the lighted window of a Boston boarding house, that a beautiful damsel might be disrobing within. Of greater interest, because of greater imaginative subtlety, are many of Sophia's apparently trivial revisions of phrasing. For Hawthorne's "animal desires" she substituted "temperament"; for "baggage," "luggage"; for "itch," "fancy"; for "vent," "utterance"; and for "caught an idea by the tail," "caught an idea by the skirts." [22] This, I submit, is the work of a dirty mind. The revisions have the effect of charging the original words with double meanings that would not have consciously occurred to us otherwise. Yet this talent for risqué puns—that is, for perceiving and then suppressing them—was shared by Hawthorne himself and by the whole culture in which he and Sophia moved. In the age of the draped piano leg, even furniture was covertly sexualized.

Compromise, euphemism, and innuendo, then, were encouraged not only by Hawthorne's temperament but by his personal and social milieu. These characteristics, however limiting they may have been in their final effect upon

21. See Stewart, *ibid.*, pp. 95, 113.
22. *American Notebooks*, Introduction, pp. xv-xvii.

his art, happened to be excellently suited to his chosen literary genre. Sentimental fiction from Richardson onward
employed an intricately developed vocabulary of high
motives and moral comforts to clothe latently titillating
situations. In one sense the writer's task consisted of manip-
ulating the clichés of the form in such a way that neither
the titillation nor the uplift would be sacrificed. Rape,
prostitution, and even incest could be treated if only the
right moral tone were sustained. Failure to sustain it, as
Melville discovered in the reception of *Pierre,* would produce shock and outrage; failure to provide the innuendo
would produce boredom.[23] Unlike his impulsive friend,
Hawthorne was shamelessly adept at keeping the rival
elements in balance, and some of his finest tales look
curiously at home in the pages of the sentimental gift-
book, *The Token.* It is wrong, therefore, to draw too sharp
a distinction between "popular" and "profound" works in
his canon. One of his subtlest tales of depravity, "The
Gentle Boy," was so admired by subscribers to *The Token*
that it was reprinted as a separate volume and became his
passport to success.

Yet the reader may accept all this without agreeing that
Hawthorne deserves to be called a psychologically profound writer. Only a few characters in all his fiction have
the solidity we think of as novelistic, and the world in
which they act is so purposefully concentrated on thematic
questions, so cluttered with symbolism, that little room
is left for individual minds to exist. If we locate Hawthorne's psychology merely in what is openly stated about
his heroes and heroines, we must agree with Marius Bewley
that this psychology is based on "some disturbingly simple
formulae" and is "often undistinguished, and sometimes

---

23. See Herbert Ross Brown, *The Sentimental Novel in America,*
1789-1860 (Durham, North Carolina, 1940), and William Wasser-
strom, *Heiress of All the Ages: Sex and Sentiment in the Genteel
Tradition* (Minneapolis, 1959).

crass." [24] For Bewley, as for most other critics, Hawthorne's art appears to turn outward toward moral simplicity rather than inward toward psychological complexity.

I would insist, however, that Henry James was originally right in saying that Hawthorne "cared for the deeper psychology," and that his works offer glimpses of "the whole deep mystery of man's soul and conscience." [25] The majority view, I feel, rests on both a misapprehension of "deep psychology" and an inattentive habit of reading Hawthorne. We must, in the first place, question the popular notion that *individuality* and *detail* are the key virtues of psychological portraiture.[26] A richly particular character, such as James's Isabel Archer, may be represented as living almost entirely in the realm of conscious moral choice, while her instinctual nature and her conflicts of feeling are hidden under an abundance of surface strokes. Hawthorne's Hester Prynne, in contrast, is rendered in terms of struggle between feelings that she neither controls nor perfectly understands. Her remorse toward her husband versus her sympathy for her lover, her desire to flee versus her compulsion to remain, her maternal instinct versus her shame at what Pearl represents, her voluptuousness versus her effort to repent and conform—these tensions are the very essence of our idea of Hester. If she is a more schematic figure than Isabel, her motives are deeper and are better known to us. It is precisely because Hawthorne is not afraid to schematize, to stress underlying patterns of

24. "Hawthorne and 'The Deeper Psychology,'" *Mandrake*, II (Autumn and Winter 1955-56), 366-73; the quoted phrases are from pp. 367 and 366.

25. *Hawthorne* (New York, 1879), p. 63.

26. Bewley, for instance, says that the deeper psychology should deal with "the shadowy subconscious world of the uniquely private, where hidden motivations and all the 'secrets' of the inmost self swim fortuitously about" (*Mandrake*, II, 366). No one who takes modern psychological theories seriously could have written these careless words.

compulsion rather than superficial eccentricities, that he is able to explore "the depths of our *common* nature." [27]

The power of Hawthorne's best fiction comes largely from a sense that nothing in human behavior is as free or fortuitous as it appears. Even with characters much less fully observed than Hester, the emphasis falls on buried motives which are absolutely binding because they are unavailable to conscious criticism. Furthermore, even the most wooden heroes bear witness to a psychological preoccupation. Whatever is subtracted from overt psychology tends to reappear in imagery, even in the physical setting itself. It is as if there were a law of the conservation of psychic energy in Hawthorne's world; as the characters approach sentimental stereotypes, the author's language becomes correspondingly more suggestive of unconscious obsession. And, in fact, one of the abiding themes of Hawthorne's work is the fruitless effort of people to deny the existence of their "lower" motives. The form of his plots often constitutes a return of the repressed—a vengeance of the denied element against an impossible ideal of purity or spirituality. Thus it is not enough, in order to speak of Hawthorne's power as a psychologist, merely to look at his characters' stated motives. We must take into account the total, always intricate dialogue between statement and implication, observing how Hawthorne—whether or not he consciously means to—invariably measures the displacements and sublimations that have left his characters two-dimensional.

Let us test this expectation on one of Hawthorne's most familiar and seemingly shallow tales. "The Maypole of Merry Mount" offers us, in Edith and Edgar, two of the

27. In the words of Thomas Mann, "Much that is extrapersonal, much unconscious identification, much that is conventional and schematic, is nonetheless decisive for the experience not only of the artist but of the human being in general." ("Freud and the Future," reprinted in *Art and Psychoanalysis*, ed. William Phillips [Cleveland, 1963], p. 381.)

most vacant sentimental characters imaginable, and its apparent theme is of no great interest: "earth's doom of care and sorrow" (I, 75) must be accepted both by the young lovers and by pleasure-seekers in general. The moral conflict between the hedonists of Merry Mount and the Puritans who finally destroy the colony is made highly obvious, both through direct debate and through such typically Hawthornian contrasts of image as sunshine versus shadow, rainbow colors versus somber black, and smiles and sighs versus disapproving frowns. The tale's conclusion, with the chastened Lord and Lady of the May heading "heavenward" (I, 84) with a just commixture of sobriety and affection, resolves this conflict so agreeably that few readers have felt impelled to ask whether anything underlies the patent banalities of theme.

Hawthorne's "philosophic romance" (I, 70) begins to seem less banal when we realize that it has more to do with the emotional qualities of Puritanism and hedonism than with the didactic example of Edith and Edgar. To the May couple the rigors of Puritanism finally appear commensurate with the hard realities of life, and are therefore morally preferable to "the vanities of Merry Mount" (I, 84). Yet everything we learn about the Puritans in the story shows that their "reality" is highly subjective and suspect. They are "dismal wretches" (I, 77) who, when not punishing themselves with toil, prayers, and fast days, are busy punishing others—slaughtering wolves and Indians, placing lighthearted colonists in the stocks, and observing the functions of "the whipping-post, which might be termed the Puritan Maypole" (I, 77). This last phrase strongly suggests an element of pleasure in legalized violence—and this is in fact the essence of the Puritan mentality as Hawthorne portrays it. Endicott, the most tolerant of the invaders, metes out penalties with great zeal, promises further "branding and cropping of ears" (I, 81), and permits himself the following significant fantasy: "I thought not to repent me of cutting down a Maypole . . . yet now I could find in my heart to plant it again, and give each of these bestial pagans one other dance round their idol. It would have served rarely for a whipping-post!" (I, 81). It is not quite correct, in view of such evidence, to say that Edith and Edgar are simply renouncing pleasure at the end of the tale. To the modest degree that they will blend into the Puritan community, they will be exchanging the overt gratifications of hedonism for the more furtive gratifications of an ascetic sadism.

It is especially ironical that Hawthorne's May couple is said to outgrow the "fantasy" and "delusion" that reign in the "magic," "airy," and "unreal" colony of Merry Mount (I, 73, 71, 74). There is less delusion at Merry Mount than meets the eye. Only the youngest colonists are taken in by the daydream of eternal play; the guiding spirits are motivated by the "gay despair" (I, 76) of middle-aged cynicism. The Puritans, in contrast, are truly victims of collective delusion. In their fanatical wish to exclude sin they have "peopled the black wilderness" with "devils and ruined souls" (I, 72)—which is to say that they have projected all their secular impulses onto imaginary foes. Their demonic view of Merry Mount in particular is contradicted by the observed facts. Which group is more enslaved to fantasy: the "sworn triflers" who "followed the false shadow [of mirth] wilfully" (I, 76), or the zealots who shoot a dancing bear because they suspect it of witchcraft?

Once we have discredited the Puritan analysis of Merry Mount, we may begin to wonder what we really know about the colony. An acquaintance with Hawthorne's sources leaves no doubt that he was aware that the chief moral complaint against Merry Mount and against May ceremonies generally was that they encouraged sexual license.[28] Yet the Puritans in the story do not raise this

28. See G. Harrison Orians, "Hawthorne and 'The Maypole of Merry Mount,' " *Modern Language Notes,* LIII (March 1938), 159-67. In Baylies's *Memoir of New Plymouth* Hawthorne must have read not only that Thomas Morton, the founder of Merry Mount, wrote

charge. We are left to suppose that they see dancing, gay costumes, and picnicking as inherently devilish without ever thinking of sex. It was Hawthorne's age, however, not that of the Puritans, which felt embarrassment at calling things by their right names; we can be sure that the historical enemies of Merry Mount did not mince their words. Though Edith and Edgar are about to begin their wedding night, and though their hearts are said to glow "with real passion" (I, 75) shortly before the Puritans intervene, the sexual aspect of hedonism is never directly mentioned. Skillful sentimentalist that he is, Hawthorne has maintained a euphemistic aloofness from themes that are inherent both in his historical sources and in the situation of his hero and heroine.

In Hawthorne's fiction, however, *suppression* always has the psychological consequences of *repression:* the denied element surreptitiously reappears in imagery and innuendo. To a modern reader, of course, the plot itself seems intrinsically symbolic in this case; its main deed is the severing of a pole which the hedonists call "their religion" (I, 77), and which is the focal object of a nuptial ceremony. We may reasonably doubt that the immemorial phallic meaning of maypoles, which was thoroughly understood in the seventeenth century, was altogether lost upon the nineteenth. But there is no need to argue on these grounds. Hawthorne's description of the costumed revelers as resembling "the crew of Comus, some already transformed

---

obscene satires and affixed them to the pole, but that the colonists performed drunken dances with Indian women and "fell into all kinds of licentiousness and profanity..." Prince's *Annals* made the same point. And in the book he openly acknowledges as a source—Joseph Strutt's *The Sports and Pastimes of the People of England*—Hawthorne found a compilation of Puritan diatribes against the "lewd men, light women...and abusers of the creature" (London, 1898, p. 46) who participated in May games. Another of Strutt's sources speaks of mass deflowerings of virgins in the branch-gathering expeditions of May Day (*ibid.,* p. 455).

to brutes, some midway between man and beast" (I, 72)
obliges us to be alert to the theme of enslavement to lust
that is found in Milton's masque. And here is the scene
itself:

> But what was the wild throng that stood hand in hand
> about the Maypole? It could not be that the fauns and
> nymphs, when driven from their classic groves and homes
> of ancient fable, had sought refuge, as all the persecuted
> did, in the fresh woods of the West. These were Gothic
> monsters, though perhaps of Grecian ancestry. On the
> shoulders of a comely youth uprose the head and branch-
> ing antlers of a stag; a second, human in all other points,
> had the grim visage of a wolf; a third, still with the trunk
> and limbs of a mortal man, showed the beard and horns
> of a venerable he-goat. There was the likeness of a bear
> erect, brute in all but his hind legs, which were adorned
> with pink silk stockings. And here again, almost as
> wondrous, stood a real bear of the dark forest, lending
> each of his fore paws to the grasp of a human hand, and
> as ready for the dance as any in that circle. His inferior
> nature rose half way, to meet his companions as they
> stooped. Other faces wore the similitude of a man or
> woman, but distorted or extragavant, with red noses
> pendulous before their mouths, which seemed of awful
> depth, and stretched from ear to ear in an eternal fit of
> laughter.... (I, 71f.)

Anyone who regards these sentences as a dispassionate
and straightforward picture of traditional May dancers is
not likely to find Hawthorne a very interesting writer.
Though most of the details appear in his sources, Hawthorne uses them with emphatic suggestiveness. The turning of classical fauns and nymphs into "Gothic monsters"
who are sporting articles of blatant symbolism indicates,
not passion, but an excessive, grotesque effort of self-conscious sophisticates to be "natural." The stag, the wolf, the
goat, and the "bear erect" have a lecherous iconographic

value, but in every description Hawthorne is careful to compromise the iconography with persisting human features. The revelers are trying with dubious success to submerge their humanity in natural power—to "stoop" to freedom. The true result is an effect of decadence. Thus the man-goat appears merely "venerable," and the man-bear with his pink silk stockings is scarcely masculine at all. I suggest that the urgency of sexual symbolism in this scene is directly proportional to the sense of sexual inhibition. Nothing could be less faunlike than the "distorted," "extravagant" faces which differ from normal ones in having "red noses pendulous before their mouths, which seemed of awful depth . . ." This is eroticism tainted with anxiety.

Now, however, we face a problem that will prove troublesome throughout this study. Assuming that the author has displaced much of his psychological interest from character onto language, are we entitled to reverse the process—to read motivation from imagery? Any answer will be an arbitrary axiom of method rather than a demonstrable inference. Yet not entirely arbitrary; one method is better than another if it can incorporate more evidence and follow the logic of plot-structure more closely. We shall find that Hawthorne's works always *take their images seriously*—that the characters behave *as if* they were disturbed by the motives we glimpse in narrative emphasis. What matters is that we too take this evidence seriously, whether we attribute it to the characters or to the author's dialogue with himself. Let it be understood, then, that in calling the Merry Mount hedonists "decadent" and "inhibited" we are making a debatable, but practically useful, choice to regard Hawthorne's descriptive nuances as psychologically pertinent. At worst we are mistaking as characterization the author's own unformulated misgivings about the freedom he has tried to depict; and we shall see, curiously, that such a confusion makes no real difference

for an understanding of the total psychological atmosphere
of his plots.

In the present case our analysis is strengthened by various indications that the Merry Mounters are engaged in
organized, frantic striving to negate the encroachments of
time. The maypole dancing takes place not on May Day
but on Midsummer Eve, which has brought "deep verdure
to the forest, and roses in her lap, of a more vivid hue than
the tender buds of Spring" (I, 70).[29] The hour is sunset,
and the bleak surrounding woods, which literally contain
the Puritan forces that will sever the pole and crop the
May Lord's "lovelock and long glossy curls" (I, 83), are
full of implicit menace. Even the maypole itself, in combining "the slender grace of youth" with "the loftiest
heights of the old wood monarchs" (I, 70), conveys an
ambiguity appropriate to people who have come to their
philosophy of pleasure only "after losing the heart's fresh
gayety" (I, 75). Thus there is an inherent melancholy at
Merry Mount that anticipates the suppression to be imposed from outside. It is little wonder that Edith and
Edgar perceive that "these shapes of our jovial friends are
visionary, and their mirth unreal" (I, 74) *before* Endicott
arrives to put the matter more strongly.

Everything we have seen in this tale urges us to conclude that the Puritans and hedonists are less different
from one another than they seem. If the Puritans, in trying to exclude sensual pleasure, nevertheless readmit it
in the form of sadism, the Merry Mounters are just as un-
successful in trying to exclude conscience. The whole plot
tends toward reconciliation. Thus, for example, Endicott
shows a surprising sympathy with the May couple; he
recognizes in them a latent sobriety, while he in turn is
"softened" by "the fair spectacle of early love" (I, 83).

29. The Shakespearian echo is significant: "Rough winds do shake
the darling buds of May, / And summer's lease hath all too short
a date." (Sonnet 18)

More strikingly, when the Puritans attack, "their darksome figures were intermixed with the wild shapes of their
foes, and made the scene a picture of the moment, when
waking thoughts start up amid the scattered fantasies of
a dream" (I, 79). Here the Puritans represent, not reality,
but "waking thoughts" which dispel fantasy; they are inhibition or censorship personified. Thus it is appropriate
that their intervention automatically produces a symbolic
impotence: "the stag lowered his antlers in dismay; the
wolf grew weaker than a lamb..." (I, 79). The motive
force in this scene is not realistic but allegorical: Inhibition has mastered Instinct. And we can, I think, take the
entire tale as a psychological allegory in which the general
mind of man has been fractured into two imperfect tyrannies of indulgence and conscience, neither of which can
entirely suppress the other. The conclusion of the tale is
a symbolic amnesty, although, as will always be the case in
Hawthorne, the party of restraint has gained the upper
hand.

Yet "The Maypole of Merry Mount" is not *entirely*
allegorical, for we are still left with the individual plight
of Edith and Edgar. But that plight now seems less euphemistic than before: "No sooner had their hearts glowed
with real passion than they were sensible of something
vague and unsubstantial in their former pleasures..."
(I, 75). The childlike lovers, who would like to conceive
of life as an endless game, feel sexual desire and realize at
once that they are surrounded by evidence of the undigni-
fied vicissitudes of Eros in middle age. Awakening to
sexual self-consciousness, the new Adam and Eve are not
unwilling to join the community of severity and shame.

We can say, therefore, that all the allegorical emphasis
of "The Maypole of Merry Mount" serves to enrich a
literal situation—a crisis of maturity. The insistent sugges-
tions of impotence and castration define this crisis for us,
even while the surface narrative remains conventionally
"pure." And the resolution of the plot, in which a for-

bidding but secretly benevolent figure of authority inter-
mixes "the moral gloom of the world" (I, 84) with the
lovers' joys, amounts to a welcome psychological strategy.
In its barest logic Hawthorne's tale informs us that if
young lovers must sooner or later understand that unchecked fantasy leads to decadence, then the only recourse
for those lovers is to a measure of asceticism. Curiously
enough, the genuine love that would have been impossible at Merry Mount is assured of survival by the Puritan
censorship of fantasy.[30]

Perhaps we have said enough about "The Maypole of
Merry Mount" to show how, in its very schematism, it
illustrates Hawthorne's "burrowing . . . into the depths of
our common nature, for the purposes of psychological
romance." Yet much remains unsaid and, at this point, un-
demonstrable. What happens in this tale, whether through
exact intention or through psychic necessity, is profoundly
typical of Hawthorne's plots throughout his career: inadmissible fantasies are unleashed in an inhibited, decadent
form and then further checked by a resurgence of authority. This authority, furthermore, always takes a more or
less openly paternal form, and Hawthorne's Ediths and
Edgars always seem as much like siblings as lovers. If this
is so, his Endicotts must be seen as preventing, not simply
disillusion, but a symbolic incest from which Hawthorne's
imagination recoils—and to which it regularly returns.
"The Maypole of Merry Mount" is, to be sure, a paltry
and dubious example of this pattern; until we have examined much corroborative evidence the reader may feel
unchallenged in regarding Hawthorne as a moralist or an
antiquarian or both. In the next few chapters, however,
we shall investigate the nature of Hawthorne's antiquar-

30. Which is not to say that the Puritans, after all, represent an
ideal of mental economy. Edith and Edgar will survive because they
can *reconcile* the instinct and conscience that tyrannize the respec-
tive colonies. Extremes are invariably destructive in Hawthorne's
fiction.

ianism; ask whether his historical themes are really separable from his psychological ones; study the nature of
family relationships, both literal and symbolic, in certain
early plots; and begin to prove that a definable, indeed
classic, conflict of wishes lies at the heart of Hawthorne's
ambivalence and provides the inmost configuration of his
plots.

The Sense of the Past

"Shall we never, never get rid of this Past?" cried he ... "It lies upon the Present like a giant's dead body! In fact, the case is just as if a young giant were compelled to waste all his strength in carrying about the corpse of the old giant, his grandfather, who died a long while ago, and only needs to be decently buried." —HOLGRAVE in *The House of the Seven Gables*

In the previous chapter we began what will prove to be an intermittent quarrel with those critics who see Hawthorne primarily as a dispenser of moral advice. His plots, we argued, follow a logic of expression and repression that bypasses or undercuts moral problems: he is more concerned with psychological necessity than with conscious virtue. If this is so, however, we find ourselves even more radically opposed to a quite different view, which I shall call the antiquarian one. This is that Hawthorne's imagination was conditioned not by inward conflicts, but by a meticulous concern with American history. In this age of "American Studies" it is fashionable to admire Hawthorne as an objective commentator on the forces that operate through history, or as the creator of a myth that distils the past's lessons for his own generation and ours. The question of private emotional meaning in his plots appears irrelevant if we see them as inspired by history itself.

We can certainly grant that Hawthorne was absorbed, particularly at the outset of his career, in native subjects and themes. His earliest intended book, along with the American romance *Fanshawe*, was to have the rather jingo-

istic title, "Seven Tales of My Native Land," and its announced themes were witchcraft and the sea. A second
abandoned collection, "Provincial Tales," points to a further interest in exploiting the traditions and legends of
New England. And a third, "The Story-Teller," was to
combine historical legend with contemporary scenes and
characters in a scheme of interlocking tales and travel
sketches. The author of these projects was not the Hawthorne who announced sadly in the Preface to *The Marble
Faun* that America had "no shadow, no antiquity, no
mystery, no picturesque and gloomy wrong, nor anything
but a commonplace prosperity, in broad and simple day-
light" (VI, 15). To judge by subject-matter alone, it seems
plausible enough to say that Hawthorne began his career
as a student and celebrant of New England's real and
fabulous past.[1]

The question, however, is one of priorities. When we
look for the thematic common denominator between the
overtly historical fiction and such equally Hawthornian,
but ahistorical, tales as "Wakefield," "Ethan Brand," and
"The Birthmark," we find that Hawthorne's interest in

1. See Nelson F. Adkins's learned article, "The Early Projected
Works of Nathaniel Hawthorne," *Papers of the Bibliographical
Society of America,* XXXIX (Second Quarter, 1945), 119-55. Recent
biographies may have exaggerated the blame that Hawthorne's prospective publishers deserve for the failure of all three collections of
tales to appear. It is evident, both from semi-autobiographical tales
like "The Devil in Manuscript" and from comments by Hawthorne
and others, that Hawthorne had deep misgivings about seeing his
work published. It was over his publisher's protest that he burned
all but two of the "Seven Tales," "in a mood half savage, half de-
spairing." (Bridge, *Personal Recollections of Nathaniel Hawthorne,*
p. 68.) The fact that every one of his works published before 1837
appeared either anonymously or pseudonymously cannot be explained entirely on circumstantial grounds. As his closest friend,
Horatio Bridge, told him in 1836, "The bane of your life has been
self-distrust." (*Ibid.,* p. 73.)

history is only a special case of his interest in fathers and
sons, guilt and retribution, instinct and inhibition. These
themes are everywhere in his fiction, from his earliest
sketches to his fragmentary unfinished romances; we shall
see that they deserve to be called obsessive. History, in
contrast, is prominent but far from universal. It can be
shown that Hawthorne's attitude toward the past springs
directly from more "primordial" concerns; the history of
the nation interests him *only* as it is metaphorical of individual mental strife. If, as I doubt, there exists a pure anti-
quarianism unaffected by the special bent of the antiquarian's mind, Hawthorne cannot be used to illustrate it.

The easiest misconception to dispel is that Hawthorne
felt a simple piety toward his Puritan ancestors. "The
Maypole of Merry Mount" is typical in reducing the Puritans to caricatures of brutal authoritarianism; if anything,
we would have to say that Hawthorne nurtured a special
animus against them. Nor did he imagine that life was
somehow grander in the early Colonial days. That age was
"ruder and rougher . . . than our own, with hardly any
perceptible advantages, and much that gave life a gloomier
tinge" (III, 534). The drabness of Puritan times appears
in Hawthorne's fiction not merely as a want of diversity
and humor, but as an oppressive starvation of life which
"could not fail to cause miserable distortions of the moral
nature" (III, 459). He is heartily glad to be two centuries
away from his first American forebears, and at times he
appears almost frightened that the distance is not great
enough. As one of his narrators concludes nervously, "Let
us thank God for having given us such ancestors; and let
each successive generation thank Him, not less fervently,
for being one step further from them in the march of
ages" (III, 460).

A society which causes miserable distortions of the moral
nature must, of course, have its appeal for the writer of
psychological romance. Only by immersing himself in Puritan history could Hawthorne satisfy his interest in buried

impulses while at the same time remaining more or less loyal to outward fact. This, I think, helps to explain the resentful tone with which he often speaks of his own bland time. For Hawthorne believes that human nature changes little from generation to generation; simply, he has no viable technique for laying bare the hearts of his contemporaries. As he says in "Endicott and the Red Cross," after cataloguing some severities of Puritan punishment, "Let not the reader argue, from any of these evidences of iniquity, that the times of the Puritans were more vicious than our own, when, as we pass along the very street of this sketch, we discern no badge of infamy on man or woman. It was the policy of our ancestors to search out even the most secret sins, and expose them to shame, without fear or favor, in the broadest light of the noonday sun. Were such the custom now, perchance we might find materials for a no less piquant sketch than the above" (I, 487f.). Hawthorne is unwilling to let us congratulate ourselves for our virtue simply because our vices are inaccessible to him.

At the same time, Hawthorne's interest in Puritan times is not to be distinguished from his sense of his own identity. In his writings Puritan leaders generally blend into the stern figures of his Salem ancestors, who, despicable as they are in their warped righteousness, are felt to stand in judgment of Hawthorne himself. He defines his meager right to an artistic career by criticizing and whimsically placating the shades of the Puritans. The most famous instances occur in "The Old Manse" and in the Preface to *The Scarlet Letter;* in both cases grim portraits—always potent forces of intimidation in Hawthorne's fiction—inspire uneasiness and self-defense. The Puritan divines who stare down at him from the walls of the Old Manse look "strangely like bad angels, or at least like men who had wrestled so continually and so sternly with the devil that somewhat of his sooty fierceness had been imparted to their own visages" (II, 13). Yet their boring sermons and pam-

phlets strike Hawthorne as a legitimate reproach to him
"for having been so long a writer of idle stories," and on
this basis he claims to have determined "at least to achieve
a novel that should evolve some deep lesson and should
possess physical substance enough to stand alone" (II, 12f.).
For such (imaginary) Puritans, art is an impermissible
indulgence in fantasy; but rather than forgo this indulgence altogether, Hawthorne hopes to effect a compromise
by making his art moral and substantial.

How seriously should we take this picture of Hawthorne
bargaining with Puritan ministers across two centuries?
As a literal account, not seriously; but very seriously as a
metaphorical statement of qualms about the moral nature
of art. Here and everywhere in Hawthorne's writing, Puritans stand in censorship of imagination. They personify
a primitive, unreasonable conscience which is none the
less tyrannical for being despised and ridiculed. Indeed,
Hawthorne's practice of disparaging, placating, and half-
heartedly joking with them is evidence that he cannot
ignore the threat of their disapproval—a disapproval which
must of course emanate from his own mind. In a word,
then, "Puritans" are the repressive side of Hawthorne
himself. That they resemble fallen angels is indicative of
the psychological irony we saw him developing in "The
Maypole of Merry Mount": the party or faculty of censorship inevitably gets attached to the impulses it is trying
to extirpate. Hawthorne is at once the artist-victim of
censorship, the Puritan censor himself, and a shrewd
analyst of the censor's dubious moral status.

This complication is sustained in the other famous passage where Hawthorne professes to be bothered by Puritan
criticism. The image of his first American ancestor, he says
in "The Custom House," "was present to my boyish imagination, as far back as I can remember" (C, I, 9). After
semi-playfully taking upon himself the "curse" of the
Hathornes' misdeeds—excesses of persecution that we shall

presently discuss—he characteristically turns about and submits himself to their supposed contempt:

> Doubtless, however, either of these stern and black-browed Puritans [William Hathorne and his son John] would have thought it quite a sufficient retribution for his sins, that, after so long a lapse of years, the old trunk of the family tree, with so much venerable moss on it, should have borne, as its topmost bough, an idler like myself. No aim, that I have ever cherished, would they recognize as laudable; no success of mine—if my life, beyond its domestic scope, had ever been brightened by success— would they deem otherwise than worthless, if not positively disgraceful. "What is he?" murmurs one gray shadow of my forefathers to the other. "A writer of story-books! ... Why, the degenerate fellow might as well have been a fiddler!" Such are the compliments bandied between my great-grandsires and myself, across the gulf of time! And yet, let them scorn me as they will, *strong traits of their nature have intertwined themselves with mine.* (C, I, 10; my italics)

Here again the modesty, whimsy, and scorn are merely ways of delaying an inevitable recognition: Hawthorne *is* his ancestors, at least in part. The word "intertwined," which points to a crippling blend of incompatible feelings whenever it occurs in Hawthorne's fiction, is here used in an overtly psychological statement: he tells us that he cannot be emotionally free from his Puritan component. What exactly does this mean? Surely it refers to a morbid fascination with guilt. As we see in the romance to which this passage is prefatory, Hawthorne is remorseless in ferreting out hidden shame; the severe concentration of *The Scarlet Letter* alarmed not only Sophia but Hawthorne himself. Through most of his career, furthermore, he reveals a special insight into the minds of characters who are absorbed in finding sin in the breasts of others. The Reverend Hooper, Ethan Brand, Young Goodman

Brown, Hester Prynne and Arthur Dimmesdale, Miriam
in *The Marble Faun* all acquire a knack (or delusion) of
seeing into their neighbors' wicked thoughts, and in each
case Hawthorne demonstrates that such hypersensitivity
springs from a personal sense of guilt. His claim of likeness to the early Hathornes, following upon an observation that they had "all the Puritanic traits, both good and
evil" (*C*, I, 9), indicates that he regards his own case with
some of the irony he applies to probers in his fiction. He
differs from his magistrate-ancestors not in his invasion of
diseased souls but in his awareness that this invasion—to
which he is committed as an artist—is itself diseased. Puritanism amounts to prurience, and Hawthorne simultaneously exercises this prurience and portrays it as morbid.

It should be apparent that Hawthorne, who influenced
the modern stereotype of Puritanism more than any other
writer, was ill-equipped to give a balanced sense of what
Puritan life was like. More important than his plentiful
rearrangements of fact for literary purposes are the distortion and simplification of moral atmosphere imposed by
his habit of involving ancestral figures in his self-criticism.
We are not surprised to learn that he exaggerated the
severity of Puritan law, and that he was, in fact, the only
American writer between 1820 and 1860 who dwelt extensively on the means of Puritan punishment.[2] We would
not go far wrong in saying that the finding and punishment of sin were *all* that he found noteworthy in the
Puritan character. It is hard to miss seeing a connection
between his reducing the Puritans to sadistic enemies of
impulse and his frequent air of replying equivocally to
unspoken accusations.

It is true, however, that much of Hawthorne's emphasis
is already present in the facts that interested him. Understandably enough, he seems to have taken as a model Puri-

2. See G. Harrison Orians, "Hawthorne and the Puritan Punishments," *College English*, XIII (May 1952), 424-32.

tan his first American ancestor, William Hathorne (1607-1681); and William Hathorne was a very Hawthornian character. As a member of the General Court of Massachusetts and later as a member of the Governor's advisory council, he was "an arbiter of conduct, a moral adviser, a confessor, and a conciliator. He was a director of police, and, above all, a prosecutor with informers ever moving among the people in search of criminals." [3] Described as the most dreaded person in Essex County, he was rebuked by Governor Winthrop and John Cotton for trying to stiffen the penal code against such crimes as swearing and lying. His duties included the detection and punishment of " 'wanton dalliance,' lascivious speech, kissing, and manifesting in any way 'unclean' desire." And his punitive sentences, many of which recur insistently in his great-great-great-grandson's fiction, have an inherent luridness about them. For a man caught in burglary he and his fellow judges prescribed the lopping off of one ear and the branding of a "B" on his forehead; for someone convicted of manslaughter they ordered that the offending hand be burned; another man who insulted the judges' dignity had his ear nailed to a pillory and then amputated, after which he was whipped and fined; a boy convicted of "bestiality" (animal contact) with a mare saw the animal bludgeoned to death and then was hanged himself; a slave was burned at the stake; and perhaps most significantly for Hawthorne, an adulteress, after receiving thirty strokes, had to stand in the market place of Boston wearing a paper with the words, THUS I STAND FOR MY ADULTEROUS AND WHORISH CARRIAGE.[4]

There is no need to speculate about the effect of such historical facts on an imagination like Hawthorne's. An ample record of his fascination and anxiety is preserved

3. Vernon Loggins, *The Hawthornes: The Story of Seven Generations of an American Family* (New York, 1951), p. 40.
4. *Ibid.,* pp. 41, 35, 45, 42, 68f.

in his fiction, from various early sketches through *The House of the Seven Gables.* One of William Hathorne's more ingenious sentences was that imposed on a shy young Quaker wife who had obeyed, so she said, a divine command to walk naked through the streets of Salem. In retribution she was tied to a cart's tail, naked to the waist, with her mother and sister also half-naked and tied to the sides, and whipped through the town.[5] In "Main Street," the sketch whose narrator thanks Heaven for not having been born a Puritan, this episode or a very similar one appears as part of an historical panorama:

> And there a woman,—it is Ann Coleman,—naked from the waist upward, and bound to the tail of a cart, is dragged through the Main Street at the pace of a brisk walk, while the constable follows with a whip of knotted cords. A strong-armed fellow is that constable; and each time that he flourishes his lash in the air, you see a frown wrinkling and twisting his brow, and, at the same instant, a smile upon his lips. He loves his business, faithful officer that he is, and puts his soul into every stroke, zealous to fulfill the injunction of Major Hawthorne's warrant, in the spirit and to the letter. There came down a stroke that has drawn blood! Ten such stripes are to be given in Salem, ten in Boston, and ten in Dedham; and, with those thirty stripes of blood upon her, she is to be driven into the forest. The crimson trail goes wavering along Main Street; but Heaven grant that, as the rain of so many years has wept upon it, time after time, and washed it all away, so there may have been a dew of mercy to cleanse this cruel blood-stain out of the record of the persecutor's life! (III, 462f.)

The extraordinary feeling of sadism in this passage seems at first to be attached solely to the constable, who frowns and smiles as he "puts his soul into every stroke." But Haw-

5. *Ibid.,* pp. 62f.

thorne has singled out his ancestor by name, and he tells us that the constable was executing the spirit as well as the letter of Major Hawthorne's sentence.[6] When intense horror gives way to a no less intense upwelling of remorse, there is a significant ambiguity about "the persecutor" who will need divine mercy; only on reflection do we see that it is Major Hawthorne, not his agent, who is ultimately responsible. This furtiveness adds to the sense of personal involvement in the whole episode—an involvement that seems quite out of place in the facetious context of "Main Street." Hawthorne is both an outraged spectator of the scene and, as its narrator and as Major Hawthorne's heir, a vicarious participant in its indecency. He is privately implicated in what he elsewhere calls the deadly sickness of sin: "Feeling its symptoms within the breast, men concealed it with fear and shame, and were only the more cruel to those unfortunates whose pestiferous sores were flagrant to the common eye" (II, 287).

Three prominent events in Hawthorne's ancestral history also became prominent elements in his fictional plots. One was the persecution of the Quakers, a policy that seemed particularly horrible to Hawthorne's rather secular generation; Hawthorne mentions it repeatedly and treats it with great subtlety in "The Gentle Boy." A second focal point was the Salem witch trials of 1692, one of whose presiding judges was Hawthorne's great-great-grandfather, John Hathorne (1641-1717), who favored the death penalty not only for witchcraft but for heresy as well. Needless to say, the coincidence of family guilt with the guiltiest public event of New England history provided Hawthorne with rich materials for his favorite themes of moral self-delusion and righteous sadism. And finally, his perusal of Felt's *Annals of Salem* must have acquainted him with a celebrated case of alleged incest. In 1680 the brother of Haw-

6. Note too that he alters the spelling of his ancestor's name to match his own—a fact of irresistible psychological interest.

thorne's maternal great-great-grandfather, Thomas Manning, was accused by his wife of incest with his two sisters.
When the accused, Nicholas Manning, fled into the forest,
not to reappear in Massachusetts for eight years, the sisters
were convicted, fined, and made to sit on a stool in the
center of the Salem meeting house with papers marked
INCEST pinned to their caps. Felt's narrative and plates discreetly suppressed the participants' names, but Vernon
Loggins has no doubt that Hawthorne knew them; and
he adds, "The effect which this dark Manning family secret
produced upon the romancer's emotions could only have
been penetrating and most poignant." [7]

It is a safe generalization, I believe, that Hawthorne
never treats his family history without a mixture of shame
and pride. The shame is obvious: all the events we have
reviewed—and to them we might add the famous White
murder case in Hawthorne's lifetime [8]—seem almost to
have been prearranged by a Hawthornian plot-maker to
illustrate the degeneracy of power. Yet Hawthorne's view
of ancestral power was highly ambiguous, not only because
he still trembled before it, but because it represented a
dignity and fame that he and his impoverished sisters could
not command.[9] To the anxiety of all unappreciated writers
Hawthorne added the snobbish nostalgia of the disinherited son; his researches into Salem history provided
him with a rival identity to that of the ineffectual, impecu-
nious, careerless young man surrounded by mercantile
nouveaux-riches.[10] Thus his commemoration of William

7. *The Hawthornes*, p. 279.
8. *Ibid.*, pp. 242-54. For a more sensational but probably less
accurate version, see Robert Cantwell, *Nathaniel Hawthorne: The
American Years* (New York and Toronto, 1948), pp. 150-54, 160-62.
9. See Loggins, p. 209.
10. Hence, by the way, Hawthorne's opposition to the Whigs of
his day. His adherence to the Democratic party, which seems odd in
view of his distrust of reform, his impatience with abolitionism, and
his involvement with the past, surely had some thwarted snobbery

and John Hathorne deserves to be seen in the light of such other pieties as his restoration of the English spelling of the family name and his attraction to the family myths of noble English ancestry and rich land-holdings in Maine. For the modern Hawthornes, as for the modern Pyncheons in *The House of the Seven Gables,* there was a greater worry than that their forefathers' bloodstains might be ineradicable; it was that they were all too eradicable.

We can summarize all this by saying that Hawthorne's evocations of Puritan times gave him *a guilty identity, which was better than none.* Hawthorne retreats into history from a contemporary world which is resistant both to his talent for finding secret guilt and to his unsteady sense of inner worthiness; yet once imaginatively engaged in history, he feels his ancestors' presence as an oppressive force of intimidation. We have not yet established why this should be so, but the reader may already agree that Hawthorne was an insecure man whose difficulties in reconciling the claims of fantasy and conscience would necessarily color his re-creations of the past.

As Roy Harvey Pearce has noted, the most compelling of Hawthorne's Colonial tales are those that make us feel a hidden oneness between the party of rebellion and the party of rule. Without accepting Pearce's moral inference from this fact,[11] we can observe that the fact itself is un-

---

behind it. He was no very profound democrat, but he felt strongly antipathetic to the new aristocracy of money that had left the Hathornes behind.

11. See "Hawthorne and the Sense of the Past, or, The Immortality of Major Molineux," *ELH,* XXI (December 1954), 327-49. This valuable essay deals with the same themes and the same tales that will concern us in the next few chapters. In my opinion Pearce aptly characterizes the spirit of Hawthorne's best historical work, but is mistaken in thinking that Hawthorne offers us the lesson that "if to become more than we are, we must destroy something in ourselves, then we cannot forget what it is we destroy" (p. 330). Pearce says

surprising. The stylized contests between sin and punishment, fancy and disillusion, in Hawthorne's plots gain their urgency from private conflict: oppressors and the oppressed are symbolically parts of a single mind. When the Puritans and hedonists in "The Maypole of Merry Mount" become "intermixed" into a picture of the moment "when waking thoughts start up amid the scattered fantasies of a dream," they are only bringing into metaphorical statement a connection that subsists between all historical enemies, and indeed between all antagonists of whatever sort, throughout Hawthorne's fiction.

It is fairly easy to show that Hawthorne's most intense and memorable historical tales obey this pattern. But if our claim about history's meaning for Hawthorne has any real validity, it should also apply to lower-keyed works which seem more genuinely antiquarian. As a test case we may take "The Gray Champion," in which, according to Pearce, history is nothing more than an "object," something to be factually recaptured.[12] Does this tale try the hypothesis that Hawthorne's Puritans always embody a brutal suppression of instinct, and that he characteristically reduces political and religious questions to elemental struggles for domination?

Without making grand claims for the importance or complexity of "The Gray Champion," we can say that it illustrates much of what we have been expounding as most Hawthornian. Its ostensible subject is a legend of demo-

---

that the discovery of guilt and righteousness in history, along with the same discovery in the present, "make the whole that is Hawthorne" (p. 339). This exaggerates not only the extent to which Hawthorne is an historical writer, but also his moral detachment from his themes. Hawthorne never so much as hints that we can be improved by recalling "what it is we destroy." When (often with irony) he does suggest that times have bettered, he always stresses the *burial* and *forgetting* of past unpleasantness. Pearce's moral is a healthy one, but it is not Hawthorne's.

12. *Ibid.*, p. 348.

cratic resistance to the power of James II, and its ostensible moral purpose is to show "the deformity of any government that does not grow out of the nature of things and the character of the people" (I, 26). Yet the tale really implies that authority can only be overmatched by greater authority. The Gray Champion who magically arrives to repel the representatives of the Crown is anything but an epitome of democracy. With his "face of antique majesty" (I, 26), his hoary beard, and his sword and staff, he is the image of a patriarch, and it is this image alone that wins the day. The whole tale could be described as a contest of paternal figures, with various powers—including Sir Edmund Andros, Governor Bradstreet, the gathered ministers of the colony, the Gray Champion himself, and by proxy the Pope and the King of England—all vying to exploit the colonists' "filial love which had invariably secured their allegiance to the mother country" (I, 21). The Gray Champion triumphs merely through his aura of being the "chief ruler" (I, 28) on the scene.

Furthermore, the people whom the Gray Champion rescues from English tyranny are deftly undermined in their pretense of standing for justice and freedom. The ministers of each parish egotistically compete to see who can assume the most "apostolic dignity" so as to deserve "the crown of martyrdom" (I, 24), while the old soldiers surviving from Cromwell's age are "smiling grimly at the thought that their aged arms might strike another blow against the house of Stuart" (I, 23). "Here, also," Hawthorne adds, "were the veterans of King Philip's war, who had burned villages and slaughtered young and old, with pious fierceness, while the godly souls throughout the land were helping them with prayer" (I, 23). The irony of this is of course overpowering. Though the tale opens on a note of indignation against those who tried "to take away our liberties and endanger our religion" (I, 21), and though it ends by declaring that New England's sons will always "vindicate their ancestry" (I, 31) by opposing domestic or

foreign tyranny, the intervening pages expose these attitudes as absurd. The ancestry of the New England colonists
is precisely what they are rejecting, and they are doing so
not by meeting tyranny with freedom but by setting up a
rival system of ancestor-worship.

Lest the reader doubt that Hawthorne could have meant
to handle a patriotic theme so disdainfully, we shall consider one further tale in which a similar situation is presented. "Endicott and the Red Cross" has been taken by
most critics as a glorification of the revolutionary spirit.
As usual, Hawthorne's opening and closing paragraphs—
and no others—provide the basis for this straightforward
reading. Our ancestors in the reign of Charles I are said to
have "resolved that their infant country should not fall
without a struggle, even beneath the giant strength of the
King's right arm" (I, 485)—a stirring formula whose characterization of America as an infant country sympatheti-
cally ignores the fact that Massachusetts was a chartered
colony of the Crown. And in a closing flight of rhetoric
Hawthorne explicitly identifies Endicott, who has cou-
rageously ripped the cross from the English banner, with
the forthcoming spirit of the Revolution. "And forever
honored be the name of Endicott!" (I, 493), cries Hawthorne. But again, the bulk of the tale imparts a Swiftian
flavor to such claims. Like the Gray Champion, Endicott is
a grizzled patriarch who displays the Puritan narrowness
and ferocity rather than the infant's helplessness or the
adolescent idealism of a Nathan Hale. Nor should we be
easily stirred by his illogical peroration against Charles I.
Appealing only to the Puritans' bigoted sense that they are
God's chosen people, he obscures their legal ties to the
King; and when he concludes grandiosely by asking, "What
have we to do with England?" (I, 493), Hawthorne's implied answer is obvious.

Though Hawthorne is superficially depicting the English and the colonists as oppressor and oppressed, he has
taken great pains to create the opposite impression. While

the Puritans are gathered in martial order, the only royalists on hand happen to be in the stocks and the pillory,
sentenced respectively for Episcopalianism and for having
toasted the King. Their cries of "sacrilegious wretch!" and
"treason!" (I, 493) are unheeded by Endicott, but surely
not by the discerning reader. Again, when Endicott pompously claims that the colony was founded "for liberty to
worship God according to our conscience" (I, 491), he is
refuted *viva voce* by another religious prisoner, a "Wanton
Gospeller" who "had dared to give interpretations of Holy
Writ unsanctioned by the infallible judgment of the civil
and religious rulers" (I, 487). The presence of the mild
and tolerant Roger Williams, who is silenced contemptuously by Endicott, serves the same function. And in this
tale Hawthorne has surpassed his own high standard in
portraying Puritan sadism. Besides the victims already
named, there are a woman wearing a cleft stick on her
tongue for having spoken against an elder of the church;
various people with cropped ears, branded cheeks, and slit
nostrils; a man condemned for life to wear a halter around
his neck; and the prototype of Hester Prynne, a handsome
and pitiable young woman wearing a capital A on the
breast of her gown. It is not by chance that Endicott's
polished breastplate reflects a bloody wolf's-head nailed to
the porch of the Salem meeting house. The atmosphere
of the town is one of intense bigotry and despotism, and
Endicott's professed love of freedom is mocked both by his
savage demeanor and by his incriminating surroundings.

These examples may suffice to show that Hawthorne was
no propagandist of the revolutionary character; they might
almost make him out to be a Loyalist in disguise. In reality,
however, he is an ironical observer of antagonists whose
self-justifying slogans are meaningless on both sides. Power,
he implies, makes a tyrant of anyone who seizes it, and
history is a series of inessential reversals in which unjust
rulers are supplanted by soon-to-be-unjust rebels. To draw
any political moral from this pattern would be to falsify its

sub-rational, automatic quality. It is the *fixed mentality* of tyrants and pretenders that gives each tale its total form; the moment of glorious defiance, of "freedom," is balanced against the massed evidence that nothing in the eternal relationship of dominators to dominated is likely to change.

If we ask why Hawthorne's imagination dwelt on these substitutions of one intolerant patriarch for another, we will not find an answer in the objective facts of American history. Hawthorne was perfectly aware that the nature of rule *had* changed since Puritan times; yet this awareness held no dramatic interest for him. It is clear that in some private way he was drawn to exaggerate the cruelty, fearsomeness, and guilt of historical personages, and to treat history more as nightmare than as panorama. We have already suggested that this must be connected to his oppressive sense of his own ancestry, and that this sense in turn is related to powerful internal inhibitions of instinct and fantasy. To substantiate and specify this latter idea, we must now turn from relatively literal historical tales to those in which Hawthorne allows himself freer license to rewrite the past in the language of his own ambivalence.

I I I

Brotherly Love

"Incest is, like many other incorrect things, a very poetical
circumstance."
—SHELLEY

At the very beginning and very end of his career Hawthorne produced halting, fragmentary works of fiction
which are of peculiar interest for their revelation of essential themes. What is subtle and even problematical in his
more polished writing leaps plainly into view in these
otherwise incoherent works; we can watch him first trying to subdue, and later trying to fend away from consciousness, obsessive attitudes that are successfully sublimated elsewhere. In a psychologically oriented study we
must ask the reader to be more patient with such works
than their aesthetic value might warrant; like other ruins,
they offer special opportunities for knowledge *because*
their inmost structure is directly exposed to us.

The chief example of such a work before the late
romances is "Alice Doane's Appeal," one of the two surviving narratives from Hawthorne's first collection, "Seven
Tales of My Native Land." [1] The story as we have it is not
the original version, which Hawthorne tells us escaped
burning only because it "chanced to be in kinder custody"
(XII, 282) when he destroyed his early works. Rather, it is

---

1. See Adkins, *Papers of the Bibliographical Society of America*,
XXXIX, 121-6. The other conjectured survivor, "The Hollow of
the Three Hills," is better controlled than "Alice Doane's Appeal"
but highly similar in theme and atmosphere.

a reworking and probably an incorporation of that version
into an autobiographical framework, so that we are now
reading a story within a story. Indeed, three distinct plot-
strands, ineptly and confusingly joined, need to be distinguished in the surviving tale. There is a legend of murder
and confession in early Salem; an historical pageant of the
Salem witch hangings, presented by the Hawthornian narrator as the final scene of his evocation of the past; and
finally, the story of the narrator's relating these episodes
to two modern young ladies on a tour of Salem's Gallows
Hill.[2]

Of the three components, the narrator's modern plot
has received the least critical attention; and even the murder plot has been dismissed as "unimportant, an incidental
means to a large end." [3] This end, according to one theory,
is to communicate to present readers a sense of inherited
historical guilt, so that they may "assume the moral responsibilities, the guilt and righteousness," stemming from our
national past.[4] If this was Hawthorne's aim, however, some
bosom serpent compelled him to thwart it at nearly every
point. His own generation of readers is represented only
by the narrator and the two ladies who, he assures us gal-
lantly, would have been at home in Paradise (XII, 279).
All the emphasis in the "storytelling" part of the plot falls
on the inapplicability of the historical material to the sentimental and complacent nineteenth century; the narrator

2. However fictional this outer frame of the tale may be, it is
clear that Hawthorne wants us to think of himself as the narrating
"I." He speaks of his Salem ancestry and the burning of his early
works, and alludes to his role as a contributor to *The Token*—which
is further grounds for believing that the narrator's part was added
at some point after the tale was submitted to *The Token* in 1830
and before it was published there in 1835.

3. Pearce, *ELH*, XXI, 337f.

4. *Ibid.*, 337. Cf. Leslie Fiedler's theory that "Alice Doane's
Appeal" is a Gothic "parable of the American Revolution" (*Love
and Death in the American Novel,* p. 43).

is hard put to keep the ladies' attention, indeed to keep them from giggling at his efforts to move them. The comic wistfulness of *The House of the Seven Gables* and the self-critical irony of *The Blithedale Romance* are thus already discernible, and these qualities undermine any moralistic lesson. Hawthorne is ultimately less interested in his story's moral effect than in the narrator's private reasons for wanting to produce such an effect. It is true that the narrator, like one side of Hawthorne, wants us to be horrified by recalling the spot "where guilt and frenzy consummated the most execrable scene that our history blushes to record" (XII, 280); but it is also true that another side of Hawthorne seems embarrassed by this rhetoric and anxious to neutralize it.

We may begin to see why such embarrassment is called for by examining the atmosphere of the historical pageant at the end of the tale. As we might anticipate by now, Hawthorne's depiction of an injustice in which his own great-great-grandfather was implicated is full of anxiety and disgust. The narrator strives to communicate "the deep, unutterable loathing and horror, the indignation, the affrighted wonder, that wrinkled every brow, and filled the universal heart" (XII, 293). As he introduces the alleged witches he stresses the vicious fantasy and projection behind the charges, which are nevertheless effective in intimidating the accused. One condemned woman does not even know why she is being marched off to execution; a once-proud man is "so broken down by the intolerable hatred heaped upon him" (XII, 293) that he yearns for death; and another woman is "distracted by the universal madness, till feverish dreams were remembered as realities, and she almost believed her guilt" (XII, 293). Again, a mother "groaned inwardly yet with bitterest anguish, for there was her little son among the accusers" (XII, 293). As in Hawthorne's scenes of accusation generally, victims and persecutors are caught up in a collective shame, a cringing before the human spirit's war upon itself.

Such scenes are never dispassionately recounted in Hawthorne's fiction; there is, invariably, a surplus of uneasiness and cruelty that spills over into the narrative tone. Whether or not the narrator is a created character, he always gets seized by the combined fear and contempt that Hawthorne customarily shows toward Puritan tyrants—especially ancestral ones. In the present case John Hathorne does not appear in person, but another figure may be said to stand in his place. Here is the climax of the procession:

Behind their victims came the afflicted, a guilty and miserable band; villains who had thus avenged themselves on their enemies, and viler wretches, whose cowardice had destroyed their friends; lunatics, whose ravings had chimed in with the madness of the land; and children, who had played a game that the imps of darkness might have envied them, since it disgraced an age, and dipped a people's hands in blood. In the rear of the procession rode a figure on horseback, so darkly conspicuous, so sternly triumphant, that my hearers mistook him for the visible presence of the fiend himself; but it was only his good friend, Cotton Mather, proud of his well-won dignity, as the representative of all the hateful features of his time; the one blood-thirsty man, in whom were concentrated those vices of spirit and errors of opinion that sufficed to madden the whole surrounding multitude. (XIII, 294)

Surely the bitterness of this paragraph was not inspired by an objective study of Cotton Mather's peripheral role in the Salem trials. This Mather is a scapegoat, an object of all the undischarged emotion that has accumulated through the episode. As a figure of tyrannical authority, he of course resembles Endicott in "Endicott and the Red Cross"; but here there is no ambiguity of patriotism, no ironic balancing-off of rival tyrannies. Rather, there is a concentrated outburst of hatred against the arch-tormentor. And the loss of control over thematic material is evidenced by the next development. The narrator, who has hitherto failed to engage the emotions of his two auditors, "plunged into my imagination for a blacker horror, and a deeper woe, and pictured the scaffold—" (XII, 294). But at this moment the two ladies begin to tremble and weep, and the historical evocation abruptly stops. The narrator has finally succeeded in his effort to find "whether truth were more powerful than fiction" (XII, 292), but the kind of truth that has reduced both him and his two friends to near-hysteria is psychological, not historical. It is the faithful reflection of repressed hostility, whatever the real object of that hostility may be.

This fact, I think, provides us with a reason—admittedly a vague one—for most of the contradictions and false starts in "Alice Doane's Appeal." Far from tutoring us about the moral meaning of our past, Hawthorne is wholly occupied in mastering an imaginative over-involvement in that past. But it is not "history" *per se* that upsets him; exactly the same emotions that color the Cotton Mather scene are apparent in the one that precedes it, ending the "Alice Doane" segment of the tale. It seems reasonable to ask whether both plots may not hold the same inner significance for Hawthorne—whether the emotional imbalance of one may not be explained by the thematic emphasis of the other. Instead of being "incidental" to the moral about history, the main plot of "Alice Doane's Appeal" suggests an explanation for Hawthorne's furtiveness about history —not just here, I would add, but everywhere in his fiction.

Here is a summary of this main plot, much of which is itself hastily summarized by the narrator. Leonard Doane, a young Salemite who as a child has been orphaned by an Indian raid, conceives a wild hatred for a stranger, Walter Brome. The cause is an affection that the wicked sophisticate Walter feels for Leonard's beautiful and virtuous sister Alice. When Walter taunts Leonard "with indubitable proofs of the shame of Alice" (XII, 286), Leonard murders him. Leonard confesses the deed to an old wizard who, it transpires, had prearranged everything that has happened thus far. In the shadowy company of the wizard, Alice and Walter make a midnight visit to a graveyard containing all the dead in Salem's history, and are treated to a spectral pageant. The sinful souls of the damned are joined by "fiends counterfeiting the likeness of departed saints" (XII, 290). The whole evil group, we learn, is assembled to revel in the wizard's successful machinations, which become doubly horrible when Walter Brome is revealed to have been Leonard's long-lost brother. But the story ends on a note of triumphant virtue: Alice gets Walter's ghost to absolve her from guilt, and the bad spirits flee "as from the sinless presence of an angel" (XII, 292).

It takes very little reflection to see that these Gothic clichés of plotting are tied to a concern with incest. Most obviously, Alice Doane may have committed incest with Walter Brome, her brother. Understandably, though, the question is thickly cloaked in ambiguity. Hawthorne assures us of Alice's spotless virtue, but then hints at her "undefinable, but powerful interest in the unknown youth" (XII, 286). Next come the "indubitable proofs of shame," but they turn out to be less than indubitable; Leonard is "now tortured by the idea of his sister's guilt, yet sometimes yielding to a conviction of her purity" (XII, 287). The wizard's fiendish laughter at Leonard's story of revenge suggests that perhaps Alice was innocent after all. Then, however, we discover that the wizard had "cunningly devised that Walter Brome should tempt his unknown sister to guilt and shame" (XII, 291f.)—seemingly a plain indication that the act took place. Yet in the very next sentence the graveyard fiends are described as eager to learn whether the wizard's plan was really consummated; and we are finally left to infer, not without misgiving, that the ghost's "absolving her from every stain" (XII, 292) includes not only a disavowal of Alice's *willingness* to commit incest, but a rejection of the idea that the act occurred at all.

However much this vacillation may be due to Hawthorne's own discomfort with the subject of incest, its immediate reference in the story is to Leonard Doane's mind. His intense affection for his sister, which he likes to think of as a "consecrated fervor" (XII, 284), verges into sexual passion, and his no less intense hatred for Walter Brome is composed at least in part of sexual jealousy. These facts are established in Leonard's confession to the wizard, which we must quote at length:

> "Searching," continued Leonard, "into the breast of Walter Brome, I at length found a cause why Alice must inevitably love him. For he was my very counterpart! I compared his mind by each individual portion, and as a whole, with mine. There was a resemblance from which I shrunk with sickness, and loathing, and horror, as if my own features had come and stared upon me in a solitary place, or had met me in struggling through a crowd. Nay! the very same thoughts would often express themselves in the same words from our lips, proving a hateful sympathy in our secret souls. His education, indeed, in the cities of the old world, and mine in this rude wilderness, had wrought a superficial difference. The evil of his character, also, had been strengthened and rendered prominent by a reckless and ungoverned life, while mine had been softened and purified by the gentle and holy nature of Alice. But my soul had been conscious of the germ of all the fierce and deep passions, and of all the many varieties of wickedness, which accident had brought to their full maturity in him. Nor will I deny that, in the accursed one, I could see the withered blossom of every virtue, which, by a happier culture, had been made to bring forth fruit in me. Now, here was a man whom Alice might love with all the strength of sisterly affection, added to that

impure passion which alone engrosses all the heart. The
stranger would have more than the love which had been
gathered to me from the many graves of our household—
and I be desolate!" (XII, 285)

Only the most gullible reader could take Leonard's reasoning at the end of this passage at face value. He tries
to discriminate between "sisterly affection," whose appropriate object is himself, and "impure passion," which can
be directed only to a stranger like Walter; yet Walter is
his "very counterpart"! In effect he attributes incestuous
feelings to his sister by saying that she must be attracted
to Walter *because* Walter resembles him. The reason
Leonard shrinks from the resemblance "with sickness, and
loathing, and horror" is that his counterpart's frankly
sexual interest in Alice points up his own surreptitious
one. The alter ego to whom all vices are permitted has
boasted of enacting Leonard's most secret wish. As so often
happens in nineteenth-century plots,[5] and as we see most
clearly in Hawthorne's own unfinished romances, incestuous desire is thinly masked by a "fortuitous" discovery of
kin relationship. The plot itself, we might say, has committed incest.

Leonard's recognition of the incestuous basis of his
hatred for Walter is not quite explicit; yet he *acts as if*
he understood this basis, and Hawthorne ensures that we
too will understand it. The brothers, he says, are "like
joint possessors of an individual nature, which could not
become wholly the property of one, unless by the extinc-
tion of the other" (XII, 286). This is to say that in murdering Walter, Leonard *becomes* Walter, and that he has
nurtured a "Walter" component of himself all along.

5. See Mario Praz, *The Romantic Agony*, tr. Angus Davidson
(New York, 1951), *passim.* This study, first published in 1930, remains a valuable guide to the less sublime side of Romantic self-
revelation.

Indeed, the first mention of Leonard is that he is a young
man "characterized by a diseased imagination and morbid
feelings" (XII, 284). Alice's excellent influence is said to be
"not enough to cure the deep taint of his nature" (XII,
284)—a mordant irony, for Alice's influence is precisely
Leonard's problem. His buried passion for her turns his
otherwise just indignation at Walter's villainy into an
"insane hatred that had kindled his heart into a volume
of hellish flame" (XII, 285f.). And most significantly, when
he has killed Walter he feels guilty not just for the murder
but for something less easily formulated. He finds himself
"shuddering with a deeper sense of some unutterable
crime, perpetrated, as he imagined, in madness or a dream"
(XII, 287). Can there be any question of what crime Hawthorne has in mind?

It appears, then, that at the outset of his effort to "open
an intercourse with the world" (I, 17) Hawthorne felt
impelled to treat the most shameful of subjects, and to do
so in a spirit of turbulent agitation—surely a strange fact
if we regard him as a gentle moralist whose essence is
repose. That he was not being sufficiently euphemistic
about his theme is registered for us by that touchstone of
popular taste, Samuel Goodrich, who wrote him in 1830
that while "The Gentle Boy" and "My Kinsman, Major
Molineux" could appear in *The Token,* "about 'Alice
Doane' I should be more doubtful as to the public approbation." [6] Hawthorne himself never collected or even
acknowledged the story, despite his padding-out of the
Twice-Told Tales, the *Mosses,* and *The Snow-Image* with
inferior work. Not until 1883 did "Alice Doane's Appeal"
get publicly linked with Hawthorne's name. As Seymour
L. Gross has argued, the incest theme must have been
especially prominent in the earlier version of the tale,
necessitating the addition of the storyteller framework and

6. Quoted by Adkins, *Papers of the Bibliographical Society of
America,* XXXIX, 128.

the summarizing of overly vivid scenes.[7] Everything indicates that Hawthorne was consciously aware that he had
hit upon dangerously unmanageable material.[8]

This brings us to consider the chief technical feature
of "Alice Doane's Appeal," its displacement of attention
from its implicit center of interest. Part of this displacement takes the form of factual obfuscation as to whether
Alice really committed incest. Another part consists in the
narrator's efforts to make the story palatable to his empty-
headed lady friends; and indeed, the ladies seem un-
troubled by the most troublesome scenes. This in turn is
made possible by a convenient ambiguity within the main
plot. Hawthorne enables the casual reader to see Leonard
in perfectly conventional terms, as the virtuous brother
who avenges his sister's honor. It is only by paying attention to innuendoes that we begin to see the appropriate-
ness of his rage against Walter to his own compromised
relationship with Alice. And thus we can say that the very
presence of Walter Brome as a stereotyped villain is a
further instance of displacement in the story. It is convenient for both Leonard and Hawthorne that Walter is
so dastardly, for—so goes the popular logic—only a fiendish
cad would relish the idea of seducing his sister. If, to the
psychologically-minded reader, Leonard has in effect murdered his personified incest wish, to every other reader
he has simply been driven to rashness by a noble fraternal
impulse.

7. "Hawthorne's 'Alice Doane's Appeal,'" *Nineteenth-Century
Fiction*, X (December 1955), 232-6.

8. We know, by the way, that Hawthorne's sister Elizabeth had
an unusually frank curiosity about incest, and that she investigated
the question of Byron's alleged incest with his sister (see Loggins,
The Hawthornes, pp. 301f.). Elizabeth is conjectured to have been
the person who rescued "Alice Doane's Appeal" from burning, and
according to Lathrop she still "retained some recollection of the
story" (XII, 9) in her last years, over half a century after its publica-
tion.

The principle of displacement also helps us to grasp the role of the wizard, which is far from admirable on aesthetic grounds. Every reader must feel cheated when he is told that the wizard has prearranged the greater part of the plot; with one blow Hawthorne thus cancels all the personal motivation he has so carefully established. Yet this strikes me as exactly why the wizard is useful. He acts as a *deus ex machina* who relieves the other characters of responsibility for their compulsions. At the same time—and this is typical of Hawthorne's circular flights from his themes—his description of the wizard shows us that he has been thinking of unconscious compulsion all along. Though fiendishly evil, the wizard is "senseless as an idiot and feebler than a child to all better purposes" (XII, 284). Under certain conditions, we learn, he "had no power to withhold his aid in unravelling the mystery" (XII, 288). He personifies that portion of the mind which drives men to do things they find abhorrent, and if we confront him honestly he will reveal his machinations.

Lastly, but most revealingly, we must examine a displacement at the very heart of the main plot—a symbolic substitution of one family figure for another. In an extraordinary passage Leonard recounts to the wizard a vision that struck him as Walter Brome lay dead at his feet:

> But it seemed to me that the irrevocable years since childhood had rolled back, and a scene, that had long been confused and broken in my memory, arrayed itself with all its first distinctness. Methought I stood a weeping infant by my father's hearth; by the cold and bloodstained hearth where he lay dead. I heard the childish wail of Alice, and my own cry arose with hers, as we beheld the features of our parent, fierce with the strife and distorted with the pain, in which his spirit had passed away. As I gazed, a cold wind whistled by, and waved my father's hair. Immediately I stood again in the lonesome

road, no more a sinless child, but a man of blood, whose
tears were falling fast over the face of his dead enemy.
But the delusion was not wholly gone; that face still wore
a likeness of my father; and because my soul shrank from
the fixed glare of the eyes, I bore the body to the lake . . .
(XII, 287)

We must thank Hyatt Waggoner for stressing the power
of these lines—and we must question his belief that they
have no relevance to the rest of the story.[9] They are irrelevant only in the sense of reaching a level of ultimate
motivation that supersedes Leonard's conscious reasoning.
Leonard shows us in this moment of vision that by killing
Walter he is symbolically reliving the murder of a prior
"dead enemy," his father. To be sure, it was an Indian
raiding party that performed the first crime; but Leonard's
fantasy ambiguously casts himself in the Indians' place.
The open murder of Walter becomes horrible to him by
virtue of Walter's resemblance to his father, and we may
surmise that this resemblance had something to do with
the urge to kill him. Leonard has seen in Walter a reincarnation of the dead parent toward whom, we perceive,
he has continued to harbor both hostility and penitence.
When he has acted upon his hostility he is free to weep
tears of remorse—tears that are inappropriate to the despicable Walter but not to the dimly remembered father for
whom he stands.

No one who is acquainted with psychoanalytic theory
will be astonished by these inferences. Leonard's evident
self-blame for a murder he did not commit is paralleled
by any number of case-histories in which the accidental
death of a consciously revered person—most often a parent
—has touched off fantasies of guilt and symptoms of neurosis.[10] Nor should we be surprised at the emergence,

9. *Hawthorne* (1963 ed.), pp. 52f.
10. As we shall argue in Chapter 5, the plot of "Roger Malvin's
Burial" turns upon exactly this principle of unconscious logic.

under great strain, of a patricidal obsession in Leonard's case. If we recognize, as Hawthorne obliges us to, that Leonard's "diseased imagination and morbid feelings" are focused upon incest wishes, we must find his unresolved filial hatred entirely appropriate. That his morbidity is directed toward a sister rather than a mother is immaterial, for—again following psychoanalytic dogma—this is the expected pattern of deflection. Just as Leonard's brother has become psychologically identical with his father, so, we might infer, Alice Doane is the recipient of feelings whose first object was her mother. The reader is entitled to reject this latter inference as extraneous to the text; yet he can hardly deny that the story's twin themes of incest and murder are connected by Leonard's classically Oedipal feelings toward a father, a brother, and a sister. There is also, of course, room for disagreement as to whether such complexity of motivation can be ascribed to so imperfectly rendered a character as Leonard. As we found in "The Maypole of Merry Mount," the implied motivation resides rather in imagery and plot-configuration than in direct authorial statements; we are free to choose between attaching it to Leonard and calling it self-revelation on Hawthorne's part.[11] Either view is acceptable so long as we recognize the nature of the feelings that govern the general atmosphere of the tale.

Given the emergence of an actual fantasy of patricide in the main plot, we are now in a better position to understand the spirit of the concluding, and supposedly irrele-

11. This is Waggoner's view; the death-memory is coherent, he says, only in the light of such circumstances as "the death of Hawthorne's own father when Hawthorne was four, the neuroticism of his mother and his elder sister, his own years of unhappy seclusion, his feeling that he had been 'saved' by his marriage, his lifelong restlessness . . ." (*Hawthorne,* p. 52). I agree with the spirit of this statement, and would only add that the whole of "Alice Doane's Appeal," not just one passage, reveals the same unresolved conflict.

vant, witch-hanging scene. For it is no exaggeration to say that Hawthorne ends his tale on a patricidal note. The arch-villain Cotton Mather is blamed for all the false incrimination of the time, including, we might repeat, the accusation of a "little son" against his mother (XII, 293). Just as Leonard Doane's dead father apparently survives in repressed fantasy, even after remorseful tears have been shed over his surrogate, so the tale abruptly ends in the shadow of a wicked tyrant, unmurdered and newly deserving of that fate. An irrational impulse of vengeance thus connects the "fictitious" part of the story to the "antiquarian" part. It would be far-fetched, of course, to say that the "deep, unutterable loathing and horror" (XII, 293) of the witch-hanging scene are really evoked by the "unutterable crime" (XII, 287) of Leonard's thoughts; the literal situation is sufficient to account for any degree of agony. What we *can* say is that Hawthorne or the narrator treats the two parts of the story in the same spirit—that the fantasy which is fairly explicit in one plot-fragment has not been wholly subdued in the narration of the other.

This fact is made especially clear by the transitional scene that separates the two fragments. We may recall that Alice is finally absolved from guilt by the ghost of Walter Brome, who appears at a midnight convocation of fiends and damned souls, representing all the early founders of Salem. Such a scene is clearly meant as fiction, yet it must also draw upon Hawthorne's sense of his early ancestors. The most striking feature of the ghostly pageant is that nearly every personage is described in terms of family relationship—"the gray ancestor," "the aged mother," "the children," "husbands and wives," "young mothers" and "their first babes" (XII, 289f.). In the place of real fathers there are seemingly admirable authorities: "old defenders of the infant colony," "pastors of the church, famous among the New England clergy" (XII, 290). When the narrator suddenly confesses that all these shapes, many of

which were loved and respected in life, are really lost souls,
the nature of their damnation is hinted:

> The countenances of those venerable men, whose very
> features had been hallowed by lives of piety, were con-
> torted now by intolerable pain or hellish passion, and
> now by an unearthly and derisive merriment. Had the
> pastors prayed, all saintlike as they seemed, it had been
> blasphemy. The chaste matrons, too, and the maidens with
> untasted lips, who had slept in their virgin graves apart
> from all other dust, now wore a look from which the two
> trembling mortals shrank, as if the unimaginable sin of
> twenty worlds were collected there. The faces of fond
> lovers, even of such as had pined into the tomb, because
> there their treasure was, were bent on one another with
> glances of hatred and smiles of bitter scorn, passions that
> are to devils what love is to the blest. (XII, 290f.)

This is the first of many such scenes in Hawthorne's fiction, where the entire population of a town will be accused
of some undefined wickedness of heart. Here the customary
circumlocution—"the unimaginable sin of twenty worlds"
—seems less euphemistic in view of the similar language
that has been applied to Leonard Doane's sense of guilt.
We must consider, as well, that the main emphasis of the
passage falls on guilty sexual thoughts; that Leonard and
Alice, the embodiments of incestuous love, are shrinking
from the spectacle; and that all these damned spectres turn
out to have gathered in order to delight in Walter and
Alice's incest. Thus the idea of past generations here is in
keeping with the story's theme; in some tentative, unformulated sense, ancestry is associated with incestry.

We may note in passing that a similar argument could
be drawn from certain images which link one part of the
tale to another. Gallows Hill, for example, where the
narrator tells his story to the giddy maidens, is said to be
covered with wood-wax, a "deceitful verdure" (XII, 279)

that simulates grass and in one season puts forth glorious yellow blossoms. From a distance the effect is quite lovely. "But the curious wanderer on the hill," says the narrator portentously, "will perceive that all the grass, and everything that should nourish man or beast, has been destroyed by this vile and ineradicable weed: its tufted roots make the soil their own, and permit nothing else to vegetate among them; so that a physical curse may be said to have blasted the spot, where guilt and frenzy consummated the most execrable scene that our history blushes to record" (XII, 280). The wood-wax bears a symbolic relevance to the story that is about to be told in its midst. Leonard's helpless subjection to incestuous feeling, resting on the apparent purity of his affection for Alice, is comparable to the usurpation of everything natural by the speciously beautiful weed; only on close inspection, Hawthorne implies, do we see that certain growths and blossoms of the personality have exacted a terrible sacrifice. But the immediate reference of the image is, of course, to the witch trials. Probably without conscious intention, Hawthorne blames his ancestors not just for theological error, but for a "guilt and frenzy" whose sources lie deep in unnatural feeling; Leonard Doane's murder of a man who shares his own motives is a psychological counterpart to what the New England magistrates did in 1692. The vile and ineradicable weed of incestuous obsession has done its utmost to choke off every rival theme in Hawthorne's tale.

No wonder, then, that Hawthorne's narrator hesitates to begin his story, backs away in disgust from his own descriptions, and vacillates between erotic insinuation, sarcasm, and apology. Hawthorne himself, we must suppose, shares his narrator's "dread of renewing my acquaintance with fantasies that had lost their charm in the ceaseless flux of mind" (XII, 283). "Alice Doane's Appeal" is striking evidence that Hawthorne's own sense of guilt, rooted in the twin themes of incest and patricide, informs his idea of history and sabotages his efforts at moral objectivity. For Hawthorne, as we shall continue to show, the sense of the past is nothing other than the sense of symbolic family conflict writ large.[12]

12. Cf. Ernest Jones: "...forefathers are psychologically nothing but fathers at a slight remove." (*Essays in Applied Psycho-Analysis,* Vol. II: *Essays in Folklore, Anthropology, and Religion* [London, 1951], p. 163.)

IV

Submission and Revolt

> From the beginning...the idea, the central legend that I
> wished my book to express—had not changed. And this central
> idea was this: the deepest search in life, it seemed to me, the
> thing that in one way or another was central to all living was
> man's search to find a father, not merely the father of his flesh,
> not merely the lost father of his youth, but the image of a
> strength and wisdom external to his need and superior to his
> hunger, to which the belief and power of his own life could
> be united.   —THOMAS WOLFE

Let us not overestimate the distance we have traveled thus
far. We have seen that the material of Puritan history has
a private and symbolic meaning for Hawthorne's imagination, and we have examined one instance of the eruption
of this meaning through the shattered surface of a fictional
plot. But to say that an obsessive theme dominates so unfinished a work as "Alice Doane's Appeal" is to have proved
very little about Hawthorne's power as a writer. The real
question is whether his acknowledged successes, with their
wholeness of effect and their real or seeming consistency
of overt theme, also amount to "psychological romance"
in the sense we have been developing. Are we justified in
declaring that Hawthorne's filial symbolism remains discernible in his most effective plots, and in fact determines
their form? With this in mind I propose to consider two
tales which, though nearly opposite in appeal, have been
accepted as masterpieces by different generations of readers.
"The Gentle Boy" was the most popular of Hawthorne's
tales in his lifetime, while "My Kinsman, Major Molineux"

was nearly ignored then and is universally praised by academic critics today. There are good reasons why a taste for one of these stories tends to exclude a taste for the other—reasons that are cultural as well as intrinsically literary. But if our approach in terms of psychological patterns is warranted, it should reveal in both works a common substratum of attitude and a common logic of motivation.

The most obvious difference between these tales is one of technique. "The Gentle Boy" is a relatively plausible, literal story that is narrated with circumstantial amplitude: in contrast, "My Kinsman, Major Molineux" has the dreamlike traits of economy, abrupt transitions, implausible scenes, and exaggerations of silence, noise, and lighting. No less important, however, is a difference in emotional effect. Emotion is frozen in symbolism in "My Kinsman," breaking through only at the climactic moment of the plot. "The Gentle Boy," however, provides a superabundance of immediate feeling—so much, in fact, that Hawthorne himself admitted that "nature here led [me] deeper into the universal heart than art has been able to follow" (cited by Lathrop, I, 11). Such a fault was more easily forgiven by Hawthorne's contemporaries than by the modern reader, who may be embarrassed by sentiment but fascinated by symbolic intricacy and ironic restraint. It was, we may imagine, largely the self-indulgent aspect of "The Gentle Boy" that made it the favorite of Sophia Hawthorne and others. Yet granted this difference, I submit that the two stories are alike in theme, and that both display Hawthorne's knack of simultaneously *analyzing* and *indulging* a psychological excess whose ultimate reference is Oedipal.

The appeal of "The Gentle Boy" seems at first to be a matter of primitive identification with a martyred hero and of cautionary emphasis on domestic, especially maternal, values. The story of a fatherless lad of six who is killed by negligence and malice is calculated to reinforce the female reader's dedication to hearth and nursery. Ilbrahim, the "sweet infant of the skies that had strayed away from his home" (I, 97) in Wordsworthian style, appears to be singularly exempt from Hawthorne's usual irony of characterization. He is a figure of incalculable worth; simply to be his mother would be the reader's most sacred privilege. At the same time, the scarcity of decent adults in the tale encourages the reader to put himself directly in Ilbrahim's place. "The others" are a contemptible lot: "all the inhabitants of this miserable world closed up their impure hearts against him, drew back their earth-soiled garments from his touch, and said, 'We are holier than thou'" (I, 97). Thus Hawthorne's tale of childhood aims a message of self-pity at the surviving child in each of us; by identifying ourselves with Ilbrahim we can renew our conviction that we have been tragically underestimated and mistreated by the world in general and by our parents in particular.

This is to say that the plot of "The Gentle Boy," with its buffeting of the child-hero from real parents to foster parents to the grave, springs from a masochistic fantasy. In this respect it partakes of the Victorian tradition of fictional childhood; one thinks especially of Dickens and Charlotte Brontë. Yet Hawthorne was temperamentally unable to exploit a cliché without also exposing its psychological basis. In a story that is clogged with gratuitous cruelty and bittersweet suffering, he subtly anatomizes the pleasures of both victimizers and victims, and eventually arrives at his usual note of philosophic irony. And I am reluctant to believe that this side of his tale was completely lost on his contemporaries; I suspect that it was some perceived interplay between indulgence and understanding that set "The Gentle Boy" apart from numberless other stories of abused innocence.

As in all Hawthorne's tales employing Puritan history, this one sets up a psychological opposition between Puritans and a dissident group, in this case the Quakers. Needless to say, the Puritans are represented as arch-sadists who

systematically banish, starve, and murder their fellow
Christians, including Ilbrahim's father. A significant point
of interest has been added, however. In showing how a
remorseless Puritan minister who preaches against the
Quakers "had practically learned the meaning of persecution from Archbishop Laud, and was not now disposed
to forget the lesson against which he had murmured then"
(I, 98), Hawthorne begins to explore the *causality* of Puritan sadism. Cruelty has begotten cruelty—a principle that
is minutely ramified through the entire story.

The real distinction of "The Gentle Boy" lies not in
Hawthorne's analysis of the Puritans but in that of the
Quakers, whose pretensions to divine guidance are under-
cut at every point. Their willingness to be martyred is
portrayed as the sheerest masochism. "The fines, imprison-
ments, and stripes, liberally distributed by our pious forefathers; the popular antipathy, so strong that it endured
nearly a hundred years after actual persecution had ceased,
were attractions as powerful for the Quakers, as peace,
honor, and reward, would have been for the worldly
minded" (I, 85). This sentence from the tale's opening
paragraph sets up an ironical mutuality of gratification
between the Puritans and the Quakers; the surface irony
of "liberally distributed" punishments is enriched by the
consideration that from the Quaker standpoint such behavior really *is* liberal; it is just what the Quakers yearn
for. Every boat from Europe brings a fresh cargo of appren-
tice sufferers, "eager to testify against the oppression which
they hoped to share" (I, 85f.); and the height of success is
reached when, in 1659, "the government of Massachusetts
Bay *indulged* two members of the Quaker sect with the
crown of martyrdom" (I, 86; my italics). When Ilbrahim's
zealous mother, having renounced her plain maternal duty,
goads the Puritans to "reward me with stripes, imprisonment, or death" (I, 101), we can no longer imagine that
Hawthorne entertains any sympathy for Quaker doctrine.
He has built his tale on the reciprocity of two fanaticisms

which are about equidistant from the "rational piety" (I, 104)—that is, normal family sentiment—cherished by his nineteenth-century readers.[1]

From the child's point of view, which is the controlling one in this story, there is little to choose between the cruel delinquency of the Puritans and the negligent delinquency of the Quakers. Both groups are locked in perversions of natural impulse; both are incapacitated for parenthood. The Quakers, "whose revengeful feelings were not less deep because they were inactive" (I, 86), are as prey to sadistic fantasies as their enemies. Ilbrahim's mother, for example, in a "flood of malignity which she mistook for inspiration" (I, 101), imagines an orgy of destruction for the Puritans: "Woe to them in their death hour, whether it come swiftly with blood and violence, or after long and lingering pain!" (I, 100). And she turns this savagery against herself—and indirectly against Ilbrahim—in suppressing her maternal feeling and abandoning Ilbrahim to his persecutors. Lest we see this merely as a personal quirk, Hawthorne offers us the example of an old Quaker leader who boasts of having overmastered the "mocking fiend" who told him not to desert his daughter on her deathbed. This zealot was aided in reaching the "peace and joy" (I, 119) of self-congratulation by a Puritan whipping. "I knelt down and wrestled with the tempter," he recalls, "while the scourge bit more fiercely into the flesh. My prayer was heard ..." (I, 119). The essence of seventeenth-century Quakerism is perceived to be a lust for punishment which significantly includes one's children as well as oneself.

Thus the exaggerated innocence of Hawthorne's child-

1. Hawthorne's revisions of "The Gentle Boy" for *Twice-Told Tales* are instructive. In the later version (which we are using here) he underplayed the political motives for religious persecution, leaving in bolder relief the strictly psychological relationship between his Puritans and Quakers. See the perceptive study by Seymour L. Gross, "Hawthorne's Revisions of 'The Gentle Boy,'" *American Literature*, XXVI (May 1954), 196-208.

victim is balanced against an especially cutting denigration
of the two societies that encircle him. As we might expect,
however, Hawthorne does not rest content with such a
melodramatic contrast. He turns much of his attention to
two characters who share with Ilbrahim an entrapment
between Puritanism and Quakerism, and whose moral role
is highly equivocal. Dorothy and Tobias Pearson are relatively sympathetic, yet as adults, and especially as foster
parents, they are not excepted from the general accusation
of unworthiness that can be felt throughout "The Gentle
Boy." In Dorothy, to be sure, we have an embodiment of
the anti-fanatical, motherly ideal that is negatively established by the other characters' excesses; Dorothy would
like to substitute Ilbrahim for her own dead children. Yet
all her ministrations cannot save him from the world's
shocks, and he finally makes a point of dying in the arms
of his own "dearest mother" (I, 125), inferior as she is.
Hawthorne's involvement in Ilbrahim's situation prevails
over his moral interest; the admirable Dorothy is finally
ineffectual because, quite simply, she is not Ilbrahim's real
mother.

In the case of Tobias Pearson, Hawthorne manages to
combine subtle characterization with fidelity to his symbolic pattern. Tobias has been much admired by critics
for his "Christian ethic" [2] in rescuing Ilbrahim from starvation and raising him as a foster son. But Hawthorne
shows us how Tobias's Christian ethic itself has derived
from a certain withdrawal of commitment, a suspect world-
weariness, that has already made him a bad provider for
his original family (see I, 94). His talent is not so much for
compassion as for failure, and his conversion to Quakerism
is presented as a psychological strategy, not a miracle.

2. See, for example, Male, *Hawthorne's Tragic Vision*, p. 47,
where this phrase occurs; Gross, *American Literature*, XXVI, 205;
and Louise Dauner, "The 'Case' of Tobias Pearson: Hawthorne and
the Ambiguities," *American Literature*, XXI (January 1950), 464-72.

Already alienated from his neighbors and burdened with an obscure feeling of guilt, he courts their disapproval of his latest aberration. He is attracted to the Quakers partly *because* he despises them: "his contempt, in nowise decreasing towards them, grew very fierce against himself; he imagined, also, that every face of his acquaintance wore a sneer, and that every word addressed to him was a gibe" (I, 114). Thus the adoption of Ilbrahim, and subsequently of Quakerism, offers Tobias an objective basis for the self-hatred he has felt all along; he will now be contemptible by virtue of being a Quaker instead of on his own deserts.

The paramount fact about Tobias is that he too, contrary to first appearance, is an unacceptable parent for Ilbrahim. His instinctive kindness toward the boy arouses a "self-suspicion" (I, 114) whose source lies in a previous failure: all his children have died, and his fellow Puritans have interpreted this as a divine judgment against his material ambition and his over-solicitude for the children's earthly happiness (see I, 94). Thus Tobias, who is hyper-sensitive to majority sentiment and anxious for religious certainty (see I, 114), has a secret motive for checking his fatherly love. At one early moment he is prevented from defending Ilbrahim by "a certain feeling like the consciousness of guilt" (I, 103f.). And this side of his nature is perceived—and approved—by Ilbrahim's mother, who is willing to commit her son to the possessor of "the hesitating air, the eyes that struggled with her own, and were vanquished; the color that went and came, and could find no resting-place" (I, 106). She correctly judges that such a weak and self-loathing foster-father will be sure to leave Ilbrahim exposed to all the purifying trials of persecution. We cannot quite say that Tobias is unconsciously committed to seeing Ilbrahim martyred; simply, he shows ambivalence toward Ilbrahim and then passively allows him to be destroyed. Yet even this much helps to correct the impression that Tobias has been rendered sentimentally; he is a peculiarly neurotic Good Samaritan.

To some extent a similar vindication can be applied to Ilbrahim's own portrait, for he too is morbid as well as angelic. "The disordered imaginations of both his father and mother," Hawthorne surmises, "had perhaps propagated a certain unhealthiness in the mind of the boy." (I, 108) This unhealthiness finds expression not merely in heightened sensitivity to pain and in a failure of self-defense, but in a perverse friendship that anticipates the relation of Arthur Dimmesdale to Roger Chillingworth in *The Scarlet Letter*. Psychically wounded by his mother's desertion, Ilbrahim conceives an affection for a brutal and deformed older child who has been physically wounded by a fall. The affection is reciprocated, and yet, as in the later case, it is turned to sado-masochistic use. The climactic scene of Ilbrahim's humiliation, when he has approached the "heavenly little band" of mock-innocent Puritan schoolmates who have previously scorned him, is extraordinarily revealing. Ilbrahim

came towards the children with a look of sweet confidence on his fair and spiritual face, as if, having manifested his love to one of them, he had no longer to fear a repulse from their society. A hush came over their mirth the moment they beheld him, and they stood whispering to each other while he drew nigh; but, all at once, the devil of their fathers entered into the unbreeched fanatics, and sending up a fierce, shrill cry, they rushed upon the poor Quaker child. In an instant, he was the centre of a brood of baby-fiends, who lifted strokes against him, pelted him with stones, and displayed an instinct of destruction far more loathsome than the blood-thirstiness of manhood.

The invalid, in the meanwhile, stood apart from the tumult, crying out with a loud voice, "Fear not, Ilbrahim, come hither and take my hand;" and his unhappy friend endeavored to obey him. After watching the victim's struggling approach with a calm smile and unabashed eye, the foul-hearted little villain lifted his staff and struck Ilbrahim on the mouth, so forcibly that the blood issued in a stream. The poor child's arms had been raised to guard his head from the storm of blows; but now he dropped them at once. His persecutors beat him down, trampled upon him, dragged him by his long, fair locks . . . (I, 112)

In this surprisingly lurid scene—a sado-masochistic nightmare if there ever was one—Hawthorne has heaped on Ilbrahim all the accumulated cruelty of his plot. For the reader who has accepted the implied invitation to put himself in Ilbrahim's place, the episode is calculated to trigger a helpless rage against the unearned malice of mankind. At the same time, we cannot ignore the fact that Ilbrahim has had a hand in his downfall. "The victim of his own heavenly nature" (I, 113) has half-willingly befriended a monster and committed himself to the mercy of known enemies. We pity him, yet we dimly recognize that he has at last found the role for which he is best suited by temperament—that of unresisting victim.

The overlong portion of "The Gentle Boy" that follows this climax consists largely of a wallowing in Ilbrahim's misery. Tension has been relaxed; we know that death is the only possible exit from the outrageous world into which the hero has been thrust. In this new atmosphere, however, an important reversal of sympathy occurs. Ilbrahim's mother, now that her negligence has done its worst, suddenly becomes an object of pity and love. Ilbrahim cries out for her in his sleep, "as if her place, which a stranger had supplied while [he] was happy, admitted of no substitute in his extreme affliction" (I, 113). When she does reappear, it is in a new mood of single-minded concern for her son. Ilbrahim is able to die happily after studying her face: he has finally succeeded—by dying—in convincing her of the importance of motherhood.

Here again we can recognize a classic self-pitying fantasy of childhood: *you'll miss me when I'm gone.* The wayward

parent is shocked out of her callousness by seeing its fatal
result. What is most significant, however, is that no amount
of misbehavior can make her ineligible for this reconciliation. Nothing, it seems, is unforgivable in a mother; the
purpose of the hero and the author is not to punish her
but to restore her to her essential role. By the end of the
tale the fanatical Catharine has been emotionally transformed, "as if [Ilbrahim's] gentle spirit came down from
heaven to teach his parent a true religion" (I, 125). She
now occupies the place that Hester Prynne will have at
the end of *The Scarlet Letter*: the ex-outcast is seen to be
spiritually better than the Puritan community which con-
descendingly offers her "that degree of pity which it is
pleasant to experience" and "the little kindnesses which
are not costly" (I, 126).

This authorial forgiveness is markedly different from
the lot of fathers in "The Gentle Boy." Ilbrahim's literal
dead father is not involved, except perhaps by neglect; no
mention is made of him after the first few pages, and his
absence from Ilbrahim's deathbed is anything but a hin-
drance to the scene's tenderness. But this tale of filial accusation seems to bring the whole category of male authorities into disrepute. The other notable fathers, Tobias
Pearson and the old Quaker leader who abandoned his
daughter, are offered no occasion to repent of their short-
comings. And from the beginning the entire cycle of persecutions is largely blamed on a single male figure, the
Colonial Governor. Without ever naming him, Hawthorne emphasizes his "brutal cruelty" and theorizes, "his
uncompromising bigotry was made hot and mischievous
by violent and hasty passions" (I, 86). Hawthorne, it
would seem, is in a good position to appreciate the "bitter
mockery" with which a Quaker historian "records the
loathsome disease, and 'death by rottenness,' of the fierce
and cruel governor" (I, 87). In a story whose Oedipal
theme is so transparent, we cannot be surprised that the

maker of orphans turns out to be a father-figure whose
guilt is evidently sexual.

Yet there is one final parent, God Himself, on whom
responsibility is placed at a sensitive moment in the plot.
When Ilbrahim's mother returns for the second time, bearing news that the persecutions are about to stop, she is
told by the Quaker leader that Ilbrahim is dying, thanks
to God's "love, displayed in chastenings" (I, 122). Even
Catharine is unequipped to appreciate such love, and her
outburst is illuminating:

> "I am a woman, I am but a woman; will He try me above
> my strength?" said Catharine very quickly, and almost in
> a whisper. "I have been wounded sore: I have suffered
> much; many things in the body; many in the mind; cruci-
> fied in myself, and in them that were dearest to me.
> Surely," added she, with a long shudder, "He hath spared
> me in this one thing." She broke forth with sudden and
> irrepressible violence. "Tell me, man of cold heart, what
> has God done to me? Hath He cast me down, never to
> rise again? Hath he crushed my very heart in His Hand?"
> (I, 122f.)

Critics who look for the redemptive side of Hawthorne's
tale would do well to ponder these Ahab-like questions,
which remain wholly unanswered. All Catharine's misdeeds, we now realize, have been performed in service to
the Father above—the arch-sadist of a lunatic universe.
Without His evil direction she would always have been
what she now becomes, "but a woman"; and by one act
of lenience He could—but does not—restore Ilbrahim to
her. It is meaningless to speculate whether Hawthorne
"really" believes this, just as it is unimportant whether
he believes that the Colonial Governor died of "rottenness." What matters is that he permits these accusations
to influence the net effect of his story. His embittered senti-

mentality is anti-paternal, even patricidal. Few of his works
are less gentle in spirit than "The Gentle Boy."

"The Gentle Boy," then, is a tale of even greater duplic-
ity than we have come to expect of Hawthorne. Its apparent historicity disguises a psychological determinism; its
banalities of characterization are in conflict with an un-
sparing study of sado-masochism; its sentimentality is per-
vaded with resentment; and its seeming conventionality
of idea is undermined by heretical doubts. If these buried
aspects of the story do not rescue it from prolixity, they
do appeal to the modern taste for intellectual tension,
irony, and depth. Yet the irony includes Hawthorne as
well as his characters; it is unlikely that he consciously
understood the extent to which masochistic fantasy governed his plot. We must make an aesthetic distinction
between works whose deepest meaning *negates* their surface pieties and those more satisfying ones in which a total
unity of effect is achieved.

"My Kinsman, Major Molineux" clearly belongs to the
latter group—which is not to say that its meaning is unambiguous. The point is that no moralizing and no idealization of the hero obstruct a "deep" interpretation, whatever that interpretation may be. The tale strikes every
reader as a tissue of symbols, a configuration whose meaning lies outside the immediate facts of the plot. The
adolescent hero, Robin Molineux, has been aptly described
as a country bumpkin, and his search for his affluent uncle
is handled in a way that seems at first to be unfeeling.
Hawthorne passes rapidly from one of Robin's vicissitudes
to the next, giving only perfunctory attention to the boy's
dismay at being continually rebuffed, and maintaining a
remarkable reticence about the absurdities of his situation.
Like Ilbrahim, Robin is largely passive; but the use Hawthorne makes of this passivity is wholly unsentimental.
Whereas Ilbrahim's victimization involves the reader in

excesses of empathy, Robin's appears to demand only an impersonal curiosity about symbolic intent.

The pertinent question for criticism is *how far* outside the literal plot of this tale we must go in order to make sense of it. One school sees Robin's gradual emancipation from his uncle as allegorical of the American Revolution; youthful and naïve America "comes of age" by assenting to the deposition of Colonial authority (Major Molineux). Others, stressing the ceremonial violence of that deposition, see the tale in mythic terms; Major Molineux in his tarring and feathering is a ritual king, "mighty no more, but majestic still in his agony" (III, 640). Both these readings have a degree of plausibility, but leave most of Robin's adventure out of account—indeed, they leave Robin himself out of account. Robin has nothing whatever to say, or even to think, about politics, but he *is* literally searching for an elder relation who will help him get on in the world, and that search is thwarted by some unnamed power. Without denying the presence of historical and mythic overtones, we would do well to ask whether Robin's own mind may not be the chief referent of Hawthorne's symbols. If every detail of the story obeys a psychological pattern, more transcendent allegorizing would seem unnecessary.[3]

Hawthorne has, indeed, offered considerable encouragement for a psychological reading. In a curious way the most insistent feature of the story is not its outward events but the anxiety they provoke in Robin. We sense his yearning for quick approbation and success, his fear of punish-

3. Of the many studies of "My Kinsman," those that are closest to the following interpretation are by Waggoner, *Hawthorne,* pp. 56-64; Franklin B. Newman, " 'My Kinsman, Major Molineux'; An Interpretation," *University of Kansas City Review,* XXI (March 1955), 203-12; Louis Paul, "A Psychoanalytic Reading of Hawthorne's 'Major Molineux': The Father Manqué and the Protégé Manqué," *American Imago,* XVIII (Fall 1961), 279-88; and Simon O. Lesser, *Fiction and the Unconscious* (Boston, 1957), pp. 212-224.

ment and failure, his resort to patently faulty rationalization when his ego is insulted, his shock in recognizing
what has been vaguely anticipated, and his final effort to
withdraw from his experience and reach a new equilibrium. These impressions are enhanced by the very absence
of superficial commentary about motives; we *must* see
psychological meaning in Robin's trials if they offer the
only clues to his nature. And there is ample reason to
believe that the whole course of the plot reflects unconscious fantasy on Robin's part. The ugly stranger who
finally locates Major Molineux for him behaves as if he
had a special foreknowledge, not only of the result of
Robin's search, but of his inner conflicts. From the first
he grins at Robin with an air of complicity, and he finally
presents the anti-Molineux procession at Robin's explicit
request. When this procession, with its "visionary air, as
if a dream had broken forth from some feverish brain"
(III, 638), stops directly before Robin, we are not surprised that "Robin's shout was the loudest there" (III,
640). At this climactic moment he joins and consummates
a process of degrading Major Molineux which has been
at work all along. As Simon O. Lesser has shown, Robin
has not been simply *prevented* from placing himself under
his uncle's authority, but *inhibited* by the enticements of
a strange town. His efforts to shed his provincialism, combined with his continual, nightmarish rebuffs at the hands
of elder authority, may be said to express and feed the
latent rebelliousness which finally bursts forth in the image
of Major Molineux's humiliation—"the foul disgrace of a
head grown gray in honor" (III, 639).

Even critics who denounce literary Freudianism have
recognized that Robin's real search is for an idealized
father—a figure of benevolent power who will shield him
from the world and lend him prestige. Robin's disappointment and recovery have been interpreted, quite correctly
in my opinion, as relating to the crisis of late adolescence
and its resolution in favor of a healthy independence from

the paternal image. It remains for us to show that the shape and details of Robin's experience fully confirm this reading. Hawthorne has not offered a case analogous to a search for a father, but has given an exact symbolic account of filial ambivalence—an account which must be symbolic because the struggle it renders is unconscious.

As we might expect, this tale of filial attitudes excludes the hero's real parents from view; that is Hawthorne's precondition for a symbolic plot. In coming to town to seek his fortune, Robin puts physical and moral distance between himself and his family: they are now available to him only in a nostalgic memory, a curiously stylized tableau suggestive of unresolved, unformulated feelings.[4] In the town, however, Robin is bombarded with father-figures who manifest extremes of contempt or benevolence toward him—usually the former. Beyond Major Molineux himself, who once hinted that he might accept him as his own son (III, 634) but is now unavailable, Robin meets a figure of male authority to match or thwart each of his moods. When he wants true fatherly guidance, it is offered by a distinguished-looking old gentleman who helps him to see that nepotistic dependence on Major Molineux will not prove useful. When he is secretly eager to see his kinsman degraded, he finds himself under the authority of the satanic leader of the procession, whose hideous physiognomy suggests aggression and death—rebellion and its reward. And when he tries to blend into the society of the town, pretending to be an accepted adult rather than a helpless young stranger, he is invariably hindered by men who evoke their superior force and threaten him with a beating or the stocks. In these encounters Robin alternates

4. In his fantasy Robin "perceived the slight inequality of his father's voice when he came to speak of the absent one; he noted how his mother turned her face to the broad and knotted trunk; how his elder brother scorned, because the beard was rough upon his upper lip, to permit his features to be moved; how the younger sister drew down a low hanging branch before her eyes . . ." (III, 632).

between a pleading deference and rash counter-threats of violence; and both strategies, the childlike and the manly, fail to gain him either the information or the respect that he needs.

Anxiety is the keynote, not only of Robin's frustrating experiences, but of the imagery that attends them. A hierarchy of wooden objects expresses Robin's inferior position. His cudgel fashioned from an oak sapling reminds us by contrast of the ancient oak tree in his family tableau —the symbol of unchallengeable paternal authority. His inability to frighten the townsmen, themselves armed with various wooden weapons, throws him back upon his fantasies of reaching instant greatness through Major Molineux; and this too is represented in wood-imagery. Facing a mansion which he takes to be his kinsman's, he finds himself unable to distinguish fancy from reality: "by turns, the pillars of the balcony lengthened into the tall, bare stems of pines, dwindled down to human figures, settled again into their true shape and size, and then commenced a new succession of changes" (III, 633). It is hard to avoid seeing a primitive phallic reference in all this uncertainty over the size and efficacy of long wooden objects—a reference that is quite appropriate to Robin's status as an anxious adolescent.[5] The power that he seeks and resents is sexual as well as social and combative.

This point is corroborated by an episode which is always scanted by "political" readers of the tale. Robin's search for the Major leads him to the doorway of a prostitute who declares significantly, "Major Molineux dwells here" (III, 626), and who tempts Robin as far as the threshold before a sleepy watchman, displaying "a long staff, spiked at the end" (III, 627), chases her inside and threatens Robin with

5. A rereading of footnote 4 above with this point in mind will cast a weird, yet not wholly unfamiliar, light on the imagined gestures of Robin's mother and sister. The barely perceptible sexual innuendo in that fantasy is developed considerably further in the scene we shall now discuss.

the stocks. This scene reveals that Robin, though he is "of the household of a New England clergyman" (III, 628), is motivated both by a powerful sexual curiosity and by a spirit of accusation. To leave one's idealized parents behind and be told that the father-surrogate Molineux "lives here" with a prostitute is to move from childlike ignorance to a state of lurid suspicion. The fantasy is a common one, according to Freud. When an adolescent can no longer believe that his parents are exempt from sexuality, "he says to himself with cynical logic that the difference between his mother and a whore is after all not so very great, since at bottom they both do the same thing." [6] The boy's contempt, furthermore, is often mixed with revived Oedipal longing, so that the "prostitute's" imagined sexual partner is a thinly disguised representative of himself. This would seem to account for Robin's temptation. In his anguished homelessness, which itself embodies his transitional phase between juvenile faith in his parents and a new autonomy, Robin has symbolically contemplated the worst suspicion a virginal young man can face, and has shown a willingness to use it as a pretext for indulging his own lust. Only an internalized paternal dissuasion, the armed guardian, has prevented the fantasy from reaching its conclusion.[7]

6. See Freud's two "Contributions to the Psychology of Love," *Collected Papers,* 5 vols. (New York, 1959), IV, 192-216. The quotation is from page 199.

7. The reader may object that Robin's encounter with the prostitute cannot bear this much meaning. Yet it is Hawthorne who implies that all Robin's acquaintances are versions of the same figures of authority. Note the following exchange between Robin, who thinks he has heard a thousand voices in the distance, and his kindly guide:

> "May not a man have several voices, Robin, as well as two complexions?" said his friend.
> "Perhaps a man may; but Heaven forbid that a woman should!" responded the shrewd youth, thinking of the seductive tones of the Major's housekeeper. (III, 636)

Without the element of dissuasion Robin would not be in the plight of an adolescent at all. Like many a later Hawthornian hero, he is as idealistic as he is prurient; indeed, idealism and prurience are complementary aspects of a single discomfort with adult reality. His ambition to supplant Major Molineux is scarcely greater than his respect for him, and the Major's final humiliation appropriately calls up both "pity and terror" (III, 639) in him. Robin has been led to this moment only through a series of initiations in which other adults have shown contempt for the Major, and it is only in their combined company that he can laugh at deposed majesty. At the end of the story he has merged himself with a jealous, jostling democracy of father-haters, but he shows no further enmity toward his kinsman. We may say that he has cathartically rid himself of both filial dependence and filial resentment, and will now be free, as his benevolent friend expects, to "rise in the world without the help of your kinsman, Major Molineux" (III, 641).

This emotional freedom is ignored by critics who want to draw a cautionary lesson from the tale. Robin, they say, has learned the moral cost of revolution, the guilt of history. In fact, however, Robin's guilt has combined with his pride to generate the entire plot, and both elements seem dissipated at the end. There is no basis for saying that he has "learned" anything besides the unreliability of nepotism. It is true, of course, that the American Revolution is prefigured in the Major's overthrow, but this merely suggests that Hawthorne, like Tom Paine, sees revolution itself in terms of filial revolt. Robin's preparedness for future success has very little to do with either history or morality; simply, he has undergone the crisis of disrespect that forms the loose social bond among democratic men.

Robin's "case," then, is very different in result from that of little Ilbrahim. One hero succumbs to morbidity while the other, less typically in Hawthorne's fiction, masters it and looks forward to adulthood. Yet in their different ways both have been orphaned, and both are concerned with repairing their dislocation from childhood security. In both stories literal fathers are supplanted by symbolic ones who are, on the whole, implicitly criticized. Ilbrahim suffers from paternal weakness and selfishness, and retreats to his mother's bosom to die; Robin acquires the confidence to challenge paternal strength, and so presumably falls heir to it.

These differences of situation only remind us of the single vision that underlies them. The doomed child and the emergent man are subject to the same "common nature" or "universal heart," with its terror of punishment, its accusations of uncleanness, and its need for respite from such inhibiting fantasies. Even the distinction between literal misfortunes and symbolic ones appears superficial: we must see that the filial resentment of Robin's fantasy-plot is precisely the controlling principle of Ilbrahim's more literal plot. What one hero tries to cast off in symbolic experience, the other suffers in the form of uninvited vicissitudes.

Thus a psychological theme is as prominent in one tale as in the other; what changes is chiefly the degree to which this theme may be reasonably viewed as operating within the hero's mind. And I find it significant that the more satisfying work is the one whose obsessiveness can be regarded as ironic characterization. If we can agree that Oedipal strife is a common denominator among Hawthorne's most intense plots, we may understand his need of a fallible protagonist whose absorption in this strife may be handled with aesthetic distance. In all his best tales, and nowhere more strikingly than in the next one we shall consider, this condition is met.

V

The Logic of Compulsion

"It don't make no difference whether you do right or wrong, a person's conscience ain't got no sense and just goes for him *anyway.*"   —HUCKLEBERRY FINN

One further story from Hawthorne's unpublished "Provincial Tales" requires our close interest, both because it has been generally misunderstood and because, once understood, it merits a high place among his fiction. In addition, "Roger Malvin's Burial" offers a classic instance of the way Hawthorne undermines questions of conscious moral choice with demonstrations of psychological necessity. As Harry Levin puts it, "Hawthorne was well aware that the sense of sin is more intimately related to inhibition than to indulgence; that the most exquisite consciences are the ones that suffer most; that guilt is a by-product of that very compunction which aims at goodness and acknowledges higher laws; and that lesser evils seem blacker to the innocent than to the experienced." [1] In previous chapters we have tried to define, not only the customary form that "exquisite conscience" takes in Hawthorne's tales, but also the primitive resentment and ambition that bring such conscience into operation. The plot of "Roger Malvin's

---

1. *The Power of Blackness,* p. 40. For another valuable formulation of Hawthorne's reduction of religious problems to psychological ones, see Melvin W. Askew, "Hawthorne, the Fall, and the Psychology of Maturity," *American Literature,* XXXIV (November 1962), 335-43.

Burial" makes sense in no other terms than these—and in these it is precisely, indeed shockingly, logical.

The story goes as follows. Roger Malvin, an old Indian-fighter who has been seriously wounded and finds himself unable to survive the homeward journey through a forest, persuades his young companion, Reuben Bourne, to leave him to die. Reuben will thereby gain a chance to survive, whereas to remain would simply mean two deaths instead of one. After promising to return some day to bury his old friend, Reuben departs and is eventually rescued by a search party. Though he marries Roger's daughter Dorcas, he is unable to explain to her that he left her father alive, preferring to let her imagine that he has already been buried. Reuben's public character and fortunes soon begin to go awry, until finally he is forced to take his wife and adolescent son off into the wilderness to seek a new life. Yet his steps bring him, not to the intended destination, but to the clearing where he left Roger Malvin many years before. There, detecting what might be a deer behind some undergrowth, he fires his musket, only to discover that he has killed his son Cyrus on the very spot where Roger died. The story ends, nonetheless, on an affirmative and extremely pious note: "Then Reuben's heart was stricken, and the tears gushed out like water from a rock. The vow that the wounded youth had made the blighted man had come to redeem. His sin was expiated,—the curse was gone from him; and in the hour when he had shed blood dearer to him than his own, a prayer, the first for years, went up to Heaven from the lips of Reuben Bourne" (II, 406).

Such language naturally leads us to interpret "Roger Malvin's Burial" as a parable of atonement, for Reuben's act of manslaughter has melted his heart and enabled him to beg God for forgiveness. But forgiveness for what? It is unclear whether Reuben has atoned merely for not bury-ing Roger or for some other failing, and critics disagree as to what he has done wrong. In Harry Levin's view, Reuben is "innocent" of Roger Malvin's death and only "inadvertently guilty" of his son's. Mark Van Doren, on the other hand, holds Reuben accountable for both the desertion of Roger and the hypocrisy of silence toward Dorcas: "he has committed a sin and he has failed to confess it when he could." A third interpretation is that of Arlin Turner, who finds that Hawthorne "relieves Reuben Bourne of any guilt for abandoning Malvin" but shows the ill effects of his failure to be honest with Dorcas. The only point of general agreement is that the slaying of Reuben's son Cyrus is accidental. For Van Doren it is "Fate" that engineers the final catastrophe, and that event strikes Levin as "one of those coincidences that seem to lay bare the design of the universe." [2]

All of these opinions, including the unquestioned one about Cyrus's death, miss the essence of Hawthorne's story by not recognizing a difference between the feeling of guilt and the state of being guilty. Turner, to be sure, makes the point that Reuben's guilt is subjective, but in regard to the desertion scene he apparently confuses a moral absolving of Reuben by Hawthorne with an absence of guilty feeling on Reuben's part. We can see, however, in this scene and throughout the story, that Hawthorne is concerned *only* with subjective guilt as Reuben's conscience manufactures it, independently of the moral "sinfulness" or "innocence" of his outward deeds. That this is so at the end of the tale is obvious, for how could we take seriously the religious notion that a man can make his peace with the Christian God by shooting his innocent son? It is clear that Reuben has not performed a Christian expiation but simply rid himself of his burden of guilty feeling. It can be shown, furthermore, that this guilty feeling was never generated by a committed sin or crime in the first place. Once we have recognized this, the task of

2. See *The Power of Blackness,* p. 55; Mark Van Doren, *Nathaniel Hawthorne* (New York, 1949), p. 80; and Arlin Turner, *Nathaniel Hawthorne: An Introduction and Interpretation* (New York, 1961), p. 31.

deciding whether Reuben has been morally absolved becomes pointless, and Reuben's own theory that his steps
have been led by "a supernatural power" (II, 402) appears
in its true light—as a delusion fostered by, and serving to
cloak, a process of unconscious compulsion that is evidenced in great detail.[3]

Everyone agrees that Reuben feels guilty after misleading Dorcas, and it seems quite evident that Reuben's behavior in that scene is governed by an inner discomfort
over his having left Roger Malvin behind. But why should
Reuben feel this discomfort? The scene of desertion is
presented in such a way as to put every justification on
Reuben's side; Roger's arguments have persuaded not only
Reuben but most of the tale's critics to feel that there is
only one reasonable decision to be made. Why, then, does
Reuben find it so difficult to explain the true circumstances to Dorcas? The answer seems to be that in some
deep way Reuben feels more responsible for Roger's death
than he actually is. "By a certain association of ideas," as
Hawthorne says of him later, "he at times almost imagined
himself a murderer" (II, 394).

How could Reuben feel himself even remotely to be
Roger's murderer? If there is no factual basis for the self-
accusation, perhaps there is a psychological basis. The
charge seems, indeed, to be true in fantasy if not true in
fact, for Reuben shows definite signs of looking forward
to deserting Roger in spite of his comradely feeling for
him. When Roger adduces the point that Dorcas must not
be left desolate, Reuben feels reminded "that there were

3. The argument that follows has been anticipated in part by
various studies. See Waggoner, *Hawthorne*, pp. 90-98; Richard P.
Adams, "Hawthorne's *Provincial Tales*," *New England Quarterly*,
XXX (March 1957), 39-57; Louis B. Salomon, "Hawthorne and His
Father: A Conjecture," *Literature and Psychology*, XIII (Winter
1963), 12-17; and Agnes McNeill Donohue, " 'From Whose Bourn
No Traveler Returns': A Reading of 'Roger Malvin's Burial,' "
Nineteenth-Century Fiction, XVIII (June 1963), 1-19.

other and less questionable duties than that of sharing the
fate of a man whom his death could not benefit. Nor,"
adds Hawthorne significantly, "can it be affirmed that no
selfish feeling strove to enter Reuben's heart, though the
consciousness made him more earnestly resist his companion's entreaties" (II, 384). This would seem to be the
source of all Reuben's trouble. It is obviously advantageous as well as reasonable for him to go on without Roger,
since he faces a prospect of married bliss if he survives.
The contrast between Roger's altruism and his own self-
seeking motives is painful to his conscience; his personal
claims must strive for recognition, and Reuben feels a
need to counter-attack them with a redoubled commitment
to remain with Roger. "He felt as if it were both sin and
folly to think of happiness at such a moment" (II, 386).
Thus we see that his feelings of guilt have already set in
before he has made a final decision to leave. He feels guilty,
not for anything he has done, but for thoughts of happiness—a happiness that will be bought at the price of a
man's life.

The more closely we look at the scene of desertion,
the more ironical Hawthorne's view of Reuben's mental
struggle appears. The mention of Dorcas marks a turning-
point between a series of melodramatic, self-sacrificing
protestations of faithfulness and a new tone of puzzlement,
self-doubt, and finally insincerity. Reuben is no longer
really combating Roger's wishes after this point, but pos-
ing objections that he knows Roger will easily refute.
"How terrible to wait the slow approach of death in this
solitude!" (II, 384) But a brave man, answers Roger, knows
how to die. "And your daughter,—how shall I dare to meet
her eye?" (II, 385) The question is already how *shall* I,
not how *would* I! When this too has been answered,
Reuben needs only to be assured of the possibility of his
returning with a rescue party. "No merely selfish motive,
nor even the desolate condition of Dorcas, could have

induced him to desert his companion at such a moment—but his wishes seized on the thought that Malvin's life might be preserved, and his sanguine nature heightened almost to certainty the remote possibility of procuring human aid" (II, 386). There follows a grim comedy in which Roger pretends to see a similarity between the present case and another one, twenty years previously, that turned out well, and Reuben fatuously allows himself to be convinced. Hawthorne leaves no doubt that Reuben is semi-deliberately deceiving himself in order to silence his conscience. "This example, powerful in affecting Reuben's decision, was aided, unconsciously to himself, by the hidden strength of many another motive" (II, 387). When he finally does leave, the act is presented as a triumph of these other motives over his human sympathy: "His generous nature would fain have delayed him, at whatever risk, till the dying scene were past; but the desire of existence and the hope of happiness had strengthened in his heart, and he was unable to resist them" (II, 389).

These citations from the story's first scene make it evident that Hawthorne, by having Reuben's self-seeking wishes concur with a morally legitimate but painful decision, has set in bold relief the purely psychological problem of guilt. Unlike his critics, Hawthorne does not dwell on the moral defensibility of Reuben's leaving; rather, he demonstrates how this act appears to Reuben as a fulfillment of his egoistic wishes, so that he is already beginning to punish himself *as if* he had positively brought about Roger's death. As in "Alice Doane's Appeal," Hawthorne has anticipated Freud's discovery that (in Freud's terminology) the superego takes revenge for unfulfilled death-wishes as well as for actual murder.[4] Indeed, Hawthorne's

4. I do not mean, however, that Reuben actively wills Roger's death at any point. The link between his prospective happiness and Roger's imminent, already inevitable death is originally a fortuitous irony of circumstance and nothing more. But Reuben's punctilious

whole rendering of Reuben's mind is based on what we
would now call psychoanalytic principles. Some of Reuben's motives, as we have seen, operate "unconsciously to
himself," which is to say that they have been repressed;
and once this repression has circumvented conscious moral
control, Reuben becomes a classic example of the man
who, because he can neither overcome his thoughts nor
admit them into consciousness, becomes their victim. The
real reason for his inability to state the outward facts of
the case to Dorcas is that these facts have become associated with the unbearable fantasy that he has murdered
his friend. Guilty feeling leads to a hypocrisy, which in
turn provides further reinforcement of guilt; "and Reuben, while reason told him that he had done right, experienced in no small degree the mental horrors which punish
the perpetrator of undiscovered crime" (II, 394).

One other inconspicuous, but absolutely decisive, element in the scene of desertion remains to be mentioned,
namely, that the relationship between Roger and Reuben
is that of a father to a son. Roger repeatedly calls him
"my boy" and "my son," and at a certain point he turns
this language to an argumentative use: "I have loved you
like a father, Reuben; and at a time like this I should have
something of a father's authority." Reuben's reply is curious: "And because you have been a father to me, should
I therefore leave you to perish and to lie unburied in the
wilderness?" (II, 384). From a strictly Freudian point of
view the answer to this rhetorical question could be *yes;*
the "son" feels murderous impulses toward the "father"
simply because he *is* the father, i.e., the sexual rival. It is
questionable whether Hawthorne's thinking has gone quite
this far. Yet it remains true that Reuben, in leaving Roger
to die, will get to have Dorcas's affections all to himself,

---

conscience turns this link into one of causality; he will no longer be
able to contemplate his own welfare without imagining, quite falsely,
that he has bought it with Roger Malvin's blood.

and we cannot say that such a consideration is not among the "many another motive" for his departure. The "father's authority" of which Roger ingenuously speaks is going to be left behind in the forest. In terms of the unconscious role he has assumed in relation to Roger, Reuben must think of himself not simply as a murderer but as a patricide.

This conclusion needs, of course, much further confirmation in order to be persuasive. Yet we may pause here to say that everything we have found in other tales—the violent and sometimes historically unfounded hatred against figures of authority, the crippling sense of guilt for unspecified criminal thoughts, and even a fairly plain fantasy of patricide in "Alice Doane's Appeal"—leads us to believe that Hawthorne was capable of taking the father-son symbolism as a basis for unconscious motivation. Nor can we quite avoid seeing that the complement to patricide, namely incest, lurks in the background of "Roger Malvin's Burial." If Roger is to be seen as Reuben's father, Dorcas becomes his sister. Without pressing this argument further, we may observe that Dorcas's later feeling for her son—"my beautiful young hunter!" (II, 404)—does not dispel the characteristic Hawthornian atmosphere of over-intimacy in this tale.

But let us return to less tenuous evidence. Reuben, who henceforth is occupied in "defending himself against an imaginary accusation" (II, 392), gradually turns his interest to his son Cyrus. "The boy was loved by his father with a deep and silent strength, as if whatever was good and happy in his own nature had been transferred to his child, carrying his affections with it. Even Dorcas, though loving and beloved, was far less dear to him; for Reuben's secret thoughts and insulated emotions had gradually made him a selfish man, and he could no longer love deeply except where he saw or imagined some reflection or likeness of his own mind. In Cyrus he recognized what he had himself been in other days . . ." (II, 396) Reuben has, in a word, projected himself into his son. And what is to be the conclusive deed of "Roger Malvin's Burial"? Reuben, who harbors an accusation of having murdered a "father" and who cannot bring this accusation up to the rational criticism of consciousness, shoots and kills the boy who has come to stand for himself. In killing Cyrus he is destroying the "guilty" side of himself, and hence avenging Roger Malvin's death in an appallingly primitive way. The blood of a "father" rests on the "son," who disburdens himself of it by becoming a father and slaying his son. This is the terrible logic of Hawthorne's tale.

Thus I would maintain, in opposition to the generally held view, that the slaying of Cyrus is not at all the hunting accident it appears to be. It is a sacrificial murder dictated by Reuben's unconscious charge of patricide and by his inability to bring the charge directly against himself. He has become the accusing Roger at the same time that he has projected his own guilty self into Cyrus. These unconscious stratagems are his means of dealing with the contradictory repressed wishes (the desire to atone and the unwillingness to accept blame) that have transformed him into an irritable, moody, and misanthropic man over the course of the years. The killing of Cyrus, by canceling Reuben's imaginary blood-debt, frees his whole mind at last for the task of making peace with God; yet this religious achievement becomes possible, as Hawthorne stresses in the closing sentence, only "in the hour when he had shed blood dearer to him than his own."

There are two main obstacles to the theory that Reuben's shooting his son is intentional. One is that Reuben has no idea that his target is Cyrus instead of a deer; he simply fires at a noise and a motion in the distance. Secondly, there is the possibility that not Reuben but God is responsible for bringing the tale to its catastrophe. The final paragraph, after all, speaks of the lifting of a curse, and Roger Malvin has imposed a religious vow on Reuben to "return to this wild rock, and lay my bones in the grave, and say a prayer over them" (II, 389). Both Roger and Reuben are religious men, and Reuben "trusted that it was Heaven's intent to afford him an opportunity of expiating his sin" (II, 402). Perhaps we are meant to read the story in divine rather than psychological terms.

The answer to this latter point is provided by Hawthorne in a single sentence describing Reuben in the final scene: "Unable to penetrate to the secret place of his soul where his motives lay hidden, he believed that a super-natural voice had called him onward, and that a super-natural power had obstructed his retreat" (II, 401f.). No one who ponders these words can imagine that Hawthorne's famous ambiguity between natural and super-natural causality is really sustained in "Roger Malvin's Burial." As for the other objection, it is certainly true that Reuben shows no conscious awareness that he is firing at his son. But does this make the act wholly unintentional? Before investigating the actual shooting we must see just what Hawthorne means by intention. His theory is evidently somewhat deeper than that of our law courts, which would surely have acquitted Reuben in a trial for murder. "Roger Malvin's Burial" discriminates from the first between surface intentions and buried ones, between outward tokens of generous concern and inward selfishness, between total ignorance and a knowledge that is temporarily unavailable to consciousness. For this last distinction we may point to the statement that Reuben cannot choose to return and bury Roger because he does not know how to find his way back: "his remembrance of every portion of his travel thence was indistinct, and the latter part had left no impression upon his mind" (II, 395). Yet we have just seen that Reuben will be guided by "his motives," residing in a "secret place of his soul." Furthermore, he has always "had a strange impression that, were he to make the trial, he would be led straight to Malvin's bones" (II, 395). We can only conclude that knowledge of the route he took in that traumatic flight from the deserted comrade has been repressed, not lost; when Reuben finally gives himself over

to the guidance of his unconscious he is led infallibly back
to the scene.

In order to see the killing of Cyrus in its true light we
must scrutinize Reuben's prior behavior. Although Cyrus
reminds him again and again that he is taking the family
in a different direction from the announced one, Reuben
keeps resuming his original course after each correction.
His thoughts are obviously dwelling on something other
than the relocation of his home. "His quick and wandering glances were sent forward, apparently in search of
enemies lurking behind the tree trunks; and, seeing nothing there, he would cast his eyes backwards as if in fear
of some pursuer." (II, 399) Reuben would appear to be
projecting his self-accusations into multiple exterior threats
to himself. The internalized Roger Malvin—the Roger
Malvin created by Reuben's unwarranted self-accusation
of murder—is evidently redoubling his demand to be
avenged as the anniversary of his death draws near. When
the fifth day's encampment is made, Dorcas reminds Reuben of the date. " 'The twelfth of May! I should remember
it well,' muttered he, while many thoughts occasioned a
momentary confusion in his mind. 'Where am I? Whither
am I wandering? Where did I leave him?' " (II, 400)
Among those "many thoughts" that have suddenly been
jolted into consciousness are probably the answers to all
three of Reuben's questions. Dorcas has accidentally
brought to the surface, though only for a moment, Reuben's feeling that he is on a deliberate mission.

Is this mission simply to bury Roger's bones? Evidently
something further is involved, for in reply to Dorcas's next
words, praising Reuben for having loyally stayed with
Roger to the end, Reuben pleads, "Pray Heaven, Dorcas,
. . . pray Heaven that neither of us three dies solitary and
lies unburied in this howling wilderness!" (II, 401). And
on this foreboding note he hastens away at once. It seems
to me obvious that Reuben's terribly sincere "prayer" is
a response to his own unconscious urge to commit the

sacrificial killing—an urge that has been screwed to the sticking place by Dorcas's unwitting irony. Like all men in the grip of a destructive obsession, Reuben hopes desperately that his own deep wishes will be thwarted; yet he rushes off in the next moment, and a few minutes later Cyrus will be dead.

We have, then, an abundance of evidence to show that one side of Reuben's nature, the compulsive side, has gained mastery over his conscious intentions. The evidence continues to accumulate as the moment of the shooting draws nearer. Reuben is assaulted by "many strange reflections" (II, 401) that keep him from governing his steps in the supposed hunt for a deer; "and, straying onward rather like a sleep walker than a hunter, it was attributable to no care of his own that his devious course kept him in the vicinity of the encampment" (II, 401). No *conscious* care, that is, for Reuben has a very good compulsive reason for his movements. Cyrus has previously set out on another deer hunt, "promising not to quit *the vicinity of the encampment*" (II, 400; my italics). Surely Hawthorne's repetition of these five words within the space of two pages is meant to strike our attention. Without quite realizing what he is doing, Reuben is stalking his son. His conscious thoughts are straying vaguely over the puzzle of his having reached this spot on this date, and he arrives at a conscious interpretation—explicitly rejected by Hawthorne, as we have already seen—that "it was Heaven's intent to afford him an opportunity of expiating his sin." The consciously accepted "sin" is that of leaving Roger Malvin unburied, but while Reuben busies himself with this lesser anxiety he is going about the business of squaring his deeper unconscious debt. Here is the deed itself:

> From these thoughts he was aroused by a rustling in the forest at some distance from the spot to which he had wandered. Perceiving the motion of some object behind a thick veil of undergrowth, he fired, with the instinct of a

hunter and the aim of a practised marksman. A low moan, which told his success, and by which even animals can express their dying agony, was unheeded by Reuben Bourne. What were the recollections now breaking upon him? (II, 402)

These are brilliantly suggestive lines. Reuben is supposedly deer-hunting, but Hawthorne leaves no implication that Reuben thinks he has spotted a deer; he fires at a "rustling" and a "motion." To say that he does this with a hunter's instinct is slyly ironical, for of course a good hunter does not shoot at ambiguous noises, particularly in "the vicinity of the encampment"! The moan that would tell Reuben of his ironic "success," if he were sufficiently in command of himself to heed it, is said to be one "by which *even* animals can express their dying agony"—a hint that animals have not been his primary target. And finally, the question at the end serves to put the blame for Cyrus's death where it properly belongs. The repressed "recollections" of the original scene are now free to become wholly conscious because the guilt-compulsion that protected them has finally completed its work.

If this argument is correct, the various interpretations of "Roger Malvin's Burial" in terms of religious symbolism must be regarded with suspicion. It is true, for example, that three of the four major characters' names are Biblical, but it is doubtful that this entitles us to say that Reuben achieves "salvation" through Cyrus.[5] Even the Abraham-

5. See W. R. Thompson, "The Biblical Sources of Hawthorne's 'Roger Malvin's Burial,'" *PMLA,* LXXVII (March 1962), 92-6. For a detailed reply to Thompson's article see p. 463 of my earlier version of this chapter in *PMLA,* LXXIX (September 1964), 457-65. The fourth principal name, incidentally, appears to be historical rather than Biblical. Two survivors of Lovewell's (or Lovell's) Fight in the Penobscot War, as Hawthorne knew, were Eleanor and David Melvin. See G. Harrison Orians, "The Source of Hawthorne's 'Roger

Isaac parallel, which seems more prominent than any other, must be taken in an ironic spirit, for Reuben's "sacrifice" of his son is dictated not by God but by self-loathing. The story's ending is heretical, to put it mildly: Reuben's alleged redemption has been achieved through murder, while the guilt from which he has thereby freed himself stemmed from an imaginary crime.[6] The real murder is unrepented yet—indeed, Reuben shows little concern for his dead son—while the fantasy-murder brings forth tears and prayer.[7] The Biblical allusions suggesting a possible redemption serve the purpose of placing in relief the merely pathological nature of the case at hand. For the idea of divine care is cruelly mocked by a plot in which all exhortations to Heaven spring from self-delusion, and in which the "redeemer" performs his redemptive function by unintentionally stopping a musket ball.

The other symbols in Hawthorne's story ought likewise to be considered in relationship to its essential savagery. The most conspicuous symbol is, of course, the oak sapling upon which Reuben places a blood-stained handkerchief, partly as a signal of rescue for Roger and partly to symbolize his own vow to return. When he does return the tree has grown into "luxuriant life," with "an excess of

---

Malvin's Burial,' " *American Literature*, X (November 1938), 313-18, and David S. Lovejoy, "Lovewell's Fight and Hawthorne's 'Roger Malvin's Burial,' " *A Casebook on the Hawthorne Question*, ed. Agnes McNeill Donohue (New York, 1963), pp. 89-92.

6. It is significant that although Reuben consciously thinks that his expiation will consist of burying Roger's bones, the actual release of his guilt-feeling comes about through the killing of Cyrus. There is no mention of burial at the end, yet the "atonement" is indeed complete; it is atonement for the imagined murder of Roger, not for the broken vow to bury him.

7. We can judge the abnormality of Reuben's reaction by contrasting it with that of Dorcas: "With one wild shriek, that seemed to force its way from the sufferer's inmost soul, she sank insensible by the side of her dead boy" (II, 406).

vegetation" on the trunk, but its "very topmost bough
was withered, sapless, and utterly dead" (II, 403). This
branch, which is the one that formerly bore the emblem
of the vow, falls in fragments upon the *tableau vivant* of
the living and dead at the very end. The symbolic meaning is, if anything, too obvious. The sapling is Reuben,
whose innocent young life has been "bent" (he bends the
sapling downward to affix the handkerchief to it) to a
sworn purpose and to a secret self-reproach; Reuben grows
as the tree grows, becoming mature in outward respects
but blasted at the top, in his soul or mind; and when the
withered bough crumbles we are doubtless meant to conclude that the guilt has been canceled and that a possibility now exists for more normal development. I would
call particular attention, however, to the *excessive* vegetation and *luxuriant* lower branches. Luxuriance in Hawthorne almost always has something sick about it, and the
word "excess" speaks for itself. I would surmise that these
aspects of the tree represent the compensatory elements in
Reuben's character, the gradual accretion of defenses
against the tormenting thoughts that he has been fighting
down for years. His peace of mind is partly restored at
the end of the tale, but he will never again be the simple
person we met in the beginning.

Finally, let us consider the symbolic value of the forest
itself. Reuben's initiation into guilt, like Young Goodman
Brown's and Arthur Dimmesdale's, occurs in the forest,
and it is in the forest that he will bring forth what his
guilty feelings have hatched. "He was," as Hawthorne says
of Reuben's desire to seek a new home, "to throw sunlight
into some deep recess of the forest" (II, 396). The forest
is of course his own mind, in which is deeply buried a
secret spot, a trauma, to which he will have to return. He
thinks he does not know the way back, he resists the opportunity to go, but ultimately he is overruled by the strength
of what he has repressed. Self-knowledge is knowledge of
what is almost inaccessibly remote, and Reuben will not

be free until he has reached this point and released what lies imprisoned there. The tale of compulsion is fittingly climaxed in "a region of which savage beasts and savage men were as yet the sole possessors" (II, 399)—the mental region of Hawthorne's best insight and highest art.

V I

Escapism

"The moment a man questions the meaning and value of life, he is sick . . ."　　—FREUD, letter to Marie Bonaparte

Hawthorne's plots, we begin to see, are very much alike in their psychological patterns—perhaps monotonously so. The monotony, however, ought to be blamed as much on our critical method as on Hawthorne's literary effects, which are notoriously ambiguous. Yet I am not quite willing to grant that our stress on sameness has kept the reader from appreciating Hawthorne's ambiguity. What, we may ask, is the source of this quality? Is it simply a matter of Hawthorne's teasing the reader with double explanations and significant omissions? Or does it rather spring from uncertainties of attitude on Hawthorne's part—uncertainties that his conscious tricks of plotting only begin to suggest? The most crucial of his ambiguities, that of moral intention, has escaped most of the critics who assure us that he is ambiguous. They say that he was ambiguous *and* Christian, ambiguous *and* didactic—in other words, that he wasn't very ambiguous at all. Let us take seriously the fact that intelligent readers have arrived at opposite notions of Hawthorne's "message," and ask if this fact cannot be explained in the terms we have previously established.

In this chapter we begin to treat a character-type who embodies the whole problem of Hawthorne's genuine moral ambiguity. This is the idealist who has determined to learn or do something that will set him apart from the

mass of ignorant men. Moral interpretations of Hawthorne's purpose invariably turn upon analysis of this
figure, for he always seems to teach a lesson. Since he
usually comes to a sorry end, and is sometimes explicitly
criticized for his pride and isolation, he is most often interpreted as a cautionary example; in his death or madness
or chagrin we are meant to see that the bonds of common
humanity are not to be severed. Yet Hawthorne sometimes
lends encouragement to an exactly contrary reading. In
his "strong and eager aspiration towards the infinite" (II,
61; the subject is Aylmer of "The Birthmark") the idealist
does succeed in differentiating himself from an ignorant
and timid humanity; and what he learns is sometimes
hinted to be a truth deeper than any that is available to
more "normal" characters. The latter are never granted
profound insights in Hawthorne's fiction, and occasionally
they are shown—by the tormented idealist—to be wilfully
self-deluded about their buried selves. Thus one critic can
plausibly find an ennobling tragic quality in a hero whose
failure is taken by another critic as a negative reminder
that we must love (and resemble) our neighbors.

This contradiction plainly has its source in Hawthorne's
mixed feelings. As an artist whose province was, as his publisher, James T. Fields, observed, "the sharp, penetrating,
pitiless scrutiny of morbid hearts," [1] he was committed to a
cynical brooding about the inner quality of human nature.
As a man who aspired to normal happiness, however, he
was committed to the opposite, a mindless contentment—
an abstention from thought. The chasm between deep
knowledge and normality is unbridgeable in his fiction;
the few "knowers" who become satisfied, such as Holgrave
in *The House of the Seven Gables,* do so by forswearing
their mental powers and surrendering themselves to timid,
conventional brides. This reflects a sense of reality on
Hawthorne's part that can only be termed neurotic: the

1. Quoted by R. H. Pearce, ed., *The Blithedale Romance and
Fanshawe, C,* III, xixn.

truth is so frightening and the process of seeking it so crippling that one had better stay well deceived. The idealist frightens Hawthorne by falling prey to obsessive ideas that are indistinguishable from Hawthorne's own, and for the same reason he has a claim on Hawthorne's sympathy. "Perhaps every man of genius in whatever sphere," Hawthorne admits, "might recognize the image of his own experience in Aylmer's journal" (II, 62)—the record of a monomaniac who is about to give a fatal potion to his wife.

Our position, then, is not that Hawthorne approves *or* disapproves of his driven heroes, but that he is ambiguously involved with them—and that he thereby has an intuitive grasp of their motives. The idealist is invariably an escapist; his quest for truth or power or immortality amounts to regressive flight from the challenges of normal adult life, and the knowledge he acquires or embodies is nothing other than an awareness of his own guilty fantasies. The nature of his inhibition, furthermore, can often be shown to coincide with the pattern we have been examining: figures of detested paternal suppression occupy a mental landscape which fairly pulsates with an unnameable, forbidden longing. As Richard P. Adams says of the early Hawthornian hero, "incest, parricide, and fear of castration" stalk him wherever he chooses to flee.[2] And yet all Hawthorne's irony of characterization cannot prevent him from secretly agreeing with what his escapists discover about the "foul cavern" (II, 455) of the human heart. His plots enact a return of the repressed, and the repressed is the truth. Neurotic terror, for Hawthorne, underlies every placid mental surface, but it reaches consciousness and corrodes sanity only when summoned forth by intolerable conflicts.

These conflicts are perhaps most fully observable in "Young Goodman Brown," a patently symbolic story

2. "Hawthorne's *Provincial Tales*," *New England Quarterly*, XXX (March 1957), 39-57; the quotation is from p. 52.

whose atmosphere and import resemble those of "My Kinsman, Major Molineux." Like Robin's, Brown's ordeal is
useful for us because it is uncomplicated by assertions of
high conscious purpose; the hero simply and "inexpli-
cably" undergoes a dreamlike or dreamed experience that
permanently alters him. Yet he becomes what other and
seemingly nobler Hawthornian escapists become: "a stern,
a sad, a darkly meditative, a distrustful, if not a desperate
man" (II, 106). This fact suggests, but of course does not
prove, that Brown's case offers a psychological paradigm
for the others; and this is just what we shall argue.

It is worth stressing that "Young Goodman Brown,"
which has teased its numerous critics with ambiguous hints
of religious allegory, has a reasonably literal starting-point
for its dream experience. If Brown loses his "faith" in
mankind or salvation, he does so by fleeing from a normal,
loving wife named Faith. These newlyweds are not yet
fully acquainted with each other's minds—and, we can
infer, not yet sure of each other's commitment to marriage.
This is established with some subtlety:

> "Dearest heart," whispered [Faith], softly and rather
> sadly, when her lips were close to his ear, "prithee put off
> your journey until sunrise and sleep in your own bed
> to-night. A lone woman is troubled with such dreams and
> such thoughts that she's afeard of herself sometimes. Pray
> tarry with me this night, dear husband, of all nights in
> the year."
>
> "My love and my Faith," replied young Goodman
> Brown, "of all nights in the year, this one night must I
> tarry away from thee. My journey, as thou callest it, forth
> and back again, must needs be done 'twixt now and sun-
> rise. What, my sweet, pretty wife, dost thou doubt me
> already, and we but three months married?" (II, 89)

Here, as so often in Hawthorne, the two-dimensionality
of the scene, with its stylized reply and its want of overt
motivation, has the effect of guiding and heightening

our psychological expectations. Faith's whispered plea to Brown, "sleep in your own bed," has a distinctly sensual overtone that Brown himself picks up in his mocking question about "doubt"; a causal connection appears to subsist between Brown's mysterious rendezvous with the Devil and his flight from his wife's embraces. The very absoluteness and seeming arbitrariness of his decision to leave makes us look for such a hidden connection. Again, Faith's confessing that "a lone woman is troubled with such dreams and such thoughts that she's afeard of herself sometimes" places the ensuing plot in a suggestive light. Brown, too, will be troubled with a "dream" that will make him afraid of himself and indeed afraid of Faith. Hawthorne is evidently implying that when a newly married pair are separated, each may become subject to unpleasant ideas that under ordinary circumstances are kept in check only by the reassuring presence of the other.

Hawthorne reminds us in various ways that Brown is facing embodiments of his own thoughts in the characters he meets in the forest. The Devil's inducements are spoken "so aptly that his arguments seemed rather to spring up in the bosom of his auditor than to be suggested by himself" (II, 95). The haunted forest is horrible to Brown, "but he was himself the chief horror of the scene . . ." (II, 99), and he races toward the witches' sabbath screaming blasphemies and giving vent to demonic laughter. Hawthorne comments: "The fiend in his own shape is less hideous than when he rages in the breast of man" (II, 100). This makes it clear that the presumptive appearance of devils in the story is meant to refer to Brown's subjective thoughts. No wonder that when he arrives at the sabbath and sees the damned congregation, "he felt a loathful brotherhood [with them] by the sympathy of all that was wicked in his heart" (II, 102). Under these conditions the appearance of Faith in this company can have no bearing on her actual virtue or lack of it; she is there because

Brown's inner *Walpurgisnacht* has reserved a special role for her.[3]

What does the Devil offer Goodman Brown? There is no ambiguity here. Having assembled likenesses of all the figures of authority and holiness in Salem village and treated them as proselytes of hell, the Devil points them out to Brown and his fellow initiates:

> "There," resumed the sable form, "are all whom ye have reverenced from youth. Ye deemed them holier than your-selves, and shrank from your own sin, contrasting it with their lives of righteousness and prayerful aspirations heavenward. Yet here are they all in my worshipping as-sembly. This night it shall be granted you to know their secret deeds: how hoary-bearded elders of the church have whispered wanton words to the young maids of their households; how many a woman, eager for widows' weeds, has given her husband a drink at bedtime and let him sleep his last sleep in her bosom; how beardless youths have made haste to inherit their fathers' wealth; and how fair damsels—blush not, sweet ones—have dug little graves in the garden, and bidden me, the sole guest, to an infant's funeral. By the sympathy of your human hearts for sin ye shall scent out all the places—whether in church, bed-chamber, street, field, or forest—where crime has been committed, and shall exult to behold the whole earth one stain of guilt, one mighty blood spot. Far more than this. It shall be yours to penetrate, in every bosom, the deep

3. Some critics have argued otherwise on the basis of Faith's pink ribbons, whose tangible reality in the forest is taken as evidence that she is "really" there. As David Levin correctly maintains, however, if the Devil is anything more than a fantasy of Brown's he can con-jure pink ribbons as easily as the more visionary part of his spectacle. See "Shadows of Doubt: Specter Evidence in Hawthorne's 'Young Goodman Brown,'" *American Literature,* XXXIV (November 1962), 344-52. Brown shares Othello's fatuous concern for "ocular proof," and the proof that is seized upon is no more substantial in one case than in the other.

mystery of sin, the fountain of all wicked arts, and which
inexhaustibly supplies more evil impulses than human
power—than my power at its utmost—can make manifest
in deeds." (II, 103f.)

Knowledge of sin, then, and most often of sexual sin,
is the prize for which Goodman Brown seems tempted to
barter his soul. In this version of the Faustian pact, the
offered power is unrelated to any practical influence in the
world; what Brown aspires to, if we can take this bargain
as emanating from his own wishes, is an acme of voyeurism, a prurience so effective in its ferreting for scandal that
it can uncover wicked thoughts before they have been
enacted.

Thus Goodman Brown, a curiously preoccupied bridegroom, escapes from his wife's embraces to a vision of general nastiness. The accusation that Brown's Devil makes
against all mankind, and then more pointedly against
Faith, clearly issues from Brown's own horror of adulthood, his inability to accept the place of sexuality in
married love. Brown remains the little boy who has heard
rumors about the polluted pleasures of adults, and who
wants to learn more about them despite or because of the
fact that he finds them disgusting. His forest journey, in
fact, amounts to a vicarious and lurid sexual adventure.
Without insisting on the extraordinary redundancy of
phallic objects in the tale, I shall merely cite the judgment of critics who do not share the bias of this study.
Roy R. Male finds that "almost everything in the forest
scene suggests that the communion of sinners is essentially
sexual . . . ," and Daniel G. Hoffman, after reminding us
that a witches' coven is, *prima facie,* an orgy with the
Devil, finds that "phallic and psychosexual associations are
made intrinsic to the thematic development of [Haw-
thorne's] story. . . . Brown's whole experience is described
as a penetration of a dark and lonely way through a

branched forest . . . At journey's end is the orgiastic communion amid leaping flames." [4]

If Brown's sexual attitude is that of a young boy rather
than a normal bridegroom, we may be permitted to wonder if parental, not wifely, sexuality is not the true object
of his prurience. This supposition is strengthened by the
virtual identity between the Devil's convocation of damned
Salem dignitaries here and the comparable scene in "Alice
Doane's Appeal." In both cases the exposé is of "all whom
ye have reverenced from youth," and in the earlier story
an Oedipal theme is made all but explicit. "Young Goodman Brown" is subtler but not essentially different. The
Devil, the carnal initiator, happens to look exactly like
Brown's grandfather, and he and Brown "might have been
taken for father and son" (II, 91). This Devil, furthermore,
persuades Brown to join the coven by feeding his cynicism
about all his male ancestors—who turn out to have a connection with Hawthorne's own ancestors. After declaring
himself to be as well acquainted with the Browns as any
other Puritan family, the Devil adds, "I helped your grandfather, the constable, when he lashed the Quaker woman
so smartly through the streets of Salem" (II, 92; see pp. 35f.
above). If forefathers are fathers at a slight remove, both
Brown and Hawthorne are leveling circuitously filial
charges of sexual irregularity here. And the charges become more pointed when the witch Goody Cloyse recognizes that the Devil is "in the very image of my old gossip,
Goodman Brown . . ." (II, 94). It is not difficult to see the
sense in which Brown's grandfather is alleged to have
been the "gossip" or confidant of a witch who is met on
the way to an orgy. If Brown must now believe this of
his grandfather, he must also have some doubts about his
father; for his earlier statement, "My father never went
into the woods on such an errand, nor his father before
him" (II, 92), has already been half-refuted.

4. *Hawthorne's Tragic Vision*, p. 78; *Form and Fable in American
Fiction*, pp. 165f.

It would seem, then, that "Young Goodman Brown" offers yet another instance of Hawthorne's practice of denigrating fathers *in absentia*. As usual, too, the missing literal father is replaced by numerous authority-figures who can be regarded as his surrogates. Few pages in the tale lack some accusatory reference to a king, a governor, a minister, a deacon, or an elder of the church. When Brown, in a frenzy of self-induced despair, cries "Come witch, come wizard, come Indian powwow, come devil himself, and here comes Goodman Brown" (II, 99), he has not simply given himself over to hell, but has done so by aligning himself with unscrupulous male authorities—the evil counterparts of "all whom ye have reverenced from youth." Having recognized in his elders the very impulses that filial respect has inhibited in himself, he declares himself free to indulge those impulses without punishment. "You may as well fear him [i.e., himself]," he tells the anti-authorities, "as he fear you" (II, 99).

Brown's fantasy-experience, like that of Robin Molineux, follows the classic Oedipal pattern: resentment of paternal authority is conjoined with ambiguous sexual temptation. In both instances, furthermore, the hero's attitude toward womankind is violently ambivalent. A general slur on women is implied when Brown sees that the forest sinners include virtually all the respectable women he has known, from the Governor's wife and her friends through "wives of honored husbands, and widows, a great multitude, and ancient maidens, all of excellent repute, and fair young girls, who trembled lest their mothers should espy them" (II, 101). The near-universality of this company reminds us of the two critical figures who are missing: Brown's mother and his wife. Yet Faith does arrive, only to disappear at the hideous moment of initiation— as if Brown were not able to stand a final confrontation of his suspicions about her. And he has been led to this moment by reflecting that the woman who taught him his catechism as a boy, Goody Cloyse, is a witch; this is to say that maternal authority is as questionable as paternal authority.[5] Like Ilbrahim, however, Brown finally absolves his mother, but not his father. Just as he is about to join the congregation of sinners, "He could have well-nigh sworn that the shape of his own dead father beckoned him to advance, looking downward from a smoke wreath, while a woman, with dim features of despair, threw out her hand to warn him back. Was it his mother?" (II, 102)

The general pattern of "Young Goodman Brown" is that fathers are degraded to devils and mothers to witches (both attributions, of course, are confirmed in psycho-analysis). Yet the outcome of that pattern, as is always true of Hawthorne's plots, is not simple degradation but a per-petuated ambivalence. Brown lives out a long life with Faith and has children by her, but entertains continual suspicions about her virtue. In retrospect we can say that the source of his uncertainty has been discernible from the beginning—namely, his insistence upon seeing Faith more as an idealized mother than as a wife. She has been his "blessed angel on earth," and he has nurtured a trans-parently filial desire to "cling to her skirts and follow her

5. Brown resembles Robin in allowing his general faith in women to be shaken by his acquaintance with one degenerate woman. In reply to his objection that Faith's heart would be broken by his joining the sabbath, the Devil says, "I would not for twenty old women like the one hobbling before us that Faith should come to any harm" (II, 93). This insinuation that the loved woman is some-how linked to the despised one is picked up by Brown. "What if a wretched old woman do choose to go to the devil when I thought she was going to heaven," he tells himself; "is that any reason why I should quit my dear Faith and go after her?" (II, 96). Like Reuben Bourne's anguished question as to whether he should desert Roger Malvin *because* Roger has been a father to him, this sentence hints at unconscious motivation. Brown is beginning to see Faith under the aspect of the evil-maternal Goody Cloyse; and he puts "a world of meaning" (II, 95) into his astonished reflection that it was she who taught him his catechism.

to heaven" (II, 90). A bridegroom with such notions is well prepared for an appointment with the Devil.

Nothing can be gained from disputing whether Brown's forest experience was real or dreamed, for in either case it serves his private need to make lurid sexual complaints against mankind. Yet the richness of Hawthorne's irony is such that, when Brown turns to a Gulliver-like misanthropy and spends the rest of his days shrinking from wife and neighbors, we cannot quite dismiss his attitude as unfounded. Like Gulliver's, his distinctly pathological abhorrence has come from a deeper initiation into human depravity than his normal townsmen will ever know. Who is to say that they are exempt from the fantasies that have warped him? The only sure point is that by indulging those fantasies Brown *has* become different; at least one case of human foul-heartedness has been amply documented, and for all we know, Salem may be teeming with latent Goodman Browns. In examining his own mind, I imagine, Hawthorne found good reasons for thinking that this might be so.

Exactly parallel to Young Goodman Brown's case is that of the Reverend Hooper in "The Minister's Black Veil"—a story that has provided much doctrinal ammunition for critics who are predisposed to see Hawthorne's ideal as a mild-mannered bachelor in clerical garb. If Hooper is not, as some maintain, "a preacher who preaches on behalf of the author," neither is he a perfect Antichrist in his pride and despair.[6] Both interpretations ignore Hawthorne's evasiveness about ultimate truth and his meticulous concern with ironies of motivation. As in Brown's case, what we learn about secret sin from Hooper is only what Hooper *becomes,* not what he believes. He is a pathetically self-deluded idealist who, goaded into monomania by a cer-

6. See Levin, *The Power of Blackness,* p. 42, and William Bysshe Stein, "The Parable of the Antichrist in 'The Minister's Black Veil,' " *American Literature,* XXVII (November 1955), 386-92.

tain incompleteness in his nature, ends by becoming the one obvious exemplar of the vice he rightly or wrongly attributes to everyone else.[7]

Perhaps the best way to see the parallelism between Hooper's case and Goodman Brown's is to remind ourselves of the religious consequences of the two revulsions against mankind. We are not likely to call Brown a religious sage, yet his attitudes are no less "holy" than Hooper's. Why should we lend a transcendent aura to Hooper's gloom while regarding Brown's, quite rightly, as pathological? The fact is that Brown's mania takes the form of a super-piety scarcely distinguishable from Hooper's:

> On the Sabbath day, when the congregation were singing a holy psalm, he could not listen because an anthem of sin rushed loudly upon his ear and drowned all the blessed strain. When the minister spoke from the pulpit with power and fervid eloquence, and, with his hand on the open Bible, of the sacred truths of our religion, and of saint-like lives and triumphant deaths, and of future bliss or misery unutterable, then did Goodman Brown turn pale, dreading lest the roof should thunder down upon the gray blasphemer and his hearers. (II, 106)

It is fairly clear that the "anthem of sin" assaulting Brown's ears is a projection of his own half-repressed fantasies. Yet in taking a radical view of man's sinfulness Brown is being an orthodox Calvinist; as several critics have noted, one of the beauties of "Young Goodman Brown" is that the Devil's role is to persuade the hero to take his religion seriously. We might therefore say that the tale is psychologically if not theologically anti-Puritan. But if this is so, it follows that we are under no obligation

7. Of all readings of the tale, that of E. Earle Stibitz does best justice to this quintessentially Hawthornian situation. See "Ironic Unity in Hawthorne's 'The Minister's Black Veil,'" *American Literature*, XXXIV (May 1962), 182-90.

to admire the same radical pessimism in Hooper simply because Hooper is a Puritan minister.

In one sense Hooper's "eccentricity" (I, 52n.) appears to be without direct motive. Like other Hawthornian monomaniacs, he points to a mysterious external necessity when asked to explain his behavior, and we are permitted no glimpse of his mind before he dons the veil. Yet Hawthorne's visual presentation of him is a distinct sketch of a familiar character-type. The minister is "a gentlemanly person, of about thirty, though still a bachelor ... dressed with due clerical neatness, as if a careful wife had starched his band, and brushed the weekly dust from his Sunday garb" (I, 53). From these few words we would expect Hooper to display a fastidiousness in his personal relations as well as in his dress. And indeed, the note of tidy womanliness here runs through the tale in a faint, suggestive undercurrent, particularly in the continual mention of the veil. As one parishioner remarks with unconscious acuteness, "How strange ... that a simple black veil, *such as any woman might wear on her bonnet,* should become such a terrible thing on Mr. Hooper's face!" (I, 56f.; my italics).

Such innuendoes become significant when we learn that Hooper is engaged to be married. His consummately normal fiancée, Elizabeth, cannot persuade him to remove the veil, with the predictable result that the marriage is called off. Hooper's reaction to Elizabeth's farewell is to smile, despite his grief, at the thought that "only a material emblem had separated him from happiness, though the horrors, which it shadowed forth, must be drawn darkly between the fondest of lovers" (I, 63f.). This smile, which recurs so often that it acquires a quality of daffy abstractedness, is Hooper's substitute for considering Elizabeth's reasonable plea. It could be plausibly argued, I think, that Hooper has donned the veil in order to prevent his marriage. On the one hand we see that he is already quite prim enough without a woman in the house, and on the other we find that he broods over dark, unspecified horrors that must separate the fondest of lovers. Where have these horrors come from, if not from his own imagination? It is possible that Hooper, who like Goodman Brown is obliged to confront the sexual aspects of womanhood, shares Brown's fears and has hit upon a means of forestalling their realization in marriage. His literal wearing of a veil, like Brown's figurative removal of it to leer at the horrid sexuality underneath, acts as a defense against normal adult love. No wonder that the topic of his first "veiled" sermon is "secret sin, and those sad mysteries which we hide from our nearest and dearest, *and would fain conceal from our own consciousness . . ."* (I, 55; my italics).

Now, I do not care to lay very much stress on the indications of sexual squeamishness in Hooper. They are there, but they command much less attention than the comparable elements in "Young Goodman Brown." But the very ambiguity in Hooper's motivation enables Hawthorne to offer us glimpses into the minds of the people who must form their own theories about their minister. This is true, for example, at the funeral of the young lady with whom Hooper seems to have had some connection, if only in his thoughts. Poe and others have made much of Hooper's uneasiness in the presence of the corpse, and have intimated that Hooper, like his later counterpart Dimmesdale, must have been tempted into sexual indulgence at least once in his career. Yet the hints of an explicit liaison are supplied by the highly suggestible bystanders to the scene. It is "a superstitious old woman" (I, 58) who thinks that the corpse has shuddered at Hooper's aspect, and it is "a fancy" (I, 58) of two parishioners that Hooper and the girl's spirit are marching hand in hand in the procession. That the fancy is shared is no sign of its truth. Simply, Hawthorne is exposing a preoccupation in the collective mind of the town.

This preoccupation might be said to be the chief object of Hawthorne's scrutiny in "The Minister's Black Veil."

From the beginning he is concerned with the telltale re-
sponses that Hooper's "ambiguity of sin or sorrow" (I, 65)
elicits from his fellow men. In the sermon on buried sin
"each member of the congregation, the most innocent girl,
and the man of hardened breast, felt as if the preacher had
crept upon them, behind his awful veil, and discovered
their hoarded iniquity of deed or thought" (I, 55). By joining young virgins with old sinners Hawthorne is placing
his customary emphasis on the universality of human
nature; no one is completely free from the urges that are
gratified by only a few. Hooper's parishioners would prefer
not to acknowledge these urges of which he has become
a visible reminder. They begin slighting him,[8] making fun
of him, fleeing his presence, calling him insane, and invent-
ing sexual rumors about him that will cancel the relevance
of the veil to their own latent thoughts. Of all the busy-
bodies in the town, including a special delegation whose
task is to uncover the mystery, no one is able to face Hooper
directly—and even Elizabeth shows herself susceptible to
the "whispers" (I, 62) of an obviously sexual scandal. When
she too is suddenly terrified by a hidden meaning in the
veil, Hawthorne has capped his demonstration of general
malaise, for Elizabeth possesses a steady, cleansing love that
seems unique in the town. Hooper is doubtless the supreme
example of isolation "in that saddest of all prisons, his own
heart" (I, 67), but his difference from the others is only a
matter of degree.

Thus the world of "The Minister's Black Veil" is one
in which a man can reasonably be "afraid to be alone with
himself" (I, 57). The real struggle in the tale is not between
Hooper and the others but between conscious and unconscious thoughts within each individual. Total repression is

8. A particularly interesting early example is Old Squire Saunders's
forgetting to invite Hooper to dinner after the Sunday service—a slip
that is said to occur "doubtless by an accidental lapse of memory"
(I, 56). It is clear that Hawthorne's interest in such "accidents" was
parallel to Freud's in *The Psychopathology of Everyday Life.*

restored in everyone but Hooper, and in his case, as in Goodman Brown's, the truth is permitted utterance only in the form of symbolism and accusation. Hooper has a sympathy with "all dark affections" (I, 65), but he lacks the courage to confess their hold upon his own imagination. He too is one of those who are frightened by the veil, and understandably so, for he has had clear intimations of what the force of civilization must contend with in its effort to remain the master. Hawthorne leaves us with the Swiftian idea that a little self-knowledge is worse than none, and that the best approximation to happiness rests in an ignorant, busy involvement with a society of unconscious hypocrites.

In proceeding from sexual fear to obsession and misanthropy, Brown and Hooper may stand for Hawthorne's escapists generally. Sometimes, as with Ethan Brand, the hint of twisted sexuality is offered almost as an irrelevant afterthought; we learn in passing that in his search for the Unpardonable Sin, which is of course finally located in his own breast, Brand has taken an innocent girl and made her "the subject of a psychological experiment, and wasted, absorbed, and perhaps annihilated her soul, in the process" (III, 489). More often, as in "Egotism; or, The Bosom Serpent," "The Birthmark," "The Artist of the Beautiful," and "The Man of Adamant," the hero is facing a matrimonial challenge like Brown's or Hooper's. Either he is evading marriage, or he has been discarded for a better lover, or he is a strangely uneasy newlywed, or his wife is simply temporarily absent. However sketchy the connection between the hero's lovelessness and his zealous project or phobia, that connection is always indicated.[9]

9. As Harry Levin remarks, Hawthorne's tales are "rife with matrimonial fears" (*The Power of Blackness*, p. 58). Levin alludes to "Mrs. Bullfrog," "The Wedding Knell," "The Shaker Bridal," "Edward Fane's Rosebud," "The Wives of the Dead," and "The White Old Maid"—a modest beginning for an inventory of the relevant works.

In all these tales it is possible, indeed traditional, to ignore the sometimes obscure hints of regressive motivation and emphasize the hero's moral achievement or failure. Cumulatively, however, the examples of sexually odd escapists amount to a virtual demonstration that Hawthorne regarded fear of normal adulthood as the *primum mobile* of all alienation, whether that alienation results in scientific study, art, or simply derangement. It is also noteworthy that the authorial moralizing in these tales is never translated into action. Hawthorne can say, for example, that Aylmer in "The Birthmark" would have done better to "find the perfect future in the present" (II, 69) than to kill his wife; but everything that precedes this final sentiment reduces it to impertinence. On the first page of the story we are warned that Aylmer's marital love could prevail only by "intertwining itself with his love of science" (II, 47), and such intertwining always points to unconscious compulsion. Hawthorne has written a tale of psychological necessity, not of moral error.[10] Similarly, Ethan Brand can interrupt his progress toward self-destruction long enough to draw a moral from his "sin of an intellect that triumphed over the sense of brotherhood with man and reverence for God" (III, 485); yet this awareness does not alter his behavior in the slightest degree. He is a passive, even a sardonically amused, spectator of his own damnation. If we ask why this must be so, the only available answer is that moral understanding does not reach low enough into the region where the hero receives his incontrovertible commands.

Our argument, however, is not that Hawthorne ingeniously constructed traps for the unwary, moralistic reader; in all likelihood he was as anxious as anyone to view his heroes superficially. Our argument is that he *represented* their motives, whether or not he meant to. And in this spirit we may remark that his tales of sexual embarrass-

10. For evidence, see p. 126 below.

ment are full of sexual symbolism. It is hard to decide whether he would have been appalled or amused at recognizing this feature of his art, but its prominence in the tales of escapism corroborates our view that sexual obsession is a governing force in those tales. The example of Young Goodman Brown is typical: flight from the marriage-bed is rendered in terms of symbolic decor whose phallic quality is apparent to most modern readers. Brown's talisman, the writhing serpent-staff he borrows from the Devil, calls to mind the bosom serpent of Roderick Elliston. The latter is invited by Elliston's "diseased self-contemplation" (II, 319) in his wife's absence, and it disappears magically at her return—a pattern that might well be characterized as masturbatory. Again, Ethan Brand, having scientifically abused an innocent girl, ends by leaping into a lime-kiln whose door "resembled nothing so much as the private entrance to the infernal regions" (III, 478). Hawthorne is paraphrasing Bunyan, but the lurid atmosphere of the tale encourages us to see a genital reference in the image.[11] And something similar may be said of the Reverend Hooper's mouth: by feeling a need to veil it he imparts a vaguely repulsive horror to it—one that is altogether in keeping with his effeminate nature.[12] Hawthorne's fastidious idealists always flee from the modest sexual demands of actuality into a world of symbolism in which sex has usurped or "intertwined" itself with every other concern.

I grant that in some cases the context is insufficiently erotic for us to insist on these readings. If we interpret "Ethan Brand" in sexual terms, it can only be by frankly applying the fallacy of analogy with similar tales. And yet

11. For a recurrence of the identical phrase in a less ambiguous context of sexual ambivalence, see the passage from "Rappaccini's Daughter" quoted on p. 118 below.

12. A more distinctly genital veiled mouth is very much at issue in *The Blithedale Romance;* see pp. 208f. below.

the analogy is a powerful one: the stamp of a single obsessed imagination lies upon all Hawthorne's stories of escapism. Roughly the same imagery and atmosphere, the same absence or absurdity of conscious motive, the same ambiguity as to whether the hero's idea of human depravity applies to others as well as to himself, the same immunity of his compulsion to moral influence, occur in every tale. Given this sameness, it seems permissible to use the obviously regressive cases as explanatory of the less obvious ones.

Hence the usefulness of the most grotesque and openly pathological of all Hawthorne's escapists, Richard Digby in "The Man of Adamant." Like his counterparts elsewhere, Digby is upset by the general wickedness of mankind, and more especially by a normal woman who offers him a prospect of married love. To escape her he sails across the ocean and searches out a special refuge—a dark cave with "so dense a veil of tangled foliage about it, that none but a sworn lover of gloomy recesses would have discovered the low arch of its entrance, or have dared to step within its vaulted chamber, where the burning eyes of a panther might encounter him" (III, 566). From this dubious bastion of purity, whose details suggest something less abstract and less exalted than communion with God, the hero delivers insults to his persistent admirer. " 'Off!' cried he. 'I am sanctified, and thou art sinful' " (III, 569). When he eventually dies, calcified by the atmosphere of his refuge, he and the cave together become more urgently symbolic than before. The mouth of the cave-sepulchre is gradually concealed by darksome pines and a further "thick veil of creeping plants" (III, 572). Over a century after Digby's death, some playful children pull aside this veil, find the petrified corpse, and race homeward "without a second glance into the gloomy recess" (III, 572). Their father is braver, yet his reaction is strangely irrational: "the moment that he recovered from the fascination of his first gaze, [he] began to heap stones into the mouth of the cavern" (III, 573). And though hardly anyone will admit to believing that the cave exists at all, "grown people avoid the spot, nor do children play there" (III, 573). "Friend-ship, and Love, and Piety," Hawthorne adds with em-phasis, "all human and celestial sympathies, should keep aloof from that hidden cave" (III, 573).

Here sexual symbolism has wrenched itself away from moral or allegorical meaning. Though Digby is a Puritan fanatic and his rejected lady a type of true religion, their theological contest is outlasted by the genital obsession that underlies it; Digby's fear is so compelling and contagious that it appalls a new generation of anxious mortals. No reading in realistic or religious terms can account for Haw-thorne's admonition that Friendship and Love and Piety should keep aloof from the cave. This tale offers an ex-treme version of the pattern we have found in others: the hero *becomes an image of what he loathes,* and his fellow men try to erase this image from their minds.

Let us understand the full implication of Hawthorne's advice to shun Digby's cave. "True religion" is not in-volved; it is simply a question of maintaining a happy ignorance of real psychic terrors. Hawthorne's counsel is not to refute or reject the monomaniac ideas that rule his plots, but to avoid them—not to light a candle in the dark, but to heap stones into the cave's mouth. This attitude, which we may call both heterodox and neurotic, will prove to be his greatest liability as an artist. Secretly entertain-ing the worst fantasies that drive his heroes to escapism, Hawthorne will begin to lose the courage necessary for creating such heroes. His entire plots, rather than merely his protagonists, will flee from themes that become more inescapable in symbolism as they become more intolerable to conscious thought. The result will be, not an ambiguous and energized study of obsession, but ingenious hypocrisy and aesthetic confusion. Before this phase of shadow-box-ing is reached, however, Hawthorne remains capable of great psychological fiction. It is no coincidence that, as the next two chapters will show, the ironic figure of the sexual escapist stands at the center of one of his richest tales and his indisputably best romance.

V I I

Giovanni's Garden

"La femme est *naturelle,* c'est-à-dire abominable."
—BAUDELAIRE

"Rappaccini's Daughter" is the rock on which theories about Hawthorne's high moral purpose regularly founder. Few of his tales invite a sweeping, transcendent interpretation more tantalizingly. Hawthorne says at the outset that he is a writer of allegories, and his plot, focused on a diabolical scientist and the courtship of his spiritually pure but chemically toxic daughter, contains absurdities that cry out for some non-literal rationale. Criticism has supplied many such rationales but has rarely been able to deal meaningfully with the story's main inconsistency. The shallow young hero, Giovanni Guasconti, is explicitly criticized for regarding Beatrice Rappaccini as monstrous, but as a potential bride she *is* monstrous. While Hawthorne takes pains to impugn the accuracy of Giovanni's observation when he is verifying her poisonousness, Giovanni turns out to have been strictly correct. Beatrice herself seems only intermittently aware of her toxic properties, and we can hardly avoid sharing some of Giovanni's eventual exasperation with her. Yet this insecticide maiden is said to be angelic perfection in fleshly form. Hawthorne's plot, in short, encourages suspicions which his explicit moralizing condemns as narrowly materialistic—a state of affairs which we are by now equipped to see as far from atypical.

The most favored reading of the tale, and one that finds

much apparent support in Hawthorne's imagery, is religious: by adopting the skepticism of Rappaccini's rival,
Baglioni, Giovanni renders himself unworthy of the Christian redemption embodied in Beatrice.[1] Such an interpretation, while lending importance to a plot whose contrivances are hard to take seriously, makes the disproportion
between vehicle and meaning especially embarrassing. The
redemption that Giovanni is said to forgo is conveyed by
a prospective marriage of two chemical freaks; to find this
symbol very appealing the reader must be inordinately
fond of religious paradoxes.

If we provisionally resist the urge to allegorize and simply consider the hero's literal situation, a more workable
interpretation suggests itself. The conflict of feelings that
Beatrice arouses in Giovanni is already familiar to us from
other tales:

> It was not love, although her rich beauty was a madness
> to him; nor horror, even while he fancied her spirit to
> be imbued with the same baneful essence that seemed to
> pervade her physical frame; but a wild offspring of both
> love and horror that had each parent in it, and burned like
> one and shivered like the other. Giovanni knew not what
> to dread; still less did he know what to hope; yet hope
> and dread kept a continual warfare in his breast, alter
> nately vanquishing one another and starting up afresh to
> renew the contest. Blessed are all simple emotions, be they
> dark or bright! It is the lurid intermixture of the two that
> produces the illuminating blaze of the infernal regions.
> (II, 123)

These are the mixed emotions whose source in other
Hawthornian heroes is sexual; and Giovanni resembles
those heroes in his inexperience, his immaturity, and his

1. This argument is most fully developed by Male, *Hawthorne's
Tragic Vision*, pp. 54-70. See also Fogle, *Hawthorne's Fiction*, pp.
91-103, and Waggoner, *Hawthorne*, pp. 111-24.

situation of erotic challenge. If Beatrice's "poisonousness" accounts for his characteristically ambivalent reaction, then that poisonousness may stand for her sexuality as it affects his contrary impulses. Hope and dread wage continual warfare in Giovanni's breast because he fears exactly what he desires. His sexual ambition triggers his fits of revulsion, for the closer he comes to Beatrice, the more he is appalled by her implied sexual power.[2]

The equation of poison with sexuality differs from more thoroughgoing allegorical theories in that it preserves the literal plot nearly intact and accounts for its seeming excesses. We need not even suppose that Beatrice's poisonousness is "really" sexuality; it suffices that both Giovanni and Beatrice herself act as if it were. The strange inconsistencies in Beatrice's behavior as well as in Giovanni's can be explained if we see that both characters, caught as they are in the first mature love affair of their lives and betrayed by their ignorance of each other's nature, use Beatrice's poisonousness as a kind of *double entendre* for what they cannot discuss or even contemplate without fear.

This theory helps to account for Beatrice's puzzling attitude toward her own toxic properties. She can confess to Giovanni in one breath, "I, it is true, am the horrible thing thou namest me," but can swear indignantly in almost the next that "it was not I" (II, 144) who poisoned him; all the blame is Rappaccini's. This self-justification appears to rest on the scarcely believable fact that Beatrice, despite her knowledge of her deadliness to other creatures and her fears for Giovanni's safety in the garden,[3] has

2. This approach is anticipated by Richard B. Hovey, "Love and Hate in 'Rappaccini's Daughter,' " *University of Kansas City Review,* XXIX (Winter 1962), 137-45. The present chapter draws on different evidence and raises further questions, but it is meant to substantiate Hovey's position.

3. At one point, in fact, she warns Giovanni away from her favorite plant because to touch it would be "fatal" (II, 132). Yet she has

never once considered that he might be taking contagion
from her. Beatrice's ignorance becomes less remarkable,
however, if we see that it refers primarily to her unawareness of her power of enticement. Though she has "instilled
a fierce and subtle poison into his system" (II, 123)—meaning, in this passage, Giovanni's mixture of emotions—she
has done so unwittingly. What she is really disavowing is
that she has deliberately exploited her attractiveness, which
has been enhanced by the mysterious aura of danger attaching to her poisonousness. That Beatrice, regardless of all
the evidence, has refused to imagine the possibility of her
infecting Giovanni until he accuses her point-blank, indicates that "poisonousness" is charged with an especially
unpleasant meaning for her with regard to Giovanni. Her
innocence consists in an almost willful ignorance of her
sexual power, and this ignorance is the foundation of her
claim to spiritual purity.

The sexual quality of Beatrice's allure has been obvious even to critics who minimize its importance. She is
repeatedly described in terms of richness, luxuriousness,
and dark gorgeousness, and her voluptuous beauty sets off
the wildest fantasies in the impressionable Giovanni. Significantly, these fantasies are linked to her poisonousness.
Again and again in the story, Giovanni's thoughts about
poison are appropriate to sexual fear, and it is noteworthy
that when he has forgotten Beatrice's poisonousness he has
also forgotten her womanly maturity. For Giovanni she
must be either childlike and innocent or poisonous and
guilty; while these are crude and unbalanced alternatives,
the important point is that they are the only ones available
to Giovanni's imagination. This narrowness in him—it is
shared, of course, in less metaphorical terms by Hawthorne's other escapists—can be explained only if we suppose that for him sexual maturity and fatal toxic power

_____

plucked a lethal blossom from it herself and worn it nonchalantly
in her bosom (II, 120).

are equally repugnant and indeed identical. The equation works, in fact, both ways: whenever Giovanni makes semi-intentional amatory advances, what literally checks him is fear of poison. Thus, for example, he yearns to touch Beatrice's hair, but "on the few occasions when Giovanni had seemed tempted to overstep the limit, Beatrice grew so sad, so stern, and withal wore such a look of desolate separation, shuddering at itself, that not a spoken word was requisite to repel him. At such times he was startled at the horrible suspicions that rose, monster-like, out of the caverns of his heart . . ." (II, 134). Here the association of "overstepping" the bounds of chaste courtship with the confronting of Beatrice's poisonousness is so patent that the effect verges on comedy.

The focus of symbolic meaning in "Rappaccini's Daughter" remains largely on the garden itself, which is not only the setting for most of the action but also a kind of moralized landscape reflecting the characters' moods and obsessions. It is noteworthy, therefore, that the garden has strong sexual connotations. Beatrice's ignorance of her own passionate nature is intricately suggested in her association with, yet repugnance for, the poisonous flowers of the garden. Several of these flowers, says Hawthorne, "would have shocked a delicate instinct" by their "commixture, and, as it were, adultery, of various vegetable species" (II, 128). Such an adultery is "the monstrous offspring of man's depraved fancy" (II, 128). The gorgeousness of these flowers "seemed fierce, passionate, and even unnatural" (II, 128) to Giovanni, and Beatrice herself confesses that they "shock and offend me when they meet my eye" (II, 129). These are strangely prudish reactions to literal flowers, however outlandish in form. One might almost accuse Giovanni and Beatrice of having read up on Freudian flower symbolism.

It is, however, precisely Beatrice's insensitivity to the flowers' relevance to her own physical nature that saves her imagination from "impurity." She does not see the ingredient of passion in her extraordinary relationship with the most poisonous shrub in the garden. "Yes, my sister, my splendor," she says to this purple plant, "it shall be Beatrice's task to nurse and serve thee; and thou shalt reward her with thy kisses and perfumed breath, which to her is as the breath of life" (II, 114). The "sisterly" quality of this affection seems questionable, and becomes more so a few pages later: "Approaching the shrub, she threw open her arms, as with a passionate ardor, and drew its branches into an intimate embrace—so intimate that her features were hidden in its leafy bosom and her glistening ringlets all intermingled with the flowers" (II, 119). We can hardly blame Giovanni if, in watching such behavior, he fearfully imagines himself in the place of the erotically smothered branches, particularly since Beatrice herself realizes that her love for him is *replacing* her love for the deadly shrub (II, 131).

That Giovanni is appalled as well as fascinated by such implications is literally plausible, but it is also symbolically pertinent to his inexperience as a lover. Hawthorne shows him to be infatuated with his own "remarkable beauty of person" (II, 109) and naïvely anxious to test out his seductiveness. His "shallowness of feeling and insincerity of character" (II, 140) demand a love-object that will merely flatter his vanity, not make sexual demands of its own. Every hint of Beatrice's complete womanliness is thus a blow to his narcissism. But beyond this, Giovanni displays an abject terror before the whole phenomenon of female sexuality. Both he and Beatrice want to perpetuate a relationship "as unreserved as if they had been playmates from early infancy—as if they were such playmates still" (II, 133f.). Beatrice, like Desdemona, has never thought of love in any other terms, but Giovanni—who will show the unjust rage of an Othello before the tale is over—has not passed his boyhood in an enclosed garden and must cope with the very reasonable suspicion that such pastoral innocence is implausible. The important thing, however, is that he does insist upon this innocence. Without recourse to analogous cases we can say that the homesick and virginal Giovanni really wants to find a surrogate mother or sister in Beatrice, for he cannot recognize her sexuality without at once degrading her spitefully to the level of a scheming prostitute.

Thus Giovanni's lurid intermixture of feelings springs not only from an ambivalence between childishness and womanliness in Beatrice, but from his own combination of fear and prurient interest with regard to her sexuality. To match his revulsion there is a nearly equal quantity of ambition to win the prize. "The instant that he was aware of the possibility of approaching Beatrice, it seemed an absolute necessity of his existence to do so" (II, 126). Hawthorne indulges in a series of blatant innuendoes to ensure that we see the nature of this necessity. The smirking crone Lisabetta, who has been interpreted in a divine light because she says such things as "For the love of Heaven, then, put your head out of the window" (II, 109f.), actually functions as a pander. She reveals to Giovanni that "there is a private entrance into the garden!" (II, 126), "where you may see all [Rappaccini's] fine shrubbery" (II, 126). That Lisabetta is not referring to a passion for botany is clinched by her next sentence: "Many a young man in Padua would give gold to be admitted among those flowers" (II, 126). Whereupon Giovanni, not to be outdone by all the other potential horticulturists, places money in Lisabetta's hand, musters his courage, and declares: "Show me the way" (II, 126). Again, we need not resort to Freudian dream-equivalences for flowers and gardens to see the sexual joke. When Giovanni is eventually led "along several obscure passages" and emerges into the garden, "forcing himself through the entanglement of a shrub that wreathed its tendrils over the hidden entrance" (II, 127), the effect, as in "The Man of Adamant," is virtually pornographic.

This is not to say, of course, that the symbolism of intercourse corresponds to a comparable deed, or even comparable knowledge, on Giovanni's part. Once within the garden he continues to act with his previous mixture of fearful curiosity and revulsion, and the remainder of the plot is borne along on these consequences of sexual ignorance. Insofar as Giovanni's admission to the "unnatural" and "artificial" flowers might register a sexual experience, that experience has taken place in fantasy only. Giovanni is well advised to step gingerly in the garden, for its unwholesomeness is just the quality of his own thoughts, and its threats to life will be matched by his own destructiveness later on. As Beatrice says in her dying words, there has been more poison in his nature than in hers from the beginning (II, 147).

It is generally true that the seemingly fortuitous circumstances of Giovanni's outward experience have a deep symbolic relevance to his character. What Beatrice, Baglioni, Lisabetta, and Rappaccini advise him to do is essentially what his own conflicting impulses of trusting love, cynical rejection, lewdness, and morbid curiosity are urging upon him. This, I think, is the source of our sense of unity in "Rappaccini's Daughter," for we see the world of this tale through the medium of Giovanni's imagination, not his eyesight. The essential action consists in the forming and resolving of his attitudes, and the personages he meets are conveniently representative of the alternatives he has proposed to himself. And thus we seem justified in calling the tale a psychological allegory. None of the action is wholly fortuitous because none of it is wholly external to the hero's private thoughts.

Recent critics have accepted this principle insofar as it applies to Baglioni, who has the Iago-like function of playing on Giovanni's lurking cynicism about the innocence of womankind. Lisabetta's equally obvious role has been slighted, perhaps because it is difficult to harmonize with a purely religious interpretation of the story. But much more important than either of these is the figure of Rappaccini, whose weird creations evidently find some echo in Giovanni's soul. No one, I believe, has attempted to define this hidden kinship. Rappaccini is always taken as an embodiment of the *libido sciendi,* a cold investigator whose nature is opposite to his daughter's—and nothing more is said. The antithesis of head and heart is so commonplace in Hawthorne criticism that the mere labeling of one character as "intellectual" and another as "sympathetic" is presumed to exhaust the subject.

It will not do to reduce "Rappaccini's Daughter" to a moral scheme resting on these excessively broad categories. Both Baglioni and Rappaccini, who are enemies in the story, would have to represent the intellect, albeit with different emphases, and the triumph of one kind of intellect over another in the administration of Baglioni's fatal antidote to Beatrice would not provide much of a "moral." Nor can we regard Rappaccini and Giovanni as neatly antithetical exemplars of two kinds of error, one springing from unchecked intellectualism and the other from unchecked emotionalism. Giovanni's emotions are anything but unchecked; at every moment they are suffering inhibition from half-submerged doubts and reservations. Even his lust contains an element of calculation. Giovanni himself wonders whether his interest in Beatrice is not "merely the fantasy of a young man's brain, only slightly or not at all connected with his heart" (II, 127). This alone might suggest that Rappaccini's flowers, which have sprung from an isolated brain and which provide the tangible basis for Giovanni's meanest suspicions of Beatrice, illustrate a quality that Giovanni and Rappaccini have in common.

Though Rappaccini has little to say, it is clear that he belongs in the gallery of Hawthorne's monomaniac investigators that includes Roger Chillingworth and Aylmer of "The Birthmark." In both these latter characters the motive force behind the fiendish passion for knowledge is sketched in for us: it is the thwarting of sexual feeling. Chillingworth's medical lore is pursued with spitefulness toward mankind only after he has failed as a husband to Hester. The true meaning of his researches is expressed in his sadistic tormenting of Dimmesdale, who cuckolded him; and *The Scarlet Letter* is full of insinuations that this relationship of investigator to investigated, of tormentor to tormented, is a kind of mock-marriage, a substitute for more normal sexual feeling in both parties. Similarly, Aylmer's desire to remove his bride's one flaw stems from revulsion against her sexuality.[4] He confesses that Georgiana's crimson birthmark "shocks" him, whereupon she cries, "You cannot love what shocks you!" (II, 48). But Aylmer, true to Hawthornian form, *can* desire the very thing that offends his squeamish mind, and his dream of plunging his knife into the birthmark until it reaches Georgiana's heart reveals a fantasy of sadistic revenge and a scarcely less obvious fantasy of sexual consummation.[5] His "medical" curiosity and his willingness to risk Georgiana's death to remove a harmless blemish are thinly disguised substitutes for his urges to *know* and *destroy* her sexuality. Before the operation is over Aylmer will have both kissed and shuddered at the suggestive birthmark, and his "scientific" murder will be concluded "in almost irrepressible ecstasy" (II, 68). The *libido sciendi,* in a word, appears to have a good deal of libido in it.

The matter at hand is whether Rappaccini is treated as Chillingworth and Aylmer are. There is, of course, no Signora Rappaccini to match Hester and Georgiana in providing an impetus to morbid experimentation, but Rappaccini does resemble his slightly mad colleagues in being allegedly willing to "sacrifice human life, . . . or what-

4. The point is made by Simon O. Lesser, *Fiction and the Unconscious,* pp. 87-90.

5. Lest we doubt the dream's significance for Aylmer's intentions toward his wife, Hawthorne adds: "Truth often finds its way to the mind close muffled in robes of sleep, and then speaks with uncompromising directness of matters in regard to which we practise an unconscious self-deception during our waking moments" (II, 52).

ever else was dearest to him, for the sake of adding so much as a grain of mustard seed to the great heap of his accumulated knowledge" (II, 116). The mutually exclusive alternatives of "pure science" and a sympathetic, normal regard for mankind are clearly present in the story, and for Hawthorne this sympathy always entails a sexual normality. We may, indeed, attach some significance to the fact that nothing whatever is said about Rappaccini's supposed former marriage. The symbolic world of the garden, tended by the pure Beatrice but laden with perverse connotations, makes up the entire realm of his affections, so that it stands as a kind of surrogate for a healthier range of feeling. And Rappaccini's mixture of attitudes toward the suggestive flowers must inevitably remind us of Giovanni's own ambivalence. On the one hand Rappaccini shows deep interest, "looking into their inmost nature" (II, 112), but on the other hand "there was no approach to intimacy between himself and these vegetable existences" (II, 112). His demeanor is that of a man "walking among malignant influences, such as savage beasts, or deadly snakes, or evil spirits, which, should he allow them one moment of license, would wreak upon him some terrible fatality" (II, 112).

This desperate self-control in defense against forces which fascinate Rappaccini and which he has himself released inevitably suggests a perverse revulsion from sexuality. His weird marital plan for Beatrice and Giovanni, which envisions the coupling of two mutually immune monsters, points to the monstrosity of his own imagination. Like Aylmer's potion, this proposed marriage appears to be at once a product of sexual disgust and a clumsy remedy for it. Indeed, regardless of his surmised feelings it is certain that Rappaccini has already had the effect of foreclosing any possibility of normal erotic life for his daughter. In terms of the world beyond his walls Rappaccini has made Beatrice untouchable; she is now available only for Gothic "experimentation" conducted at home under the auspices of the "disinterested scientist." [6]

This, then, is why Rappaccini's garden is also Giovanni's garden: for both characters it appears to represent sexuality as seen through morbid inquisitiveness. In terms of the tale's psychological allegory this inquisitiveness is the alternative to normality that Rappaccini holds out to Giovanni. Unlike Baglioni's advice to stay away from Beatrice and Lisabetta's implicit urging of sexual conquest, this alternative offers both an escape *and* a conquest. To be a human pesticide married to another is, for Rappaccini, to overcome normality with sadistic triumph. This is succinctly expressed in his final speech to Beatrice: "Dost thou deem it misery to be endowed with marvellous gifts against which no power nor strength could avail an enemy—misery, to be able to quell the mightiest with a breath—misery, to be as terrible as thou art beautiful? Wouldst thou, then, have preferred the condition of a weak woman, exposed to all evil and capable of none?" (II, 147). Here it is seen that Rappaccini's tampering with his daughter's metabolism has had a positively sadistic intent which he is now irrelevantly placing at her own command; with the control of poison one can surmount one's humanity, like the unsexed Lady Macbeth, and devastate one's imagined enemies. The real enemy, of course, is "the condition of a weak woman," which both Rappaccini and Giovanni seem to find unbearable.

This is not to say that Giovanni adopts Rappaccini's

6. In a fascinating article Charles Boewe has shown how Rappaccini's cross-pollination of plants must have had overtones of sexual irregularity for Hawthorne and his contemporaries (we might add, for his characters as well). Boewe concludes that in Hawthorne's time hybridization was closely associated with sterility; the "adultery," as Hawthorne calls it, of one plant with another would necessarily produce a botanical freak incapable of further reproduction. Rappaccini has had a comparable effect on Beatrice as well as on his flowers. See "Rappaccini's Garden," *American Literature,* XXX (March 1958), 37-49.

attitude as his own conclusive response, for Giovanni continues to vacillate until the end. The point is that there
is a "Rappaccini" ingredient in his psyche, a streak of
sadism originating in his fear of Beatrice. Giovanni will
act with malicious fury at the crucial moment in his relationship with her. The objective basis for his rage is his
discovery that his own veins are becoming filled with poison, but the manner of his reaction expresses a positive zest
in administering torment. Note his "scientific" behavior
just before this meeting:

> Recovering from his stupor, he began to watch with
> curious eye a spider that was busily at work hanging its
> web from the antique cornice of the apartment, crossing
> and recrossing the artful system of interwoven lines—as
> vigorous and active a spider as ever dangled from an old
> ceiling. Giovanni bent towards the insect, and emitted a
> deep, long breath. The spider suddenly ceased its toil;
> the web vibrated with a tremor originating in the body
> of the small artisan. Again Giovanni sent forth a breath,
> deeper, longer, and imbued with a venomous feeling out
> of his heart; he knew not whether he were wicked, or
> only desperate. The spider made a convulsive gripe with
> his limbs and hung dead across the window.
>
> "Accursed! accursed!" muttered Giovanni, addressing
> himself. "Hast thou grown so poisonous that this deadly
> insect perishes by thy breath?"
>
> At that moment a rich, sweet voice came floating up
> from the garden.
>
> "Giovanni! Giovanni! It is past the hour! Why tarriest
> thou? Come down!"
>
> "Yes," muttered Giovanni again. "She is the only being
> whom my breath may not slay! Would that it might!"
> (II, 140f.)

In this subtle passage we see that Giovanni's resentment
now extends to life in general. Note especially how he
attributes deadliness to a "vigorous," "active," and literally

constructive spider, the innocuous victim of his experiment. The deadliness lies in his own poisoned mind, which, whether "wicked, or only desperate," is now ready to direct its hatred against Beatrice in person.

We should not be surprised, then, that Giovanni's delayed rendezvous with Beatrice is a vicious one. She is now to suffer for having "enticed me into thy region of unspeakable horror!" (II, 143)—an accusation of rather graphic ambiguity. Giovanni's diatribe against Beatrice is characterized by both disgust and brutal cruelty:

> "Yes, poisonous thing!" repeated Giovanni, beside himself with passion. "Thou hast done it! Thou hast blasted me! Thou hast filled my veins with poison! Thou hast made me as hateful, as ugly, as loathsome and deadly a creature as thyself—a world's wonder of hideous monstrosity! Now, if our breath be happily as fatal to ourselves as to all others, let us join our lips in one kiss of unutterable hatred, and so die!" (II, 143)

Giovanni will quickly repent of this mood when his fury is spent, but for a few moments he has shown us the true emotional meaning of his poison. Ultimately he has cared only for his own attractiveness, and when this has been threatened—not destroyed, for presumably Baglioni's antidote will succeed with him—he revels histrionically in a bittersweet fantasy of annihilation. His concluding sentence is worthy of Swinburne in combining a perverted lust with a sadistic longing to destroy the woman who has both inspired and inhibited that lust. And the effect of his words is genuinely murderous. Beatrice appears to realize that the antidote which he next offers will be fatal to her, and she drinks it willingly, for she *has* lived for someone else's love and has found it transformed to an unbearable cruelty.

Beatrice thus takes her place beside the other full-blooded heroines, Hester, Zenobia, and Miriam, with whom her name is justly linked in Hawthorne criticism.

Like them, she must suffer for the implicit threat that her
sexual aura bears to the timid men who surround her.
Her case, however, is more crucially ambiguous than theirs,
for while they realize their womanliness and flaunt it before their tormentors, Beatrice's conscious attitude remains
girlish to the end. This consistent disparity between her
purity of soul and her physical allure might be said to be
allegorically invoked by Giovanni's own contradictory
demands of her, but it is thematically meaningful as a
literal fact. Both Beatrice and Giovanni, like the Lord and
Lady of the May at Merry Mount, cherish the impossible
illusion of a childlike unself-conscious love between physically mature adults. The course of the plot may be defined
as the gradual dispelling of that illusion.

It is in this context that we should interpret Hawthorne's playful references to Rappaccini's garden as "the
Eden of the present world" (II, 112). Indeed, we may now
reconsider the whole question of religious meaning in the
tale. To describe the garden as an emblem of postlapsarian
nature is certainly correct, yet it barely approximates the
complex effect Hawthorne has created. The "fall" in this
case is from the child's unawareness of sex, not from virtue.
Unlike Adam and Eve, Giovanni and Beatrice are destined,
not to sin, but to become cognizant of sin—and even this
formulation needs revising in Beatrice's case. She is simply victimized by the consequences of Giovanni's inability
to assimilate the discovery of sexuality in her, a discovery
she never really makes herself. Hawthorne has implicitly
emptied the concept of sin of its ordinary meaning, for in
this tale evil is produced, not by overt wrongdoing, nor
even by sinning in thought, but by the conflict between
lustful wishes and an ideal of sexless virtue. Hence the
sincerity—and the heresy—of Hawthorne's exclamation,
"Blessed are all simple emotions, be they dark or bright!"
(II, 123).

The reading of "Rappaccini's Daughter" that translates
Giovanni's problem merely into the accepting or rejecting

of Christian faith is at once over-simple and over-refined: it simplifies Giovanni's psychological plight and it departs unnecessarily from the given situation. Yet the problem of faith does get entangled in Giovanni's dilemma. Wherever he renews his "faith" in Beatrice's moral innocence, the language of his thoughts seizes upon religious metaphors. Thus, for example, Beatrice's presence can bring him

> ... recollections of the delicate and benign power of her feminine nature, which had so often enveloped him in a religious calm; recollections of many a holy and passionate outgush of her heart, when the pure fountain had been unsealed from its depths and made visible in its transparency to his mental eye; recollections which, had Giovanni known how to estimate them, would have assured him that all this ugly mystery was but an earthly illusion, and that, whatever mist of evil might seem to have gathered over her, the real Beatrice was a heavenly angel. (II, 141f.)

The reader will note that the imagery here is itself a kind of antidote to doubts about Beatrice's girlishness; Giovanni's mental eye sees that "the depths" of the "pure fountain" are unpolluted. Hawthorne invokes Beatrice's "passion" only to show that it is not passionate in the ordinary sense at all. Elsewhere Giovanni's own "passion" is treated in the same beneficent terms: "But now his spirit was incapable of sustaining itself at the height to which the early enthusiasm of passion had exalted it; he fell down, grovelling among earthly doubts, and defiled therewith the pure whiteness of Beatrice's image" (II, 139). Such passages implicitly make religious faith contingent on a "passionate" recognition of absolute, unambiguous purity in Beatrice. It is thus apparent that for Giovanni, religious faith must rest on self-deception, for his "faith" is a faith in Beatrice's non-poisonousness. And the same point seems to hold on the symbolic level: if supernatural

belief must depend on a denial of sexual feeling in Beatrice, and specifically on denying that she has (albeit un-
thinkingly) enticed Giovanni with her sexual appeal, then
supernatural faith is made possible by a lie.

It is significant, therefore, that when Giovanni has
reached the nadir of belief in Beatrice he achieves the
height of blasphemy:

> "Thou,—dost thou pray?" cried Giovanni, still with the
> same fiendish scorn. "Thy very prayers, as they come from
> thy lips, taint the atmosphere with death. Yes, yes; let
> us pray! Let us to church and dip our fingers in the holy
> water at the portal! They that come after us will perish
> as by a pestilence! Let us sign crosses in the air! It will be
> scattering curses abroad in the likeness of holy symbols!"
> (II, 144)

This urge to perform Black Masses, which we shall meet
again at a critical point in *The Scarlet Letter,* expresses a
momentary upsurging of sexual feeling against a self-control which has been based on the effort to exclude "impure
thoughts." A demonic energy is released at the price of
being perversely wedded to the religious values it opposes.

Though Giovanni wavers between blaming Rappaccini
outright for his daughter's condition and deciding that
she has shared in his scheme, both interpretations locate
the original source of evil in Rappaccini. It is thus a
"father" who is ultimately responsible in Giovanni's eyes,
and in Beatrice's as well. This is highly pertinent to Giovanni's loss of religious faith, for Hawthorne has set up
ample parallels between Rappaccini and God. Rappaccini
has "created" (II, 142) the central shrub in his new Eden,
and he presides over everything that happens between its
Adam and Eve. This is not to say, however, that Rappaccini is identifiable with the Christian God. He is a parody
of divinity, a creator whose productions are "no longer of
God's making, but the monstrous offspring of man's de-

praved fancy, glowing with only an evil mockery of beauty"
(II, 128). Recalling that all of Giovanni's acquaintances
in the tale reflect aspects of himself, we may say that Rappaccini is the God of Giovanni's latent atheism, the God
of a godless world. To believe in him—to find nothing in
existence that has not been touched by his polluting influence—is to disbelieve in goodness.

If Giovanni must be counted as yet another Hawthornian
protagonist who regresses to juvenile nausea over female
sexuality, we cannot ignore the fact that blame for this
sexuality is laid upon a father. The situation is metaphorically an Oedipal one, for we recall that Giovanni and
Beatrice have wanted to remain like "playmates from early
infancy," and at one point Giovanni wonders how he could
be "conversing with Beatrice like a brother" (II, 131) despite his knowledge of her deadliness. Rappaccini has
already committed a kind of incest by polluting Beatrice
with his chemicals, and the ultimate horror of his marriage
scheme for Giovanni is that it will be, not just freakish,
but vicariously incestuous. Giovanni's religious crisis, like
that of Melville's Pierre, emerges from the ambiguity of
his response to an opportunity which entails powerful
innuendoes of incest.

We must beware, however, of overpraising Hawthorne
for the objectivity of his characterization. Like Melville,
though less conspicuously, he is entangled in his hero's
sophistries. For it is Hawthorne, not Giovanni, who has
resorted to the explanatory device of making Rappaccini
the arch-villain. Like the wizard in "Alice Doane's Appeal,"
Rappaccini serves as a check upon frankness, an escape-
valve for dangerous autobiographical meaning. The Oedipal configuration of "Rappaccini's Daughter," as well as
its religious confusion, may be traced through Giovanni's
mind to Hawthorne's. Hence we can *almost* credit Hawthorne with a pitiless symbolic anatomy of an adolescent
mind. We cannot call it entirely pitiless when the hero's

vacillations and fantasies are so urgently those of the author.

In turning now to *The Scarlet Letter* (1850), we do not move as far from the psychological allegory of "Rappaccini's Daughter" as might appear. The romance deserves high praise for its symbolic consistency and symmetry, its dignity and pathos, its rare completeness as a literal action; yet these are the result, not of Hawthorne's bypassing the former concerns of his fiction, but of his assimilating them to a steady tragic sense of reality. If Hester Prynne is no Beatrice, blurred by the author's contradictory feelings toward her, those feelings remain nonetheless contradictory. Simply, Hawthorne has succeeded for once in containing his anxieties almost entirely within an ironic portrait of the mind for whom his heroine is awesomely provocative. Whatever objectivity *The Scarlet Letter* attains is reached through self-transcendence—the disengagement of a fictional reality from a very Hawthornian hero's mode of perceiving it. For Hawthorne that disengagement can never be total; the famous ambiguities of *The Scarlet Letter* spring directly from his uncertain degree of involvement with Dimmesdale. Thus the given world of the romance, while by no means a product of Dimmesdale's mind, is perhaps best understood when viewed as a challenge and reply to that mind. It is through Dimmesdale, then, that we shall approach Hawthorne's masterpiece.

VIII

The Ruined Wall

"The golden sands that may sometimes be gathered (always, perhaps, if we know how to seek for them) along the dry bed of a torrent, adown which passion and feeling have foamed, and past away. It is good, therefore, in mature life, to trace back such torrents to their source."

—HAWTHORNE, *American Notebooks*

Hester Prynne and Arthur Dimmesdale, in the protective gloom of the forest surrounding Boston, have had their fateful reunion. While little Pearl, sent discreetly out of hearing range, has been romping about in her unrestrained way, the martyred lovers have unburdened themselves. Hester has revealed the identity of Chillingworth and has succeeded in winning Dimmesdale's forgiveness for her previous secrecy. Dimmesdale has explained the agony of his seven years' torment. Self-pity and compassion have led unexpectedly to a revival of desire; "what we did," as Hester boldly remembers, "had a consecration of its own" (*C*, I, 195), and Arthur Dimmesdale cannot deny it. In his state of helpless longing he allows himself to be swayed by Hester's insistence that the past can be forgotten, that deep in the wilderness or across the ocean, accompanied and sustained by Hester, he can free himself from the revengeful gaze of Roger Chillingworth.

Hester's argument is of course a superficial one; the ultimate source of Dimmesdale's anguish is not Chillingworth but his own remorse, and this cannot be left behind in Boston. The closing chapters of *The Scarlet Letter* demonstrate this clearly enough, but Hawthorne, with characteristic license, tells us at once that Hester is wrong. "And be the stern and sad truth spoken," he says, "that the breach which guilt has once made into the human soul is never, in this mortal state, repaired. It may be watched and guarded; so that the enemy shall not force his way again into the citadel, and might even, in his subsequent assaults, select some other avenue, in preference to that where he had formerly succeeded. But there is still the ruined wall, and, near it, the stealthy tread of the foe that would win over again his unforgotten triumph" (*C*, I, 200f.).

This metaphor is too striking to be passed over quickly. Like Melville's famous comparison of the unconscious mind to a subterranean captive king in Chapter XLI of *Moby-Dick*, it provides us with a theoretical understanding of behavior we might otherwise judge to be poorly motivated. Arthur Dimmesdale, like Ahab, is "gnawed within and scorched without, with the infixed, unrelenting fangs of some incurable idea," and Hawthorne's metaphor, inserted at a crucial moment in the plot, enables us to see the inner mechanism of Dimmesdale's torment.

At first, admittedly, we do not seem entitled to draw broad psychological conclusions from these few sentences. Indeed, we may even say that the metaphor reveals a fruitless confusion of terms. Does Hawthorne mean to describe the soul's precautions against the repetition of overt sin? Apparently not, since the "stealthy foe" is identified as *guilt* rather than as the forbidden urge to sin. But if the metaphor means what it says, how are we to reduce it to common sense? It is plainly inappropriate to see "guilt" as the original assailant of the citadel, for feelings of guilt arise only in *reaction against* condemned acts or thoughts. The metaphor would seem to be plausible only in different terms from those that Hawthorne selected.

We may resolve this confusion by appealing to Arthur Dimmesdale's literal situation. In committing adultery he has succumbed to an urge which, because of his ascetic beliefs, he had been unprepared to find in himself. Nor, given the high development of his conscience and the sincerity of his wish to be holy, could he have done otherwise than to have violently expelled and denied the sensual impulse, once gratified. It was at this point, we may say— the point at which one element of Dimmesdale's nature passed a sentence of exile on another—that the true psychological damage was done. The original foe of his tranquility *was* guilt, but guilt for his thoughtless surrender to passion. In this light we see that Hawthorne's metaphor has condensed two ideas that are intimately related. Dimmesdale's moral enemy is the forbidden impulse, while his psychological enemy is guilt; but there is no practical difference between the two, for they always appear together. We may understand Hawthorne's full meaning if we identify the potential invader of the citadel as a libidinal impulse, *now necessarily bearing a charge of guilt.*

This hypothesis helps us to understand the sophisticated view of Dimmesdale's psychology that Hawthorne's metaphor implies. Dimmesdale's conscience (the watchful guard) has been delegated to prevent repetition of the temptation's "unforgotten triumph." The deterrent weapon of conscience is its capacity to generate feelings of guilt, which are of course painful to the soul. Though the temptation retains all its strength (its demand for gratification), this is counterbalanced by its burden of guilt. To readmit the libidinal impulse through the guarded breach (to gratify it in the original way) would be to admit insupportable quantities of guilt. The soul thus keeps temptation at bay by meeting it with an equal and opposite force of condemnation.

But let us consider the most arresting feature of Hawthorne's metaphor. The banished impulse, thwarted in one direction, "might even, in his subsequent assaults, select some other avenue, in preference to that where he had formerly succeeded." Indeed, the logic of Hawthorne's figure seems to assure success to the temptation in finding another means of entrance, since conscience is massing all its defenses at the breach. This devious invasion would evidently be less gratifying than the direct one, for we are told that the stealthy foe would stay in readiness to attack the breach again. Some entry, nevertheless, is preferable to none, especially when it can be effectuated with a minimum resistance on the part of conscience. Hawthorne has set up a strong likelihood that the libidinal impulse will change or disguise its true object, slip past the guard of conscience with relative ease, and take up a secret dwelling in the soul.

In seeking to explain what Hawthorne means by this "other avenue" of invasion, we must bear in mind the double reference of his metaphor. It describes the soul's means of combating both sin and guilt—that is, both *gratification* of the guilty impulse and *consciousness* of it. For Dimmesdale the greatest torment is to acknowledge that his libidinous wishes are really his, and not a temptation from the Devil. His mental energy is directed, not simply to avoiding sin, but to expelling it from consciousness—in a word, to repressing it. The "other avenue" is the means his libido chooses, given the fact of repression, to gratify itself surreptitiously. In psychoanalytic terms this is the avenue of compromise that issues in a neurotic symptom.

Hawthorne's metaphor of the beseiged citadel cuts beneath the theological and moral explanations in which Dimmesdale puts his faith, and shows us instead an inner world of unconscious compulsion. Guilt will continue to threaten the timid minister in spite of his resolution to escape it, and indeed (as the fusion of "temptation" and "guilt" in the metaphor implies) this resolution will only serve to upset the balance of power and enable guilt to conquer the soul once more. Hawthorne's metaphor demands that we see Dimmesdale not as a free moral agent but as a victim of feelings he can neither understand nor control. And the point can be extended to include Chillingworth and even Hester, whose minds have been likewise altered by the consequences of the unforgotten act, the permanent breach in the wall. If, as Chillingworth asserts, the awful course of events has been "a dark necessity" from the beginning, it is not because Hawthorne believes in Calvinistic predestination or wants to imitate Greek tragedy, but because all three of the central characters have been ruled by motives inaccessible to their conscious will.

The implications we have drawn, perhaps over-subtly, from Hawthorne's metaphor begin to take on substance as we examine Arthur Dimmesdale in the forest scene. His nervousness, his mental exhaustion, and his compulsive gesture of placing his hand on his heart reveal a state that we would now call neurotic inhibition. His lack of energy for any of the outward demands of life indicates how all-absorbing is his internal trouble, and the stigma on his chest, though a rather crass piece of symbolism on Hawthorne's part, must also be interpreted psychosomatically. Nor can we avoid observing that Dimmesdale shows the neurotic's reluctance to give up his symptoms. How else can we account for his obtuseness in not having recognized Chillingworth's character? "I might have known it!" he murmurs when Hester forces the revelation upon him. "I did know it! Was not the secret told me in the natural recoil of my heart, at the first sight of him, and as often as I have seen him since? Why did I not understand?" (C, I, 194) The answer, hidden from Dimmesdale's surface reasoning, is that his relationship with Chillingworth, taken together with the change in mental economy that has accompanied it, has offered perverse satisfactions which he is even now powerless to renounce. Hester, whose will is relatively independent and strong, is the one who makes the decision to break with the past.

We can understand the nature of Dimmesdale's illness by defining the state of mind that has possessed him for seven years. It is of course his concealed act of adultery that lies at the bottom of his self-torment. But why does he lack the courage to make his humiliation public? Dimmesdale himself offers us the clue in a cry of agony: "Of penance I have had enough! Of penitence there has been none! Else, I should long ago have thrown off these garments of mock holiness, and have shown myself to mankind as they will see me at the judgment-seat" (C, I, 192). The plain meaning of this outburst is that Dimmesdale has never surmounted the libidinal urge that produced his sin. His "penance," including self-flagellation and the more refined torment of submitting to Chillingworth's influence, has failed to purify him because it has been unaccompanied by the feeling of penitence, the resolution to sin no more. Indeed, I submit, Dimmesdale's penance has incorporated and embodied the very urge it has been punishing. If, as he says, he has kept his garments of mock holiness *because* he has not repented, he must mean that in some way or another the forbidden impulse has found gratification in the existing circumstances, in the existing state of his soul. And this state is one of morbid remorse. The stealthy foe has re-entered the citadel through the avenue of remorse.

This conclusion may seem less paradoxical if we bear in mind a distinction between remorse and true repentance. In both states the sinful act is condemned morally, but in strict repentance the soul abandons the sin and turns to holier thoughts. Remorse of Dimmesdale's type, on the other hand, is attached to a continual re-enacting of the sin in fantasy and hence a continual renewal of the need for self-punishment. Roger Chillingworth, the psychoanalyst *manqué,* understands the process perfectly: "the fear, the remorse, the agony, the ineffectual repentance, the backward rush of sinful thoughts, expelled in vain!"

(C, I, 139). As Hawthorne explains, Dimmesdale's cow-ardice is the "sister and closely linked companion" (C, I, 148) of his remorse.

Thus Dimmesdale is helpless to reform himself at this stage because the passional side of his nature has found an outlet, albeit a self-destructive one, in his present miser-able situation. The original sexual desire has been granted recognition *on the condition of being punished,* and the punishment itself is a form of gratification. Not only the overt masochism of fasts, vigils, and self-scourging (the last of these makes him laugh, by the way), but also Dimmes-dale's emaciation and weariness attest to the spending of his energy against himself. It is important to recognize that this is the same energy previously devoted to passion for Hester. We do not exaggerate the facts of the romance in saying that the question of Dimmesdale's fate, for all its religious decoration, amounts essentially to the question of what use is to be made of his libido.

We are now prepared to understand the choice that the poor minister faces when Hester holds out the idea of escape. It is not a choice between a totally unattractive life and a happy one (not even Dimmesdale could feel hesita-tion in that case), but rather a choice of satisfactions, of avenues into the citadel. The seemingly worthless alterna-tive of continuing to admit the morally condemned im-pulse by the way of remorse has the advantage, appreciated by all neurotics, of preserving the status quo. Still, the other course naturally seems more attractive. If only re-pression can be weakened—and this is just the task of Hester's rhetoric about freedom—Dimmesdale can hope to return to the previous "breach" of adultery.

In reality, however, these alternatives offer no chance for happiness or even survival. The masochistic course leads straight to death, while the other, which Dimmes-dale allows Hester to choose for him, is by now so foreign to his withered, guilt-ridden nature that it can never be

put into effect. The resolution to sin will, instead, necessarily redouble the opposing force of conscience, which
will be stronger in proportion to the overtness of the
libidinal threat. As the concluding chapters of *The Scarlet
Letter* prove, the only possible result of Dimmesdale's attempt to impose, in Hawthorne's phrase, "a total change
of dynasty and moral code, in that interior kingdom"
(*C*, I, 217), will be a counter-revolution so violent that it
will slay Dimmesdale himself along with his upstart libido.
We thus see that in the forest, while Hester is prating of
escape, renewal, and success, Arthur Dimmesdale unknow-
ingly faces a choice of two paths to suicide.

Now, this psychological impasse is sufficient in itself to
refute the most "liberal" critics of *The Scarlet Letter*—
those who take Hester's proposal of escape as Hawthorne's
own advice. However much we may admire Hester and
prefer her boldness to Dimmesdale's self-pity, we cannot
agree that she understands human nature very deeply. Her
shame, despair, and solitude "had made her strong," says
Hawthorne, "but taught her much amiss" (*C*, I, 200).
What she principally ignores is the truth embodied in the
metaphor of the ruined wall, that men are altered irrepa-
rably by their violations of conscience. Hester herself is
only an apparent exception to this rule. She handles her
guilt more successfully than Dimmesdale because, in the
first place, her conscience is less highly developed than his;
and secondly because, as he tells her, "Heaven hath granted
thee an open ignominy, that thereby thou mayest work
out an open triumph over the evil within thee, and the
sorrow without" (*C*, I, 67). Those who believe that Hawthorne is an advocate of free love, that adultery has no
ill effects on a "normal" nature like Hester's, have failed
to observe that Hester, too, undergoes self-inflicted punishment. Though permitted to leave, she has remained in
Boston not simply because she wants to be near Arthur
Dimmesdale, but because this has been the scene of her

humiliation. "Her sin, her ignominy, were the roots which she had struck into the soil," says Hawthorne. "The chain that bound her here was of iron links, and galling to her inmost soul, but never could be broken" (C, I, 80).

We need not dwell on this argument, for the liberal critics of *The Scarlet Letter* have been in retreat for many years. Their place has been taken by subtler readers who say that Hawthorne brings us from sin to redemption, from materialistic error to pure spiritual truth. The moral heart of the novel, in this view, is contained in Dimmesdale's Election Sermon, and Dimmesdale himself is pictured as Christ-like in his holy death. Hester, in comparison, degenerates spiritually after the first few chapters; the fact that her thoughts are still on earthly love while Dimmesdale is looking toward heaven is a serious mark against her.

This redemptive scheme, which rests on the uncriticized assumption that Hawthorne's point of view is identical with Dimmesdale's at the end, seems to me to misrepresent the "felt life" of *The Scarlet Letter* more drastically than the liberal reading. Both take for granted the erroneous belief that the novel consists essentially of the dramatization of a moral idea. The tale of human frailty and sorrow, as Hawthorne calls it in his opening chapter, is treated merely as the fictionalization of an article of faith. Hawthorne himself, we might repeat, did not share this ability of his critics to shrug off the psychological reality of his work. *The Scarlet Letter* is, he said, "positively a hell fired story, into which I found it almost impossible to throw any cheering light." (See p. 6 above.)

All parties can agree, in any case, that there is a terrible irony in Dimmesdale's exhilaration when he has resolved to flee with Hester. Being, as Hawthorne describes him, "a true religionist," to whom it would always remain essential "to feel the pressure of a faith about him, supporting, while it confined him within its iron framework" (C, I, 123), he is ill-prepared to savor his new freedom for what it is.

His joy is that of his victorious libido, of the "enemy" which is now presumably sacking the citadel, but this release is acknowledged by consciousness only after a significant bowdlerization:

> "Do I feel joy again?" cried he, wondering at himself. "Methought the germ of it was dead in me! O Hester, thou art my better angel! I seem to have flung myself—sick, sin-stained, and sorrow-blackened—down upon these forest leaves, and to have risen up all made anew, and with new powers to glorify Him that hath been merciful! This is already the better life! Why did we not find it sooner?" (C, I, 201f.)

Hawthorne's portrayal of self-delusion and his compassion are nowhere so powerfully combined as in this passage. The Christian reference to the putting on of the New Man is grimly comic in the light of what has inspired it, but we feel no more urge to laugh at Dimmesdale than we do at Milton's Adam. If in his previous role he has been only, in Hawthorne's phrase, a "subtle, but remorseful hypocrite" (C, I, 144), here he is striving pathetically to be sincere. His case becomes poignant as we imagine the revenge that his tyrannical conscience must soon take against these new promptings of the flesh. To say merely that Dimmesdale is in a state of theological error is to miss part of the irony; it is precisely his theological loyalty that necessitates his confusion. His sexual nature must be either denied with unconscious sophistry, as in this scene, or rooted out with heroic fanaticism, as in his public confession at the end.

On one point, however, Dimmesdale is not mistaken: he has been blessed with a new energy of body and will. The source of this energy is obviously his libido; he has become physically strong to the degree that he has ceased directing his passion against himself and has attached it to his thoughts of Hester. But as he now returns to town,[1] bent upon renewing his hypocrisy for the four days until the Election Sermon has been given and the ship is to sail, we see that his "cure" has been very incomplete. "At every step he was incited to do some strange, wild, wicked thing or other, with a sense that it would be at once involuntary and intentional; in spite of himself, yet growing out of a profounder self than that which opposed the impulse" (C, I, 217). The minister can scarcely keep from blaspheming to his young and old parishioners as he passes them in the street; he longs to shock a deacon and an old widow with arguments against Christianity, to poison the innocence of a naïve girl who worships him, to teach wicked words to a group of children, and to exchange bawdy jests with a drunken sailor. Here, plainly, is a return of the repressed, and in a form which Freud noted to be typical in severely holy persons.[2] The fact that these impulses have reached the surface of Dimmesdale's mind attests to the weakening of repression in the forest scene, while their perverse and furtive character shows us that repression has not ceased altogether. Hawthorne's own explanation, that Dimmesdale's hidden vices have been awakened because "he had yielded himself *with deliberate choice*, as he had never done before, to what he *knew* was deadly sin" (C, I, 222; my italics), gives conscience its proper role as a causative factor. Having left Hester's immediate influence behind in the forest, and having returned to the society where he is known for his purity, Dimmesdale already finds his "wicked" intentions constrained into the form of a verbal naughtiness which he cannot even bring himself to express.

Now Dimmesdale, presumably after a brief interview

1. Note, incidentally, the implicit sexuality of his cross-country run, as he "leaped across the plashy places, thrust himself through the clinging underbrush, climbed the ascent, plunged into the hollow . . ." (C, I, 216).

2. See, for example, *Collected Papers*, III, 331, 599f.

with the taunting Mistress Hibbins, arrives at his lodgings. Artfully spurning the attentions of Roger Chillingworth, he eats his supper "with ravenous appetite" (*C*, I, 225) and sits down to write the Election Sermon. Without really knowing what words he is setting on paper, and wondering to himself how God could inspire such a sinner as himself, he works all night "with earnest haste and ecstasy" (*C*, I, 225). The result is a sermon which, with the addition of spontaneous interpolations in the delivery, will impress its Puritan audience as an epitome of holiness and pathos. Nothing less than the descent of the Holy Ghost will be held sufficient to account for such a performance.

Yet insofar as the Election Sermon will consist of what Dimmesdale has recorded in his siege of "automatic writing," we must doubt whether Hawthorne shares the credulous view of the Puritans. Dimmesdale has undergone no discernible change in attitude from the time of his eccentric impulses in the street until the writing of the sermon. Though he works in the room where he has fasted and prayed, and where he can see his old Bible, he is not (as Male argues) sustained by these reminders of his faith. Quite the contrary: he can scarcely believe that he has ever breathed such an atmosphere. "But he seemed to stand apart, and eye this former self with scornful, pitying, but half-envious curiosity. That self was gone! Another man had returned out of the forest; a wiser one; with a knowledge of hidden mysteries which the simplicity of the former never could have reached" (*C*, I, 223). In short, the Election Sermon is written by the same man who wants to corrupt young girls in the street, and the same newly liberated sexuality "inspires" him in both cases. If the written form of the Election Sermon *is* a great Christian document, as we have no reason to doubt, this is attributable not to Dimmesdale's holiness but to his libido, which gives him creative strength and an intimate acquaintance with the reality of sin.

Thus Dimmesdale's sexual energy has temporarily found

a new alternative to its battle with repression—namely, sublimation. In sublimation, we are told, the libido is not repressed but redirected to aims that are acceptable to conscience. The writing of the Election Sermon is just such
an aim, and readers who are familiar with psychoanalysis
will not be puzzled to find that Dimmesdale has passed
without hesitation from the greatest blasphemy to fervent
religious rhetoric.

The writing of the Election Sermon is just such
covered his piety in the three days that intervene between
the writing of the sermon and its delivery. Both Hester and
Mistress Hibbins "find it hard to believe him the same
man" (C, I, 241) who emerged from the forest. Though
he is preoccupied with his imminent sermon as he marches
past Hester, his energy seems greater than ever and his
nervous mannerism is absent. We could say, if we liked,
that at this point God's grace has already begun to sustain
Dimmesdale, but there is nothing in Hawthorne's description to warrant a resort to supernatural explanations. It
seems likely that Dimmesdale has by now felt the full
weight of his conscience's case against adultery, has already
determined to confess his previous sin publicly, and so is
no longer suffering from repression. His libido is now
free, not to attach itself to Hester, but to be sublimated
into the passion of delivering his sermon and then expelled forever.

The ironies in Dimmesdale's situation as he leaves the
church, having preached with magnificent power, are extremely subtle. His career, as Hawthorne tells us, has
touched the proudest eminence that any clergyman could
hope to attain, yet this eminence is due, among other
things, to "a reputation of whitest sanctity" (C, I, 249).
Furthermore, Hester has been silently tormented by an
inquisitive mob while Dimmesdale has been preaching,
and we feel the injustice of the contrast. And yet Dimmesdale has already made the choice that will render him
worthy of the praise he is now receiving. If his public

hypocrisy has not yet been dissolved, his hypocrisy with himself is over. It would be small-minded not to recognize that Dimmesdale has, after all, achieved a point of heroic independence—an independence not only of his fawning congregation but also of Hester, who frankly resents it. If the Christian reading of *The Scarlet Letter* judges Hester too roughly on theological grounds, it is at least correct in seeing that she lacks the detachment to appreciate Dimmesdale's final act of courage. While she remains on the steady level of her womanly affections, Dimmesdale, who has previously stooped below his ordinary manhood, is now ready to act with the exalted fervor of a saint.

All the moral ambiguity of *The Scarlet Letter* makes itself felt in Dimmesdale's moment of confession. We may truly say that no one has a total view of what is happening. The citizens of Boston, for whom it would be an irreverent thought to connect their minister with Hester, turn to various rationalizations to avoid comprehending the scene. Hester is bewildered, and Pearl feels only a generalized sense of grief. But what about Arthur Dimmesdale? Is he really on his way to heaven as he proclaims God's mercy in his dying words?

> "He hath proved his mercy, most of all, in my afflictions. By giving me this burning torture to bear upon my breast! By sending yonder dark and terrible old man, to keep the torture always at red-heat! By bringing me hither, to die this death of triumphant ignominy before the people! Had either of these agonies been wanting, I had been lost for ever! Praised be his name! His will be done! Farewell!" (*C*, I, 256f.)

This reasoning, which sounds so cruel to the ear of rational humanism, has the logic of Christian doctrine behind it; it rests on the paradox that a man must lose his life to save it. The question that the neo-orthodox interpreters of *The Scarlet Letter* invariably ignore, however, is whether Hawthorne has prepared us to understand this scene only in doctrinal terms. Has he abandoned his usual irony and lost himself in religious transport?

The question ultimately amounts to a matter of critical method: whether we are to take the action of *The Scarlet Letter* in natural or supernatural terms. Hawthorne offers us naturalistic explanations for everything that happens, and though he also puts forth opposite theories—Pearl is an elf-child, Mistress Hibbins is a witch, and so on—this mode of thinking is discredited by the simplicity of the people who employ it. We cannot conscientiously say that Chillingworth *is* a devil, for example, when Hawthorne takes such care to show us how his devilishness has proceeded from his physical deformity, his sense of inferiority and impotence, his sexual jealousy, and his perverted craving for knowledge. Hawthorne carries symbolism to the border of allegory but does not cross over. As for Dimmesdale's retrospective idea that God's mercy has been responsible for the whole chain of events, we cannot absolutely deny that this may be true; but we can remark that if it *is* true, Hawthorne has vitiated his otherwise brilliant study of motivation.

Nothing in Dimmesdale's behavior on the scaffold is incongruous with his psychology as we first examined it in the forest scene. We merely find ourselves at the conclusion to the breakdown of repression that began there, and which has necessarily brought about a renewal of opposition to the forbidden impulses. Dimmesdale has been heroic in choosing to eradicate his libidinal self with one stroke, but his heroism follows a sound principle of mental economy. Further repression, which is the only other alternative for his conscience-ridden nature, would only lead to a slower and more painful death through masochistic remorse. Nor can we help but see that his confession passes beyond a humble admission of sinfulness and touches the pathological. His stigma has become the central object in the universe: "God's eye beheld it! The angels were for ever pointing at it! The Devil knew it well, and fretted it continually with the touch of his burning finger!" (*C*, I, 255). Dimmesdale is so obsessed with his own guilt that he negates the Christian dogma of original sin: "behold me here, the one sinner of the world!" (*C*, I, 254). This strain of egoism in his "triumphant ignominy" does not subtract from his courage, but it casts doubt on his theory that all the preceding action has been staged by God for the purpose of saving his soul.

However much we may admire Dimmesdale's final asceticism, there are no grounds for taking it as Hawthorne's moral ideal. The last developments of plot in *The Scarlet Letter* approach the "mythic level" which redemption-minded critics love to discover, but the myth is wholly secular and worldly. Pearl, who has hitherto been a "messenger of anguish" to her mother, is emotionally transformed as she kisses Dimmesdale on the scaffold. "A spell was broken. The great scene of grief, in which the wild infant bore a part, had developed all her sympathies; and as her tears fell upon her father's cheek, they were the pledge that she would grow up amid human joy and sorrow, nor for ever do battle with the world, but be a woman in it." (*C*, I, 256) Thanks to Chillingworth's bequest—for Chillingworth, too, finds that a spell is broken when Dimmesdale confesses, and he is capable of at least one generous act before he dies—Pearl is made "the richest heiress of her day, in the New World" (*C*, I, 261). At last report she has become the wife of a European nobleman and is living very happily across the sea. This grandiose and perhaps slightly whimsical epilogue has one undeniable effect on the reader: it takes him as far as possible from the scene and spirit of Dimmesdale's farewell. Pearl's immense wealth, her noble title, her lavish and impractical gifts to Hester, and of course her successful escape from Boston all serve to disparage the Puritan sense of reality. From this distance we look back to Dimmesdale's egocentric confession, not as a moral example which Hawthorne

would like us to follow, but as the last link in a chain of
compulsion that has now been relaxed.

To counterbalance this impression we have the case of
Hester, for whom the drama on the scaffold can never be
completely over. After raising Pearl in a more generous
atmosphere she voluntarily returns to Boston to resume,
or rather to begin, her state of penitence. We must note,
however, that this penitence seems to be devoid of theological content; Hester has returned because Boston and
the scarlet letter offer her "a more real life" (C, I, 262)
than she could find elsewhere, even with Pearl. This simply confirms Hawthorne's emphasis on the irrevocability
of guilty acts. And though Hester is now selfless and
humble, it is not because she believes in Christian sub-
missiveness but because all passion has been spent. To the
women who seek her help "in the continually recurring
trials of wounded, wasted, wronged, misplaced, or erring
and sinful passion" (C, I, 263), Hester does not disguise
her conviction that women are pathetically misunderstood
in her society. She assures her wretched friends that at
some later period "a new truth would be revealed, in order
to establish the whole relation between man and woman
on a surer ground of mutual happiness" (C, I, 263). Hawthorne may or may not believe the prediction, but it has
a retrospective importance in *The Scarlet Letter*. Hawthorne's characters originally acted in ignorance of passion's strength and persistence, and so they became its
slaves.

"It is a curious subject of observation and inquiry,"
says Hawthorne at the end, "whether hatred and love be
not the same thing at bottom. Each, in its utmost development, supposes a high degree of intimacy and heart-knowl-
edge; each renders one individual dependent for the food
of his affections and spiritual life upon another; each leaves
the passionate lover, or the no less passionate hater, forlorn
and desolate by the withdrawal of his object" (C, I, 260).
These penetrating words remind us that the tragedy of

The Scarlet Letter has chiefly sprung, not from Puritan society's imposition of false social ideals on the three main characters, but from their own inner world of frustrated desires. Hester, Dimmesdale, and Chillingworth have been ruled by feelings only half perceived, much less understood and regulated by consciousness; and these feelings, as Hawthorne's bold equation of love and hatred implies, successfully resist translation into terms of good and evil. Hawthorne does not leave us simply with the Sunday-school lesson that we should "be true" (*C*, I, 260), but with a tale of passion through which we glimpse the ruined wall —the terrible certainty that, as Freud put it, the ego is not master in its own house. It is this intuition that enables Hawthorne to reach a tragic vision worthy of the name: to see to the bottom of his created characters, to understand the inner necessity of everything they do, and thus to pity and forgive them in the very act of laying bare their weaknesses.

IX

The Sin of Art

"And in his old age the sweet lyrics of Anacreon made the girls
laugh at his white hairs the more."
—HAWTHORNE, "Fragments from the Journal of a Solitary Man"

There is general agreement that Hawthorne's career after
The Scarlet Letter turns toward self-consciousness, im-
paired dramatic illusion, and prolix elaboration of symbolism. All three developments must strike the psychologically-minded critic as partaking of a single retreat from
painful themes. Hawthorne, always a self-doubting writer
who mingled his own preoccupations with those of his
characters, becomes at once more obsessed and less capable
of studying obsession as a detached analyst. Characterization, in other words, gets more seriously eroded by the
meaning of the whole work for Hawthorne's imagination.
Like his own monomaniac heroes, Hawthorne finds himself unable to suppress the fantasies he no longer cares to
recognize as belonging to "our common nature." The fantasies return in symbolism—just as they did for his heroes—
with such heightened urgency that Hawthorne becomes
anxious to disown his whole fictional world. His recourse
is to ironic self-criticism, comic digression, and finally an
unwillingness to bring his blatantly incestuous plots to
any conclusion at all. That is the melancholy pattern we
shall be tracing in the closing chapters of this book.

For a Freudian, of course, there is nothing startling in
the idea that fictional plots may gratify fantasies and strike
subtle compromises with obsession. Yet the reader may

justly wonder whether this theory could have occurred to Hawthorne—indeed, could have so appalled him that he had to sabotage his late romances when their surreptitious meaning became increasingly plain. As it happens, though, his works prior to 1851 abound with indications of this very sense of the fantasy-meaning of art. Artists, pseudo-artists, and self-conscious narrators in every stage of Hawthorne's career are made to embody authorial misgivings about the source, purpose, and latent content of art. These misgivings are glancingly noted by some students of Hawthorne's allegedly Romantic or Transcendental theory of creativity, but they are never taken very seriously.[1] For us they are of much greater interest than the flatly conventional statements of enthusiasm which they contradict and undermine. If the artist-figure, as I believe, is threatened by the same temptations that destroy the escapist generally, we may come to understand why art-theory is subject to Hawthorne's familiar ambivalence between ideality and cynicism. Nor will we be surprised when, in the late romances, guilt for psychological self-revelation takes the form of tireless symbolic debate about the propriety of one's being an artist at all.

1. In *Hawthorne's View of the Artist* (New York, 1962), the fullest treatment of the subject, Millicent Bell declares that Hawthorne entertained two opposite theories of art, one "ideal" and one derogatory and debunking. In our terms this is simply Hawthorne's customary ambivalence—an ambivalence that renders questionable any effort to speak of his deliberate theory or theories. On her final page Miss Bell says that "one must ask why" Hawthorne's fictional treatment of art seems "obsessed with the theme of guilt" (p. 204). The various explanations that are scattered through her book—explanations in terms of Hawthorne's social and economic conservatism, his allegiance to an eighteenth-century view of the imagination, his intimidation by Yankee materialism—only remind us that his susceptibility to such ideas remains unexplained. Miss Bell's final answer, "Is it not simply that he would be an artist when every sign from man and Heaven indicated that the choice was a cursed one?" (p. 204), is as meaningless as it is melodramatic.

Evidence that Hawthorne associates art with escapism is offered not only in his tales of artistic striving but also in the tales of monomania that we have already examined. Ethan Brand, with his pride in the twin powers of exposing the truth and governing human destinies, is a proto-artist, and Hawthorne significantly chooses to mock him through a parody of art. Brand is made to recognize his kinship with the old Jew who shows him his Unpardonable Sin in a diorama, which also happens to contain "the most outrageous scratchings and daubings, as specimens of the fine arts, that ever an itinerant showman had the face to impose upon his circle of spectators" (III, 490). The point is that Brand too is an itinerant showman, purporting to reveal the essence of human nature but really "converting man and woman to be his puppets, and pulling the wires that moved them to such degrees of crime as were demanded for his study" (III, 495).

Again, Aylmer in "The Birthmark" compares himself favorably to Pygmalion—whose sculpting, of course, brought a woman to life rather than to death. In preparing Georgiana's chambers prior to the operation, and in producing optical displays to absorb her interest, Aylmer uses skills that are unmistakably artistic: "The scenery and the figures of actual life were perfectly represented, but with that bewitching, yet indescribable difference which always makes a picture, an image, or a shadow so much more attractive than the original" (II, 57). This is the language that Hawthorne characteristically uses in praise of great art; and yet Aylmer's magic show is a prelude to murder, a distraction covering psychopathic intentions. In the tale's schematic opposition of the earthly and the spiritual, Georgiana's chambers represent an extreme of bodiless fantasy no less unwholesome than the bowel-like laboratory where Aylmer's dream will be consummated.

Aylmer's art may thus be regarded as serving the cause of repression. It is meaningful in this light that *conceal-*

ment is the dominant motif in Georgiana's chambers. They were formerly used for Aylmer's "recondite pursuits"; they are fitted to be "the secluded abode of a lovely woman"; their curtains, "concealing all angles and straight lines, appeared to shut in the scene from infinite space"; Aylmer has succeeded in "excluding the sunshine"; and he feels able to "draw a magic circle around [Georgiana] within which no evil might intrude" (II, 55f.). Such emphasis, combined with the chambers' lavish artiness, dimness, and heavy perfumes, implies that something very gross needs to be hidden; it is, as we recall, Georgiana's sexuality. Like Rappaccini's garden, Aylmer's interior decoration incorporates eroticism into what was meant as a refuge from sex. The "penetrating fragrance," "gorgeous" adornment, "rich" fabrics, and "soft, impurpled radiance" (II, 55f.) of the apartments remind us of the garden's erotic suggestiveness. In both cases the artificer reveals himself at last to be sadistically vengeful toward the womanliness he can neither accept nor perfectly exclude. And Rappaccini, incidentally, contemplates his poisoned lovers "as might an artist who should spend his life in achieving a picture or a group of statuary and finally be satisfied with his success" (II, 146).[2]

These examples might lead us to suppose that Hawthorne sees some necessary connection between frustrated sexuality and art. The point is oddly corroborated by Hester Prynne, whose nature would seem to be opposite to Aylmer's. Hawthorne leaves no doubt that her artistic embroidery, with its "fertility and gorgeous luxuriance

2. Lest the reader see no resemblance between Rappaccini and his creator, we may cite Hawthorne himself on the "gross, gross, gross" older women of England: "Surely, a man would be justified in murdering them—in taking a sharp knife and cutting away their mountainous flesh, until he had brought them into reasonable shape, as a sculptor seeks for the beautiful form of woman in a shapeless block of marble." Hawthorne, *The English Notebooks,* ed. Randall Stewart (New York, 1962), p. 88.

of fancy" (*C*, I, 53), expresses her sexuality. "She had in her nature a rich, voluptuous, Oriental characteristic,—a taste for the gorgeously beautiful, which, save in the exquisite productions of her needle, found nothing else, in all the possibilities of her life, to exercise itself upon." (*C*, I, 83) Her needlework "might have been a mode of expressing, and therefore soothing, the passion of her life" (*C*, I, 84). This passion is, to be sure, normal rather than fugitive. Yet even Hester feels guilty about the modest degree of fulfillment she has found in her art, and Hawthorne notes, "This morbid meddling of conscience with an immaterial matter betokened, it is to be feared, no genuine and stedfast penitence, but something doubtful, something that might be deeply wrong, beneath" (*C*, I, 84). Even for the most bounteously passionate of Hawthorne's characters, then, art and guilt are intertwined. Only by following the implication that Hester's art is sexually gratifying can we understand why "she rejected it as sin" (*C*, I, 84).

Insofar as Hester differs from the Brand-Aylmer-Rappaccini type of proto-artist, she also differs from most of the real artists in Hawthorne's fiction. For Hawthorne is, not surprisingly, fascinated by failure—both artistic failure and the failure of maturity that makes art necessary as a psychological recourse. Hester's example indicates that art emerges from sexuality and is called upon to substitute for it, but in most cases the substitution is not merely inadequate, but neurotic.

No one can fail to be impressed by the frequency with which Hawthorne's artists, and especially his vaguely autobiographical narrators, are characterized as self-indulgent peepers. The *locus classicus* occurs in "Sights from a Steeple," whose narrator, "all-heeding and unheeded" in his lofty perch, envisions an ecstasy of voyeurism: "The most desirable mode of existence might be that of a spiritualized Paul Pry, hovering invisible round man and woman, witnessing their deeds, searching into their hearts, borrowing brightness from their felicity and shade from their sorrow, and retaining no emotion peculiar to himself" (I, 220).[3] The prefiguration here of such cold-hearted observers as Ethan Brand and Miles Coverdale is obscured by the lack of criticism or irony on Hawthorne's part, but already we see the root ideas of investigation, vicarious and hoarded power, and emotional withdrawal. A little later this same narrator finds himself fascinated by two girls who meet a young man, and he is quite content to see the young man show a preference for the girl "to whom I—enacting, on a steeple top, the part of Paris on the top of Ida—adjudged the golden apple" (II, 223). What separates the narrator from the chosen lady is not simply physical distance but aesthetic distance, i.e., the wish to substitute contemplation for involvement.

"The Toll-Gatherer's Day" opens with a similar fantasy about a man "whose instinct bids him rather to pore over the current of life than to plunge into its tumultuous waves" (I, 234)—an arresting metaphor. The toll-gatherer who is said to be ideally situated for such activity might find "grotesque merriment" (I, 238) in the passing of newlyweds in their bridal carriage. It is the Hawthornian narrator, however, who truly relishes this scene. He fancies that the bride's "blushing cheek burns through the snowy veil" (I, 238), and he mentally offers the pair an extravagant honeymoon wish that concludes: "May the hot sun kindle no fever in your hearts! May your whole life's pilgrimage be as blissful as this first day's journey, and its close be gladdened with even brighter anticipations than those which hallow your bridal night!" (I, 238) The narrator's apostrophe, following upon his vicarious sensing of the bride's erotic expectations, may not be altogether free of the cynical irony that was directly expressed in the notebook entry from which Hawthorne took the incident: "It would be pleasant to meet them again next summer," Haw-

3. Hawthorne's allusion is to John Poole's farce of 1825, *Paul Pry*.

thorne had recorded, "and note the change" (*American Notebooks*, p. 34).

Without a knowledge of Hawthorne's later career we might not lay much stress on these passages, for they show little or no moral criticism of the voyeuristic tendency. Sometimes, as in "Sunday at Home," the peeping narrator is presented as a thoroughly charming and amiable fellow whose detachment has nothing to do with sex and is positively a virtue (see I, 37). Sometimes Hawthorne surprises us with scenes of overtly lascivious voyeurism which he himself seems to regard as blandly innocent; "Sketches from Memory" provides the most outstanding example.[4] And the adolescently indulgent "Fragments from the Journal of a Solitary Man," which idealizes a tragically wasted young writer, ends with a deathbed journal entry which is meant to convey a surpassing moral sympathy but which again is plainly an exalted voyeurism: "Soon to be all spirit, I have already a spiritual sense of human nature, and see deeply into the hearts of mankind, discovering what is hidden from the wisest. The loves of young men and virgins are known to me, before the first kiss, before the whispered word, with the birth of the first sigh" (XII, 41). The "Oberon" of this tale (the name is Hawthorne's own nickname from college days) has the customary lack of rapport with women that we expect of all Hawthorne's

4. And curiously enough, this frank scene is pure autobiography, referring to Hawthorne's overnight passage on an Erie Canal boat: "My head was close to the crimson curtain,—the sexual division of the boat,—behind which I continually heard whispers and stealthy footsteps; the noise of a comb laid on the table or a slipper dropped on the floor; the twang, like a broken harpstring, caused by loosening a tight belt; the rustling of a gown in its descent; and the unlacing of a pair of stays. My ear seemed to have the properties of an eye; a visible image pestered my fancy in the darkness; the curtain was withdrawn between me and the western lady, who yet disrobed herself without a blush" (II, 491).

isolated figures,[5] and we are left to infer that art has replaced normal love in his mental economy.

Thus we can say that Hawthorne's early works frequently provide a basis for ironic criticism of the emotionally deprived artist, but rarely engage in this criticism —for obvious autobiographical reasons. The often neglected example of *Fanshawe* is characteristic. Hawthorne makes it clear that Fanshawe's temporary hope of winning Ellen Langton's love is an either-or alternative to his "dream of undying fame, which, dream as it is, is more powerful than a thousand realities" (*C*, III, 350). The transparently projective romance eventually brings its virtuous but consumptive hero a fairly direct offer of marriage from the heroine—an offer he refuses with a quixotic logic worthy of Henry James.[6] Fanshawe's manly alter ego, the class poet Edward Walcott, marries Ellen and significantly puts poetry aside; "and he never regretted the worldly distinction of which she thus deprived him" (*C*, III, 460). Fanshawe, having morbidly assured his lady love that she will not be to blame for the shortness of his life, literally studies to death at the age of nineteen; like many

5. "Even a young man's bliss has not been mine," he reveals. "With a thousand vagrant fantasies, I have never truly loved, and perhaps shall be doomed to loneliness throughout the eternal future, because, here on earth, my soul has never married itself to the soul of woman" (XII, 26). This tale is especially noteworthy for its recounting of a dream which represents Oberon as horrifying everyone by promenading on Broadway in a shroud. The general theme of morbid exhibitionism and alienation from humanity throws an interesting light not only on the hidden meaning of Oberon's art, but also on a parallel hero, the Reverend Hooper. Hooper is the degenerate Hawthornian artist *par excellence* in asserting vicarious control over his fellow men by withdrawing from a woman and making a public but ambiguous display of his fantasies.

6. " 'You have spoken generously and nobly, Ellen,' he said. 'I have no way to prove that I deserve your generosity, but by refusing to take advantage of it.' " (*C*, III, 458)

another Hawthornian bystander, he has escaped a relationship for which he was temperamentally unsuited. Yet
Hawthorne's emphasis is one of sacrificial self-pity rather
than irony. If we see (as many critics have seen) that Walcott and Fanshawe are complementary sides of Hawthorne,
we may say that the romance satisfies two fantasies, one of
heroism and amorous success and another of throbbing
self-abnegation. The net effect is more or less what we
gather from Hawthorne's early letters and journals: he
continues to cherish his own dream of undying fame but
senses that it would be dissipated by a happy marriage.

If the artist as a character-type is invariably loveless and
frequently self-inhibited, we cannot be astonished if his
art sometimes becomes a symbolic outlet for eroticism.
Take, for instance, the narrator of "Footprints on the Sea-
Shore," whose entire meditation is an equivocal defense
of artistic vicariousness. His solitary activities are those
of a man who needs to express his fantasies but who fears
the public's intruding gaze and doubts his ability to
achieve fame (see especially I, 508). Three girls, who
"mingle like kindred creatures with the ideal beings of
my mind" (I, 511), taunt him by appearing and disappear-
ing on various parts of a beach, evoking his peeping tendency and challenging his vow to solitude. Finding one
suggestive recess after another in which to linger, the narrator lets his mind "disport itself at will":

> There is a magic in this spot. Dreams haunt its precincts
> and flit around me in broad sunlight, nor require that
> sleep shall blindfold me to real objects ere these be
> visible. Here can I frame a story of two lovers, and make
> their shadows live before me and be mirrored in the tran-
> quil water, as they tread along the sand, leaving no foot-
> prints. Here, should I will it, I can summon up a single
> shade, and be myself her lover. Yes, dreamer,—but your
> lonely heart will be the colder for such fancies. (I, 513)

This narrator understands that it would be best to keep his fancies private, and that their effect will be to weaken his emotional ties to reality. Literary imagination, like other workings of fantasy in Hawthorne's protagonists, is a result of sexual cowardice, and reality often intrudes to deride it—as the three girls in this tale later deride the peeper by peeping at *him* with "stifled laughter" (I, 514).

The pattern of furtive erotic gratification through artistic fancy is a recurrent one. Thus the narrator of "The Vision of the Fountain," who has glimpsed and then lost an enticing female apparition, tells us how he accommodated himself to his loss:

> I withdrew into an inner world, where my thoughts lived and breathed, and the Vision in the midst of them. Without intending it, I became at once the author and hero of a romance, conjuring up rivals, imagining events, the actions of others and my own, and experiencing every change of passion, till jealousy and despair had their end in bliss. Oh, had I the burning fancy of my early youth, with manhood's colder gift, the power of expression, your hearts, sweet ladies, should flutter at my tale!
> (I, 246)

In this passage the motive for fiction is vicariously erotic in a triple sense: as creator, hero, and storyteller the artist gains control over a love-situation, successfully competes within that situation, and causes ladies' hearts to flutter at the narrative.[7]

7. Only one tale, so far as I know, contradicts the theory that art results from a withdrawal from sexual reality. This is "Drowne's Wooden Image," whose sculptor-hero is inspired by genuine love. Yet here the art-work's role is more startling than elsewhere: it is a direct object of desire. Drowne is seen "bending over the half-created shape, and stretching forth his arms as if he would have embraced and drawn it to his heart; while, had such a miracle been possible, his countenance expressed passion enough to communicate warmth and sensibility to the lifeless oak" (II, 353). And the real existence of

If art is to be interpreted as compensation for sexual failure, we cannot be surprised when we come across certain Hawthornian artists who would like to use their plots spitefully. In "Night Sketches," for example, the ubiquitous narrator spies upon a man and woman who have slipped into a rain-swollen street. "Luckless lovers!" he muses. "Were it my nature to be other than a looker-on in life, I would attempt your rescue. Since that may not be, I vow, should you be drowned, to weave such a pathetic story of your fate as shall call forth tears enough to drown you both anew" (I, 482). The tone is whimsical, yet this "looker-on in life" unmistakably *wants* the observed lovers to perish—and for the sake of his emotional power over his readers. We may recall at this point the aggressive intentions of the narrator of "Alice Doane's Appeal," who wants timid maids to tremble on a spot "where so many had been brought to death by wilder tales than this" (XII, 289). Not only does he feel a need to unburden himself of the inner story's theme, but he succeeds in breaking down his listeners' indifference in a suggestive way: "Their bright eyes were fixed on me; their lips apart" (XII, 289). The trembling and tears that ensue attest to the narrator's rapacious intent; he has used his art to simulate what he dare not try in reality.

The artist's self-pity, like that of other thwarted lovers, easily verges into fantasies of destruction. The nervous poetaster who is joining an austere Shaker community in "The Canterbury Pilgrims" is vexed by his anonymity: "But I have my revenge! I could have given existence to a thousand bright creations. I crush them into my heart, and there let them putrefy! I shake off the dust of my feet against my countrymen!" (III, 522).[8] And the theme

---

Drowne's beloved model is left in doubt until the final paragraph of the story.

8. This passage bears comparison to a letter of Hawthorne's to Longfellow in which he says that if his neglectful readers "will not

of malice against both the artist's characters and his public is consummated in "The Devil in Manuscript," which re-introduces us to a different, but more closely auto-biographical, Oberon as he is about to burn his tales. First he notes with satisfaction that the fire is consuming his fictional personages:

> "They blaze," said he, "as if I had steeped them in the intensest spirit of genius. There I see my lovers clasped in each other's arms. How pure the flame that bursts from their glowing hearts! And yonder the features of a villain writhing in the fire that shall torment him to eternity. My holy men, my pious and angelic women, stand like martyrs amid the flames, their mild eyes lifted heavenward. Ring out the bells! A city is on fire. See!—destruction roars through my dark forests, while the lakes boil up in steaming billows, and the mountains are volcanoes, and the sky kindles with a lurid brightness! All elements are but one pervading flame! Ha! The fiend!" (III, 581)

Then, in a joyful frenzy bordering on madness, Oberon sees that the flame from his chimney has started a general fire: "The Fiend has gone forth by night, and startled thousands in fear and wonder from their beds! Here I stand,—a triumphant author!" (III, 583). Doubtless this is meant to be a comic ending, but its spirit is vengeful. If the burning of Oberon's art releases a "Devil" of malice, are we not entitled to say that the malice was latent in that art all along? The fire acts as a cancellation of reticence; what was formerly covert is now allowed to work

---

be grateful for [the imagination's] works of beauty and beneficence, then let them dread it as a pervasive and penetrating mischief..." Turning satirist, Hawthorne will "select a victim, and let fall one little drop of venom on his heart, that shall make him writhe before the grin of the multitude for a considerable time to come..." (Quoted by Stewart, *American Notebooks*, p. 298n.) Here Hawthorne becomes in fantasy a Hawthornian experimenter; see, for example, p. 129 above for a literal enactment of the metaphor.

its intended effect. And Oberon is, of course, once again a
bachelor who has been "surrounding myself with shadows,
which bewilder me, by aping the realities of life" (III,
576)—exactly the language with which Hawthorne repeatedly characterized his own bachelorhood.[9]

One-sided though it is, our survey of artist-figures may
help to explain the most curious aspect of Hawthorne's
treatment of art. This is that he appears both to mock the
impotence of fantasy and to fear its power. While he often
regards the artist as a Faustian necromancer who has gained
illegitimate control over other lives, he can also see him
as a charlatan—a fraudulent puppeteer, as in "Main Street,"
"A Select Party," and "Feathertop." The contradiction
makes sense only if we realize that the Hawthornian artist
is trapped in erotic vicariousness. As the first Oberon realizes, the world will scorn a middle-aged man who is "still
telling love-tales, loftily ambitious of a maiden's tears, and
squeezing out, as it were, with his brawny strength, the
essence of roses" (XII, 28). When thwarted, however, the
artist is left with a residue of aggression that may not
always take the trivial form we see in "The Canterbury
Pilgrims" and "The Devil in Manuscript." In certain plots
—most notably "The Prophetic Pictures" and, we shall
argue, *The Blithedale Romance*—Hawthorne explores the
possibility that the artist may truly destroy the real-life
models of his art. If we are left to wonder how literally
this is meant, we are at least convinced that retreat into
fantasy is emotionally dangerous. In an Ethan Brand the
extremes of Devil and charlatan are compatible; the man
who is willing to exaggerate human defects for dramatic
éclat is already fiendish in his isolation and pride.

Our argument is not that Hawthorne consciously depicted his artists as sexual escapists, but that they belong

9. The most famous example occurs in another letter to Longfellow, where Hawthorne self-effacingly declares: "Sometimes, through
a peep-hole, I have caught a glimpse of the real world..." (quoted
by Lathrop, I, 11.)

in this category regardless of his intention. The best illustration of this principle—and the last work we shall consider before turning all our interest to the romances—is "The Artist of the Beautiful," a tale which superficially argues the superiority of art to life.[10] Owen Warland, the ingenious watchmaker who succeeds in creating a rather absurd mechanical butterfly, achieves a transcendent exaltation which cannot even be affected by the butterfly's destruction. "When the artist rose high enough to achieve the beautiful, the symbol by which he made it perceptible to mortal senses became of little value in his eyes while his spirit possessed itself in the enjoyment of the reality" (II, 535f.). This ending, along with the rhetoric of eternity and ideality that precedes it, is sincerely meant as a rebuke to the earthly characters who have misunderstood and discouraged the artist. Yet Owen's triumph, if we examine it closely, is seen to be a direct result of his frustrations; rather than simply aspiring to the ideal and persevering in spite of temporal interference, he has turned to the ideal only as a refuge from his weakness of temperament and physique.

We must note in the first place that Owen is conspicuously wanting in masculinity. The tale abounds in sexual innuendo about his penchant for chaste and miniature beauty. Most obviously, Owen

> ...looked with singular distaste at the stiff and regular process of ordinary machinery. Being once carried to see a steam-engine,...he turned pale and grew sick, as if something monstrous and unnatural had been presented to him. This horror was partly owing to the size and terrible energy of the iron laborer; for the character of Owen's mind was microscopic, and tended naturally to the

10. Useful studies of this tale are Rudolph Von Abele, "Baby and Butterfly," *Kenyon Review,* XV (Spring 1953), 280-92, and William Bysshe Stein, " 'The Artist of the Beautiful': Narcissus and the Thimble," *American Imago,* XVIII (Spring 1961), 36-44.

minute, in accordance with his diminutive frame and the marvellous smallness and delicate power of his fingers. (II, 507)

The hero who looks with distaste at the stiff and regular process of ordinary machinery is, not surprisingly, treated with mocking condescension by the object of his love in the tale. Owen detects in Annie Hovenden "a secret scorn —too secret, perhaps, for her own consciousness" (II, 532). She quite literally prefers "the size and terrible energy of the iron laborer," for she marries the potent blacksmith, Robert Danforth, and is perfectly happy with him.

The crucial fact about Owen is not that he is scorned by Annie, Danforth, and Annie's cynical father, Peter Hovenden, but that he feels himself vulnerable to their criticism. He confesses that Danforth's "hard, brute force darkens and confuses the spiritual element within me..." (II, 511), and under Peter's influence "everything was converted into a dream except the densest matter of the physical world. Owen groaned in spirit and prayed fervently to be delivered of him" (II, 514). This suggests that the hero's "spiritual element" is far from self-sufficient; the other characters embody a principle of reality that he can neither achieve nor repress.

Owen's supposedly autonomous artistic power is remarkably dependent on the progress of his courtship. Competition for Annie's love is the motive, and she herself is the muse, of his artistic plans. Only she, furthermore, is capable of altering those plans, first by literally shattering his work and later by becoming engaged to Danforth. On the second occasion Owen's reaction is especially meaningful: he breaks the product of many months' labor and begins to turn fleshly, plump, and babyish—in a word, eunuch-like. This can only mean that Owen's sexuality, such as it is, has expressed itself in his art and is being further thwarted by Annie's refusal to regard that art as an adequate substitute for masculinity. Outwardly, Hawthorne explains,

Owen "had been no ardent or enterprising lover"; his passion has been confined "entirely within the artist's imagination" (II, 522). The Annie who has inspired his art is
"a creature of his own" (II, 523)—in less polite terms, a
masturbatory daydream. Only the forcible interruption of
that daydream frees Owen to give himself to a genuinely
ideal art at the end.

Even at the end, however, Hawthorne cannot keep from
subverting his Platonic theme. Owen, who has expressed
his preference for art over utility by telling Danforth that
he is "not ambitious to be honored with the *paternity* of
a new kind of cotton machine" (II, 511; my italics), finds
Annie "admiring her own infant, and with good reason,
far more than the artistic butterfly" (II, 534). As soon as
we take Owen's brainchild as the real baby's rival—and this
becomes unavoidable when the baby eventually crushes
the butterfly in his hand—the contrast is damaging to
Owen from both a human and an artistic standpoint.
Whereas the ethereal Owen is constrained to design imita-
tions of life, the baby is introduced as "a little personage
who had come mysteriously out of the infinite, but with
something so sturdy and real in his composition that he
seemed moulded out of the densest substance which earth
could supply" (II, 528). The baby, that is, fulfills Hawthorne's criterion for the highest art, and thus constitutes
a living reproach to Owen's flight into sheer "spirituality."
The baby's destruction of the butterfly is superficially
presented as one last act of ungrateful disbelief on the part
of the world, before Owen's Platonism has the final say;
but Hawthorne has taken pains to remind us that the
source of that Platonism is impotence.

We may observe, finally, that Owen's gradual sublimation of instinct follows a regressive pattern. Owen is childlike and becomes more so as his amorous hopes are
dimmed; correspondingly, he makes his artistic muse
Annie-as-mother after he has been deprived of Annie-as-
possible-wife (see II, 527). In his last phase he has managed

to erase the female ideal from consciousness, but he has reached this point only by withdrawal from a failed attempt at normal love through a subsequent worship of a mother-figure. The victory of pure art coincides with a total failure of manhood and a repudiation of the emotional ties which Hawthorne elsewhere treats as the necessary condition for sanity.

We are not permitted to doubt Hawthorne's word that Owen's new "reality" is a great solace to him. But this is very different from saying that art is worth making sacrifices for. Both Owen and Hawthorne show every sign of preferring the human reality which art imperfectly, ineffectually, and guiltily simulates, but which is unattainable for certain temperaments. We shall hardly be amazed when Hawthorne, unlike Owen, finds it impossible to be an artist any longer without making embarrassed apologies to imaginary critics. The end is already discernible when artistic beauty is represented by a mechanical butterfly that is fashioned by an effeminate failure and crushed in a baby's tiny fist.

X

Homely Witchcraft

"A thought may be present to the mind, so distinctly that no
utterance could make it more so; and two minds may be conscious of the same thought, in which one or both take the
profoundest interest; but as long as it remains unspoken, their
familiar talk flows quietly over the hidden idea, as a rivulet
may sparkle and dimple over something sunken in its bed. But,
speak the word; and it is like bringing up a drowned body out
of the deepest pool of the rivulet, which has been aware of the
horrible secret all along, in spite of its smiling surface."
                         —HAWTHORNE, *The Marble Faun*

Anyone who is following Hawthorne's romances in order
must review his methodology when he reaches *The House
of the Seven Gables* (1851). From this book through *The
Blithedale Romance, The Marble Faun,* and the four romances that remained unfinished, Hawthorne's fictional
world is beset with incongruities. Characters sincerely explain their motives, apparently with Hawthorne's concur-
rence, and then reveal quite opposite motives that are
never discussed. They sometimes raise the social and moral
questions that came to preoccupy Hester Prynne, but instead of answering those questions they bend all efforts to
not thinking about them any more; and when they succeed
in this blackout Hawthorne seems relieved. Relief, indeed,
is the desired end-point of each romance—not a solution
to its thematic issues but oblivion to them. As we suggested at the start of the previous chapter, it is Hawthorne
himself and not his characters for whom this oblivion can
be understood as meaningful. No wonder the characters

are so inarticulate when they try to explain why they feel troubled; the trouble lies more in their meaning for Hawthorne than in their somewhat flimsy literal dilemmas. The critic must decide whether to go on trying to explain the characters' reticences and oddities without referring to this private symbolism. Once committed to the seemingly unexceptionable premise that Hawthorne and his late characters consciously know what they are doing, the critic is helpless to account for an art that becomes progressively more cryptic, bizarre, and self-defeating.

The problem is, to be sure, relatively inconspicuous in *The House of the Seven Gables,* which can engage the reader successfully either in its love story, its picturesque Salem history, its Yankee humor, its romantic legend, its modern realism, its melodrama, or even its few moments of Gothic terror. Only when he tries to find aesthetic order in these motley effects does the critic begin to see that there is something fundamentally contradictory in Hawthorne's romance. Why does the announced moral purpose of showing that "the wrong-doing of one generation lives into the successive ones, and . . . becomes a pure and uncontrollable mischief" (III, 14) get dissolved in the "dear home-loveliness and satisfaction" that Sophia Hawthorne discerned in the final pages? Is it because Hawthorne's true intention was comic and sentimental all along? But if so, how do we account for the primitive intensity with which both Hawthorne and his "good" characters seem to despise and fear the villain of the story, Judge Jaffrey Pyncheon? Why is Holgrave, the daguerreotypist, author, and social radical, represented as being both self-sufficient and in desperate need of marriage to the busy little conformist, Phoebe Pyncheon? Why does the mere death of Jaffrey Pyncheon, rather than any conscious moral penance, free the modern Pyncheons from the real or metaphorical curse that has dogged their family for two centuries? Why does Hawthorne feel obliged to dwell whimsically, but at disconcerting length, on a number of largely trivial symbols—a house, an elm, a well, a spring, a mirror, some posies, a garden, some hens, some bees? Why must he apologize over and over for being tedious or inconsistent in tone? Why does he use his plot for an extensive yet partly covert review of all the scandals and weaknesses in his own family history? And why, in his avowed attempt at writing a popular romance, does he give such prominence to two characters, Hepzibah and Clifford Pyncheon, for whom nearly all the possibilities of life are already exhausted?

In order to take a sufficiently inclusive view of *The House of the Seven Gables* we must both examine and look beyond Hawthorne's surface emphasis. The book is not a diabolical exercise in deceit; Hawthorne means, or would like to mean, what he says about his characters and their doings. But his deeper hints of characterization, his imagery, and the direction of his plot all bespeak an overriding concern with an unstated theme. The ending, which strikes the modern reader as morally complacent, is in fact psychologically urgent, an ingeniously ambiguous gesture of expiation for a dominant idea that has been warping the book's direction. When the obsessed Holgrave, the character who most nearly resembles Hawthorne-as-artist, swears to Phoebe that he has already turned conservative for her sake, he is making a declaration on behalf of the entire romance. *The House of the Seven Gables* "turns conservative" as a way of evading its deepest implications —the same fantasy-implications we have noted elsewhere.

Looking forward to Hawthorne's creative breakdown as well as backward to the tales mentioned in Chapter 9, we shall argue that on its autobiographical level *The House of the Seven Gables* is "about" the risks of artistic imagination, which are simply the risks of seizure by unconscious wishes. Roughly the same debate between fantasy and inhibition recurs in each of the late romances, and always with the same outcome. Since forbidden thoughts inevitably smirk through the best efforts at conventionality, the whole enterprise of fiction must be symbolically renounced—or, in the case of the four abortive romances, quite literally renounced. We shall be able to show that those last plots are not broken off because Hawthorne became sick or weary or morally confused, but because they too frankly embody the theme which is barely kept under control in the book at hand.

In one respect it is generally agreed that this romance has an autobiographical significance. The Pyncheon forebears, whose history opens the plot and is resumed at several points, are unmistakable representatives of the Hathornes; hence the mixture of nostalgia and resentment in their portrayal. Hawthorne's customary charges against his ancestors—of religious hypocrisy, social tyranny, and moral abuse—are leveled against the Pyncheons, and specific family shames such as the Salem witch hangings are exploited for the announced theme of inherited guilt. The decline of the Pyncheons is half-seriously attributed to a curse which is closely modeled on one that the accused witch Sarah Good supposedly laid upon John Hathorne (really upon Nicholas Noyes). And the disinherited modern Pyncheons resemble Hawthorne in regretting the gradual loss of the authority under which their family's historic crimes were perpetrated. In this light it is significant that the plot works toward a symbolic expiation and a reversal of bad fortune for the sympathetic Pyncheons. Hawthorne can laugh at the worthless "eastern claims" of the Pyncheon-Hathornes, but his satire is blunted by the fact that Hepzibah and Clifford come into easy circumstances, while the "guilty" remnant of Puritan days, the arch-villain Jaffrey Pyncheon, is conveniently and mysteriously put to death. The providential ending, in other words, amounts to a wishful settling of old scores on Hawthorne's part.[1]

1. It is also noteworthy that Clifford Pyncheon has been imprisoned for a crime resembling the White murder case—a page of recent history that Hawthorne found particularly shameful—but is

The very fact that Jaffrey Pyncheon *is* a villain—one who is treated even less generously than Roger Chillingworth—deserves pondering in view of the meaning of ancestral tyrants throughout Hawthorne's fiction. Jaffrey is a slightly attenuated reincarnation of the original Colonel Pyncheon, the family's father; and the entire romance prior to his death is oppressed with a sense of fierce authority and inhibition. Jaffrey's effect on his cousins is exactly that of Colonel Pyncheon's portrait, which, with its "stern, immitigable features," acts as "the Evil Genius of his family," ensuring that "no good thoughts or purposes could ever spring up and blossom" (III, 36) under his gaze. By now we might feel entitled to surmise from such phrases that Jaffrey's role in *The House of the Seven Gables* is paternal, and that the two sets of characters who survive him are symbolically his children. There is in fact more than sufficient evidence for this reading. At present, however, let us rest content with the observation that Jaffrey's death is the central event of the plot, enabling one couple to have a euphoric escape and another couple to marry and become rich. Nor should we omit the effect of Jaffrey's death on Hawthorne himself. Whether or not Jaffrey is recognized as a father figure, the reader must surely acknowledge the clogged passion, the vindictive pleasure, expressed in that extraordinary chapter (18) which is given over to a fearful taunting of Jaffrey's corpse.

A mixture of awe and hatred is discernible through the entire rendering of Judge Pyncheon. His villainy is separated from his conscience by layers of self-esteem and public honor which seem to impress Hawthorne despite his moral disapproval of them. For Hawthorne as for Clifford and Hepzibah, Jaffrey is an imminent presence, an unspecified threat, rather than an active criminal. While he is alive his specific guilt can only be suggested in an elabo-

---

later vindicated by the discovery that no murder took place at all. See note 8 on p. 37 above.

rate, highly tentative metaphor. In some forgotten nook
of the "stately edifice" of an important man's character,
says Hawthorne,

> may lie a corpse, half decayed, and still decaying, and
> diffusing its death-scent all through the palace! The in-
> habitant will not be conscious of it, for it has long been
> his daily breath! Neither will the visitors, for they smell
> only the rich odors which the master sedulously scatters
> through the palace ... Now and then, perchance, comes
> in a seer, before whose sadly gifted eye the whole structure
> melts into thin air, leaving only the hidden nook, the
> bolted closet, ... or the deadly hole under the pavement,
> and the decaying corpse within. Here, then, we are to
> seek the true emblem of the man's character, and of the
> deed which gives whatever reality it possesses to his life.
> And, beneath the show of a marble palace, that pool of
> stagnant water, foul with many impurities, and, perhaps,
> tinged with blood,—that secret abomination, above which,
> possibly, he may say his prayers, without remembering it,
> —is this man's miserable soul! (III, 274)

Hawthorne makes it sufficiently clear that Jaffrey's case
is being described here, yet the deviousness and Gothic
gruesomeness of the accusation show a reluctance to approach the matter very closely. The metaphor, in declaring
that only the sadly gifted eye of the seer can perceive
Jaffrey's real nature, encourages us to look for repressed
guilt or be left with specious appearances; yet Hawthorne
himself is less willing than formerly to explain the nature
and operation of that guilt. Even in death Jaffrey remains
inscrutable and terrifying, resistant to the autopsy of motives that Hawthorne does not yet feel ready to undertake.
    We do, of course, finally learn the exact circumstances
that make Hawthorne "almost venture to say ... that a
daily guilt might have been acted by [Jaffrey], continually
renewed ... without his necessarily and at every moment
being aware of it" (III, 273). Jaffrey has robbed his uncle,

named Clifford; his uncle, witnessing the deed, has consequently died of shock; and Jaffrey has framed his cousin, young Clifford Pyncheon, for this supposed murder. Thus the ex-convict Clifford is, in the sense of Hawthorne's metaphor, Jaffrey's "corpse"—or, to use another word that is much emphasized, his "ghost." In this light the manner of Jaffrey's own death becomes ironically appropriate. As Alfred H. Marks persuasively argues, Hawthorne implies that Jaffrey's mysterious death is caused by the unexpected sight of the "ghost" Clifford Pyncheon.[2] It is likely that Jaffrey dies in the same way as his uncle. A Clifford, in this event, has caused the death of Jaffrey after Jaffrey has caused the death of a Clifford—a symmetry of justice reminiscent of "Roger Malvin's Burial."

To mention "Roger Malvin's Burial," however, is to measure the distance Hawthorne has traveled from the early 1830's. Jaffrey's guilt, unlike Reuben Bourne's, is never rendered in terms of observable behavior; at the moment of his death he is as imposing and impenetrable as ever. It would seem that Hawthorne is more anxious to avoid him than to understand him. Surely it is meaningful that Jaffrey dies offstage through no one's intention, and is only gingerly approached in death by the morbidly scornful narrator. We are nearing the strange world of the unfinished romances, where figures of authority receive sudden outbursts of unexplained authorial hatred and are savagely killed, not by their antagonists, but by "innocent" mischances of plotting. Filial obsession, in other words, is beginning to destroy objective characterization and moral interest.[3]

2. See "Who Killed Judge Pyncheon? The Role of the Imagination in *The House of the Seven Gables*," *PMLA*, LXXI (June 1956), 355-69.

3. The privacy of Hawthorne's filial concern may be gauged from another piece of veiled family biography. Jaffrey's death is immediately, we might almost say causally, followed by the death by cholera, in a foreign port, of his last direct heir. Hawthorne's own father

Yet in a cryptic way *The House of the Seven Gables* deals extensively with moral and psychological affairs. Its "necromancies," we are told, may one day find their true meaning within "modern psychology" (III, 42). In various ways Hawthorne allows us to see the entire historical, social, and symbolic framework of the romance as pertaining to the question of individual guilt. The focal symbol of the House is endowed from the opening page with "a human countenance" (III, 17), and the struggle for possession of it follows familiar Hawthornian lines. The falsely accused wizard Matthew Maule has not been simply executed by his enemy, Colonel Pyncheon; he has been incorporated into the subsequent life of the House. The new structure "would include the home of the dead and buried wizard, and would thus afford the ghost of the latter a kind of privilege to haunt its new apartments..." (III, 21). Like the more strictly figurative "ruined wall" of *The Scarlet Letter,* the Pyncheon estate embodies a mental condition in which an uneasy re-enactment of guilt will be made necessary by the effort to avoid responsibility for that guilt. For all its political and social ramifications, the Maule-Pyncheon antagonism is chiefly a metaphor of imperfect repression.[4]

This imperfect repression is the agent of all the ironic

---

died of a fever (first reported to be cholera) in Surinam—a fact that could hardly have been generally known to readers of *The House of the Seven Gables.* Thus Hawthorne stamps a paternal significance on Judge Pyncheon not for any instructive purpose, but because that is what secret fantasy demands.

4. Note, for example, that the hereditary mesmeric power of the Maules, who are said to dominate the Pyncheons in "the topsy-turvy commonwealth of sleep" (III, 42), directly depends on the Pyncheons' continuing bad conscience. Holgrave, the last of the Maules, tells us this (III, 64), and Hawthorne himself speculates "whether each inheritor of the property—conscious of wrong, and failing to rectify it—did not commit anew the great guilt of his ancestor, and incur all its original responsibilities" (III, 34).

justice in *The House of the Seven Gables*. Every tyrant
is psychologically at the mercy of his victim; or, as Hawthorne puts it in his notebook, "All slavery is reciprocal"
(*American Notebooks*, p. 107). The rule is first applied to
the original Colonel Pyncheon, who dies while inaugurat-
ing the House he has built on the executed Matthew
Maule's property. It is clear that the Colonel's "curse" of
susceptibility to sudden death is nothing other than his
guilt toward Maule. The pattern is repeated for Gervayse
Pyncheon in the story told by Holgrave; this Pyncheon's
greed makes him tacitly co-operate when the second Matthew Maule, supposedly in exchange for a valuable document, takes mesmeric control over his daughter and subsequently causes her death. And if Marks's theory is correct,
Jaffrey Pyncheon is similarly enslaved to the oppressed
Clifford, who is able to cause Jaffrey's death merely by
entering his field of vision. In all these cases it is bad conscience, rather than arbitrary plotting on Hawthorne's
part, that has exacted punishment for abuses of power.

It is not possible, however, to say that perfect justice is
done. If the authoritarian characters suffer from a secret
malaise and eventually come to grief, they nevertheless
have their full stomachs and public dignity for compensation; revenge is sudden and therefore incomplete. The
meek victims, by contrast, are in continual misery (if they
survive at all) until the reversal occurs, and even then they
retain their internalized sense of persecution. Hepzibah
and Clifford, who are presented as figures of infantile innocence, are more pathetic in trying to enjoy their freedom
after Jaffrey's death than in their former state of intimidation. "For, what other dungeon is so dark as one's own
heart! What jailer so inexorable as one's self!" (III, 204)
These sentences, applied to two characters who have done
nothing wrong and indeed have been virtually incapable
of feeling temptation, may remind us that Hawthorne's
focus is not on moral guilt but on a broader phenomenon
of psychological tyranny. The very prominence of Hep-

zibah and Clifford in the plot, along with the somewhat ponderous emphasis on the wasting-away of the Pyncheon energies from generation to generation, suggests that impotence rather than guilt may be Hawthorne's true theme.

I mean the term *impotence* in both a social and sexual sense. It is implied that in some way the Pyncheons have become effete by continuing to deny the claims of the vigorous and plebeian Maules. We could say that a failure of adaptation to modern democratic conditions has left the Pyncheons socially and economically powerless. Clearly, however, this failure has a sexual dimension. Not the least of the Maules' secret privileges is to "haunt . . . the chambers into which future bridegrooms were to lead their brides" (III, 21f.)—a fairly direct reference to some interference with normal sexuality. Just as denial of the earthy Maule element in society leads eventually to a loss of social power, so the same denial in emotional nature—symbolized by refusal to intermarry with the Maule line—leads to a loss of sexual power. Hepzibah and Clifford are the embodied result of these denials, as we shall see.

The conjunction of the sexual and social themes is best illustrated in Holgrave's legend of Alice Pyncheon. The aristocratic Alice, who "deemed herself conscious of a power—combined of beauty, high, unsullied purity, and the preservative force of womanhood—that could make her sphere impenetrable" (III, 242), is in effect seduced by the second Matthew Maule. The language of the entire episode is transparently sexual, and Alice is drawn not merely by mesmeric prowess but by "the remarkable comeliness, strength, and energy of Maule's figure" (III, 240). The outcome of this seduction, however, is not a union of any sort. Having been socially insulted by Alice's arrogant father, Maule uses his sexual mastery only to demonstrate sadistic control over Alice. "A power that she little dreamed of had laid its grasp upon her maiden soul. A will, most unlike her own, constrained her to do its grotesque and fantastic bidding." (III, 249)

This is to say that Maule is perversely toying with Alice's unladylike susceptibility to his erotic appeal, much as the other Maules exploit the Pyncheons' unpaid debt to them. The purpose is exactly opposite to healthy fulfillment, as the final event of Alice's life makes especially clear. The still-virginal Alice, who "would have deemed it sin to marry" because she is "so lost from self-control" (III, 250), is hypnotically summoned to attend Matthew Maule's wedding to a laborer's daughter. Alice's former "purity" and her class-consciousness—they are really a single fastidiousness—are thus successfully flouted; she is spurned and mocked by a man who supposedly had no claim on her interest. Significantly, the only "penetration" of Alice's "sphere" occurs on the way home from this wedding, when a fatal dose of consumption makes its entry into "her thinly sheltered bosom" (III, 250). Alice becomes a romantic prototype of the later, more realistically inhibited Pyncheons who find themselves removed from the possibility of sexual fulfillment. The warfare between repression and the repressed will end only with the marriage of a Pyncheon to a Maule, and this will occur only after the chief impediment to both social and sexual democracy is removed.

What is that impediment? In Alice Pyncheon's case it is a father who imposes his elite pretensions on her, prevents her from considering marriage to a workingman, and half-willingly barters her away for a greedy purpose of his own. Each detail recalls the peculiarly unhealthy situation of Beatrice Rappaccini. When we turn to the modern Pyncheon "children," Hepzibah and Clifford, we find that the role of Gervayse Pyncheon or Dr. Rappaccini is played by cousin Jaffrey. Jaffrey is after the very same document that Gervayse Pyncheon was, and he too has made a "child" —the childlike Clifford—pay for his own criminality. Most strikingly, Jaffrey has hoarded to himself the dwindling sum of Pyncheon eroticism. Though he is not completely immune to the family enervation (see III, 148f.), Jaffrey is still characterized by "a kind of fleshly effulgence" (III,

144) and by "brutish ... animal instincts" (III, 368). In his hypocritical gesture of family affection toward Phoebe, "the man, the sex, somehow or other, was entirely too prominent ..." (III, 146). And it is suggested more than once that Jaffrey, like his first Puritan ancestor, "had fallen into certain transgressions to which men of his great animal development, whatever their faith or principles, must continue liable ..." (III, 151). We begin to understand that the theory of Pyncheon decline—a decline that seems to apply only to real or metaphorical children—is inseparable from the recurrence in each generation of a licentious and selfish male Pyncheon—a caricature of the Freudian child's imagined father.

Two lines of a familiar triangle are thus discernible as un underlying configuration in *The House of the Seven Gables:* an overbearing, terrifying, and guilty "father" is matched against innocent but emotionally withered "children." The third line, which we could infer equally well from Hawthorne's previous work or from psychoanalytic doctrine, should be incest fear—the fantasy-terror which goes into the very idea of an all-forbidding and self-indulging Jaffrey Pyncheon. The Oedipal villain, in other words, is an embodied idea of paternal punishment for thoughts of incest, and the form actually taken by such punishment is impotence.

As it happens, *The House of the Seven Gables* abounds in ambiguous innuendo about both incest and impotence. Thus, for example, Holgrave uses the Pyncheons to illustrate a caution against too prolonged a family dynasty: "in their brief New England pedigree, there has been time enough to infect them all with one kind of lunacy or another!" (III, 222) What cannot quite be uttered about human inbreeding can be said of the family chickens, who are explicit emblems of their owners (see III, 184): "It was evident that the race had degenerated, like many a noble race besides, in consequence of too strict a watchfulness to keep it pure" (III, 113). Whether incest has been liter-

ally committed is as open a question for the Pyncheons
as it was for the Mannings (see p. 36f. above); the real
significance of the incest hints lies in their connection to
the other Oedipal features of the total work. Those features do not encourage us to look for evidence of actual
incest, but on the contrary for the emotional starvation
that ensues from a morbid dread of incest. And this is
exactly what we find in the decrepit siblings, Hepzibah and
Clifford.

Hepzibah is of course a classic old maid, and Hawthorne
keeps the sexual implications of her state before our minds.
He introduces her in mock-erotic terms ("Far from us be
the indecorum of assisting, even in imagination, at a
maiden lady's toilet!" [III, 46]), and he repeatedly characterizes her feelings as those of an aged virgin. He also
supplies us with what might be an etiological suggestion
as to why Hepzibah has remained virginal. Unlike the
other modern Pyncheons, she willingly submits herself to
the imposing portrait of the first Colonel Pyncheon: "She,
in fact, felt a reverence for the pictured visage, of which
only a far-descended and time-stricken virgin could be
susceptible" (III, 50). The father of the Pyncheon dynasty
has acquired some of the affection that would normally be
reserved for a husband. And this admittedly dim suggestion of incestuous feeling is greatly heightened by Hepzibah's secret and tender absorption in another portrait,
whose subject might well have been "an early lover of Miss
Hepzibah" (III, 48)—but is in truth her brother Clifford
as a young man!

Clifford in turn is effeminate and attached to the image
of his mother. His physical traits alone are emphatically
revealing: "full, tender lips, and beautiful eyes" (III, 48),
a face "almost too soft and gentle for a man's" (III, 117),
"thin delicate fingers" (III, 174), and so on. His portrait
not only shows "feminine traits, moulded inseparably with
those of the other sex"; it also makes one think inevitably
"of the original as resembling his mother, and she a lovely

and lovable woman, with perhaps some beautiful infirmity of character . . ." (III, 80). And later we hear of Clifford's dreams, "in which he invariably played the part of a child, or a very young man. So vivid were they . . . that he once held a dispute with his sister as to the particular figure or print of a chintz morning-dress, which he had seen their mother wear, in the dream of the preceding night" (III, 205). Clifford's dream-memory turns out to be exact.

If Clifford's mother is his dream, I find it significant that Jaffrey, who is blamed for his passage directly "from a boy into an old and broken man" (III, 205), is called his "nightmare" (III, 299, 371). Here again the strictest Freudian expectations are fulfilled. The melodramatic villainy of the "father" is blamed for a failure of manhood whose sources are clearly temperamental, and which antedates that villainy. The power of intimidation which Jaffrey has come to symbolize is explained by the manner of Clifford's brief release from it at Jaffrey's death. In a wild exhilaration that contrasts sharply with Hepzibah's more anxious response, Clifford simultaneously tosses off Oedipal rivalry, the Puritan past, and moral restraint; they are all revealed to be emotionally identical. Rocketing to an unknown modern destination on a railroad train that is leaving Jaffrey's corpse ever farther behind, the timid eunuch Clifford suddenly becomes a universal Eros. By means of the telegraph, he predicts excitedly, "Lovers, day by day,— hour by hour, if so often moved to do it,—might send their heart-throbs from Maine to Florida, with some such words as these, 'I love you forever!'—'My heart runs over with love!'—'I love you more than I can!' and, again, at the next message, 'I have lived an hour longer, and love you twice as much!' " (III, 313). This is the Clifford who feared to venture outside his home while Jaffrey lived.

Clifford is perhaps the supreme example in Hawthorne's fiction of a man whose feelings have become polarized between an exquisite aestheticism and frustrated sensuality. His worship of the beautiful and his hypersensitivity

are matched by his huge appetite for food and his rather
prurient titillation in the company of the developing
virgin, Phoebe. Though his interest in her is described as
chaste, Hawthorne adds that

> He was a man, it is true, and recognized her as a woman.
> ... He took unfailing note of every charm that apper-
> tained to her sex, and saw the ripeness of her lips, and
> the virginal development of her bosom. All her little
> womanly ways, budding out of her like blossoms on a
> young fruit-tree, had their effect on him, and sometimes
> caused his very heart to tingle with the keenest thrills
> of pleasure. At such moments,—for the effect was seldom
> more than momentary,—the half-torpid man would be full
> of harmonious life, just as a long-silent harp is full of
> sound, when the musician's fingers sweep across it. (III,
> 171f.)

Significantly, Phoebe's company enables Clifford to retreat
more easily into a state of childhood (see III, 180)—one in
which his "gentle and voluptuous emotion" (III, 48) need
meet no challenges from mature sexual reality.

To understand why Phoebe produces just this effect on
Clifford, it is now necessary to consider her general symbolic role in the romance. It is, of course, a redemptive
role, though by no means a theological one. To the social
and psychological decadence of the House she brings one
supreme virtue that has thus far been lacking: "There was
no morbidness in Phoebe" (III, 166). Her function is to
dispense symbolic sunshine (note her name) where hereditary gloom prevailed before. This is very obvious; but as
always in Hawthorne's serious work, the banal theme is
rooted in psychological relationships of considerable
subtlety.

On the patent level Phoebe represents a kind of innocent energy and prettiness, a domestic competence un-
hindered by any brooding over the meaning of things.

Her Pyncheon blood endows her marriage to Holgrave-
Maule with familial symbolism, but in fact she is antithetical to most of the Pyncheon traits, and her effect on the
ancestral property is to cancel or reverse many of its dark
implications. Thus in the Pyncheon garden, "unctuous
with nearly two hundred years of vegetable decay" (III,
93), she discovers a perfect rose, with "not a speck of blight
or mildew in it" (III, 137). This "nice girl" and "cheerful
little body" (III, 96, 97) aligns herself with all the symbols
of persisting purity amid the general collapse—with the
singing birds and above all with the unpolluted fountain
in the garden. She is even able to neutralize the suggestive
implications of her very bedroom, where "the joy of bridal
nights had throbbed itself away." Hawthorne assures us
that "a person of delicate instinct would have known at
once that it was now a maiden's bedchamber, and had been
purified of all former evil and sorrow by her sweet breath
and happy thoughts. Her dreams of the past night, being
such cheerful ones, had exorcised the gloom, and now
haunted the chamber in its stead" (III, 95).

Now, this passage shows us Phoebe's chief part in the
romance, which is not simply to stand for innocence but
to refute or "exorcise" sexual cynicism. Hepzibah and
Clifford, after all, are innocent enough; but Phoebe's
purity has thematic weight because she is seen at the brink
of womanhood. Hawthorne deliberately puts her within
a sexual perspective in order to declare her exempt from
erotic inclinations. She dreams, but cheerfully; she has
"brisk impulses" (III, 209), but they urge her to hike in
the countryside; her "ordinary little toils," unlike Hester
Prynne's, do not register unfulfilled desire but merely
"perfect health" (III, 167). She is even observed by Clifford at the moment of recognizing the existence of her
emergent sexual appeal, yet she pays for this recognition
with nothing more than a maidenly blush and a slight
modification of her forthrightness (see III, 263).

Phoebe's role is epitomized at one point in a striking oxymoron. In neutralizing the morbidity of her surroundings she is said to wield a "homely witchcraft" (III, 94)—that is, a marriage of spiritual power and tidy domesticity. In Hawthorne's usual world this is unthinkable; one can be either a conventional nobody or a moral outlaw with a special potency of spirit. The "limit-loving" (III, 161) Phoebe, in contrast, derives her power of exorcism precisely from her ignorant conventionality—indeed, from her unwillingness to face unpleasant truths. This is especially apparent in her relations with Clifford: "whatever was morbid in his mind and experience she ignored; and thereby kept their intercourse healthy..." (III, 173). So, too, she innocently evades the lecherous Jaffrey's kiss (see III, 145) and fails to confirm Hepzibah's original fears that she will be a rival for Clifford's love (see III, 91, 98). When she finally confesses that her sentiments toward Hepzibah and Clifford have been maternal (see III, 258), this exemption from sexuality takes on an Oedipal significance. Despite her youth Phoebe stands in the place of an ideal parent, a selfless breadwinner and moral guide who can replace the tyrannical parent of guilty fantasy.

The real test of this role is provided by Holgrave, whose interest in Phoebe is necessarily amorous. Like Jaffrey, he is both haunting and haunted. As a Maule he owns the mesmeric power which seduces and destroys, yet this power leaves him prone to self-destructive monomania. By marrying Phoebe after virtually hypnotizing her and then allowing her to go free after all, he offers a model of self-restraint from the morbid "experimentation" upon womankind that is so tempting for Hawthornian males generally. He and Phoebe together—he having renounced his unconscious, she scarcely having noticed hers—finally embody a contradictory but necessary vision of mature love combined with indefinitely protracted childhood.

It is noteworthy that Hawthorne strains verisimilitude

in order to work Holgrave into his concern for fathers and sons. Without any apparent reason the resourceful and independent daguerreotypist is oppressed by the figure of Jaffrey Pyncheon in death. As he tells Phoebe,

> "The presence of yonder dead man threw a great black shadow over everything; he made the universe, so far as my perception could reach, a scene of guilt and of retribution more dreadful than the guilt. The sense of it took away my youth. I never hoped to feel young again! The world looked strange, wild, evil, hostile; my past life, so lonesome and dreary; my future, a shapeless gloom, which I must mould into gloomy shapes! But, Phoebe, you crossed the threshold; and hope, warmth, and joy came in with you!" (III, 362)

Here the theme of patricidal guilt, again as in "Roger Malvin's Burial," is being stretched to include a wholly symbolic father who has not been murdered at all. Holgrave's fear of "retribution" has no basis in stated motives, yet it reminds us that his view of society and history has been metaphorically Oedipal. The cruel world in his estimate is "that gray-bearded and wrinkled profligate, decrepit, without being venerable" (III, 215); and the tyranny of the past is "just as if a young giant were compelled to waste all his strength in carrying about the corpse of the old giant, his grandfather, who died a long while ago, and only needs to be decently buried" (III, 219). Jaffrey's death thus satisfies a patricidal strain in Holgrave's nature—a fact which is corroborated by his "unmotivated" anxiety before Jaffrey's corpse.

The best indication that the "happy" outcome of *The House of the Seven Gables* was not cathartic for its contriver is an omnipresent uneasiness about the propriety, the honesty, and the quality of fictive art. From the defensively humble Preface onward Hawthorne seems to despair of sustaining the picturesque effects which he simultaneously equates with artistic value and denigrates as trickery. The ending to his plot confirms his pessimism: modern ordinariness triumphs over a compulsive and romantic addiction to the past. To a certain extent this pattern is put to good comic use; in the world of homely witchcraft the only ghosts are "the ghosts of departed cook-maids" (III, 124), and Maule's well is no more bewitched than "an old lady's cup of tea" (III, 120). Especially in his treatment of Hepzibah, who resembles him in trying to sell to "a different set of customers" such traditional wares as "sugar figures, with no strong resemblance to the humanity of any epoch . . ." (III, 53), Hawthorne manages to take a whimsical view of his artistic plight. Like her creator in his post-college years, Hepzibah, "by secluding herself from society, has lost all true relation with it" (III, 257f.) and must now try to "flash forth on the world's astonished gaze at once" (III, 57). And yet her failure to do so—her bondage to an anachronistic stock-in-trade—has a desperate autobiographical meaning for Hawthorne. He as well as Hepzibah, if they are to stay in business at all, must follow the cynical advice on modern salesmanship offered by the earthbound Yankee, Uncle Venner: "Put on a bright face for your customers, and smile pleasantly as you hand them what they ask for! A stale article, if you dip it in a good, warm, sunny smile, will go off better than a fresh one that you've scowled upon" (III, 87).[5]

5. The Hawthorne-Hepzibah parallel can be carried further. In her devotion to the past Hepzibah is said by Holgrave to be "peopling the world with ugly shapes, which you will soon find to be as unreal as the giants and ogres of a child's story-book" (III, 62). The prediction comes true: Hepzibah and Clifford eventually "bade a final farewell to the abode of their forefathers, with hardly more emotion than if they had made it their arrangement to return thither at tea-time" (III, 377). While this is pleasant for Hepzibah, from Hawthorne's point of view it is entirely too easy. He is committed as an artist to the realm of picturesque ancestral guilt which even Hepzibah finds outdated and indeed imaginary.

If Hepzibah illustrates the futility of Hawthornian art in the nineteenth century, Clifford and Holgrave may be said to illustrate the flaws and dangers of the artistic temperament. Clifford, the artist *manqué*, is both squeamish and vicariously sensual, both "ideal" and secretly voracious. At times he is merely irritable and dull, but occasionally his fantasy is given symbolic rein, as when he blows artistic bubbles to be pricked by unappreciative passers-by (see III, 206f.). In either capacity, however, he remains enveloped in a robe of moonshine, "which he hugged about his person, and seldom let realities pierce through" (III, 205). Thus he is an extreme version of the withdrawn Hawthornian artist, and it is not difficult to see what he has withdrawn from. His "images of women," says Hawthorne, "had more and more lost their warmth and substance, and been frozen, like the pictures of secluded artists, into the chillest ideality" (III, 170). As usual, ideality and coldness toward women are the same thing, and are associated with "secluded artists." Only Phoebe, the embodied negation of all unpleasant fantasies about women, can persuade Clifford that "the world was no longer a delusion." [6]

6. One of Hawthorne's miniature allegories of art is especially revealing in this connection. Clifford finds himself aesthetically delighted by an organ-grinder's puppets, until he notices the lewd and greedy monkey who is collecting coins. He is especially struck by the monkey's "wrinkled and abominable little visage" and his "thick tail curling out into preposterous prolixity from beneath his tartans" (III, 197). This tail, "too enormous to be decently concealed," betokens a "deviltry of nature" that is particularly offensive to Clifford-as-artist; for the monkey is seizing pennies on behalf of a parody of art. Clifford "had taken childish delight in the music, and smiled, too, at the figures which it set in motion. But, after looking a while at the long-tailed imp, he was so shocked by his horrible ugliness, spiritual as well as physical, that he actually began to shed tears..." (III, 198). Clifford weeps for his own secret feeling that the aesthetic realm is polluted by greed and lust.

Similarly, Phoebe aids Holgrave in restraining his tendency to be an "all-observant" (III, 189) peeper. His interest
in his companions has essentially been an author's over-
view of his characters, and at one point he actually makes
a literary work out of Pyncheon history. Alice Pyncheon's
legend and the circumstances of its narration sum up
everything Hawthorne has to say about the secret meaning
of art. The legend itself, says Holgrave, "has taken hold
of my mind with the strangest tenacity of clutch . . ." and
he is telling it "as one method of throwing it off" (III, 223).
Authorship, including the intention to publish the work
in a magazine, is presented as a way of mastering obsession. Yet Holgrave has a more immediate purpose as well,
to impress Phoebe with his talent. The covert eroticism of
the story is evidently communicated to its listener, for at
the end she "leaned slightly towards [Holgrave], and
seemed almost to regulate her breath by his":

> A veil was beginning to be muffled about her, in which
> she could behold only him, and live only in his thoughts
> and emotions. His glance, as he fastened it on the young
> girl, grew involuntarily more concentrated; in his attitude
> there was the consciousness of power, investing his hardly
> mature figure with a dignity that did not belong to its
> physical manifestation. It was evident that, with but one
> wave of his hand and a corresponding effort of his will, he
> could complete his mastery over Phoebe's yet free and
> virgin spirit: he could establish an influence over this
> good, pure, and simple child, as dangerous, and perhaps
> as disastrous, as that which the carpenter of his legend
> had acquired and exercised over the ill-fated Alice. (III,
> 252f.)

The thinly euphemistic nature of this scene presumably
enabled its first readers to ignore, or at least to perceive
indistinctly, the implication that cheery little Phoebe is
endowed with sexual desire. She unconsciously welcomes

her seducer, and he "involuntarily" tightens his hold on her. This hold has been won through the mesmeric power of art, and motivated not simply by desire but by the prying and rapacious tendency which in Hawthorne's harsh view constitutes the artistic character. That tendency must be "cured," at least in symbolism, if a satisfactory resolution is to be reached. And thus Holgrave obligingly steps out of his Maule identity and reforms both himself and the spirit of the romance. He relaxes his spell over Phoebe and allows her deliberate obtuseness to have the final say: "But for this short life of ours, one would like a house and a moderate garden-spot of one's own" (III, 188). At the end, though the revitalized Pyncheon chickens have begun "an indefatigable process of egg-laying" (III, 372), art has been tacitly set aside and forgotten.

The logic of this conclusion is impeccable. If the image of Jaffrey Pyncheon in death makes Holgrave's future appear to be "a shapeless gloom, which I must mould into gloomy shapes," and if Phoebe alone can erase that image from his mind, then marriage to Phoebe obviates the need for moulding further "gloomy shapes." To become free of anxiety is to lose all reason for creativity. For Holgrave it cannot matter that Phoebe is in fact a tissue of symbolic contradictions: motherly child, sisterly bride, fertile and prolific virgin. It is Hawthorne for whom this subtle compromise is finally meaningful. And in a broader sense the incongruities of his plot—the yoking together of ancestral guilt, of maladaptation to modern reality, and of a villain's death which produces unholy erotic glee and a therapeutic marriage—find their rationale in Hawthorne's struggle to disbelieve that the world is indeed "a scene of guilt and of retribution more dreadful than the guilt." Not Holgrave but Hawthorne, who called his wife Phoebe, has set Phoebe-ism as the steep ransom from obsession. And it is Hawthorne, ultimately, who with secret and wistful irony measures the consequence of this surrender for his

own later career. "The world owes all its onward impulses
to men ill at ease," he has Holgrave tell Phoebe with great
truthfulness; and shortly thereafter Holgrave adds, "If we
love one another, the moment has room for nothing more"
(III, 363).

XI

Turning the Affair into a Ballad

"Le dessin est une espèce d'hypnotisme: on regarde tellement
le modèle, qu'il vient s'asseoir sur le papier." —PICASSO

If *The Blithedale Romance* (1852), despite a good deal of
recent explication, remains the least admired of Hawthorne's longer narratives, the reason is not far to seek.
The House of the Seven Gables represented a drop in
intensity from the sustained tragedy of *The Scarlet Letter,*
but this next book seems to be divided between a drab
chattiness and episodes of facile melodrama. Numerous
passages are lifted, with scarcely any revision, from Hawthorne's Brook Farm notebooks. The narrator, Miles Coverdale, resembles his creator not only in superficial respects
but in his fears about the unromantic, unpicturesque
nature of modern life; his prose transcribes an incessant
and labored effort to keep our interest. We are tempted
to say that the book would have been better if it had been
wholly devoted either to the autobiographical record of
Hawthorne's disillusionment with Brook Farm utopianism
or to the melodramatic and legendary events which are
conjectured to form the prehistory of Coverdale's friends.

It would be wrong to sweep away these misgivings about
The Blithedale Romance simply on the basis of a theory
about its covert meaning; if the book has struck nearly
all its readers as confused, then it is blameworthy. We are
not surprised to learn that it was extensively rewritten and
that Hawthorne, when he had finished, wondered whether
to call it "Hollingsworth," "Zenobia," "Priscilla," "Miles

194

Coverdale's Three Friends," "The Veiled Lady," "Blithedale," "The Arcadian Summer," or—his choice "in lack of
a better"—"The Blithedale Romance." [1] Such indecision
corresponds all too well to the indecisiveness of the story
itself. *The Blithedale Romance* is a book in which Hawthorne's customary equivocation about social and moral
ideas has been extended to include such apparently ele-
mentary matters as his moral estimate of his characters,
his notion of their feelings about one another, and even
his factual knowledge of their previous lives.

The view we have been taking of Hawthorne's career,
however, leads us to expect that beneath the surface confusion of *The Blithedale Romance* there may be an inner
coherence of self-debate. In the past we have found that
Hawthorne's hesitations and implausibilities have always
been the best indicators of obsessive thematic content; as
the surface world becomes less intelligible its symbolic
value becomes clearer. That this principle applies to the
seeming chaos of the unfinished romances will be amply
demonstrated. Yet *The Blithedale Romance* is just coherent enough to permit its critics to call it failed utopian
satire or failed melodrama or failed autobiography. The
necessity has rarely been perceived of putting the various
imperfect parts within a single rationale that would explain Hawthorne's inability to make any one of them his
focus of interest.

Our position is that *The Blithedale Romance* is, in an
almost incredibly cryptic way, an intelligible product of
the obsessed Hawthorne whose private themes have become so predictable. I believe we can justify the supposition that Hawthorne, finding his literal plot hopelessly
distorted by irrational fantasy, turned the book into a
self-critical comedy by attributing that distortion to his

1. See *The Memoirs of Julian Hawthorne,* ed. Edith Garrigues
Hawthorne (New York, 1938), p. 34, and Hawthorne's *American
Notebooks,* pp. 308f.

narrator. Like James in *The Sacred Fount,* perhaps, he partially rescued a doomed story by stressing the principle of self-delusion inherent in the narrator's—and ultimately in his own—prying concern with other lives. In neither case is the irony sufficiently unambiguous or sufficiently discernible to the reader; the most we can say is that it is consistently available to close scrutiny.

Certainly it is difficult to take the bewildering "romance" among Hollingsworth, Zenobia, and Priscilla as the heart of the book as it now stands. No narrator ever had worse luck than Coverdale in learning the most essential facts about the figures whose story we are supposed to enjoy. Late in the plot he summarizes the points he has yet to settle, and indeed will never get straight at all: "Zenobia's whole character and history; the true nature of her mysterious connection with Westervelt; her later purposes towards Hollingsworth, and, reciprocally, his in reference to her; . . . the degree in which Zenobia had been cognizant of the plot against Priscilla, and what, at last, had been the real object of that scheme" (*C,* III, 215). Most of the important scenes he describes, furthermore, are observed from an inconvenient distance, or are not observed at all. Two of his chapters—Zenobia's legend of the Veiled Lady and the autobiography of her father, old Moodie—are imaginative reconstructions of someone else's words, and for the most crucial meeting of Hollingsworth, Zenobia, and Priscilla he arrives "half-an-hour too late" (*C,* III, 212).

These puzzling difficulties become significant when we realize that Hawthorne, and indeed Coverdale himself, have taken considerable pains to suggest that the story as we read it is not to be altogether trusted.[2] Repeatedly the narrator warns us that his descriptions may interest us not merely for their element of truth but "as exemplifying the

2. Some of the evidence for this and following statements may be found in my article, "A New Reading of *The Blithedale Romance,*" *American Literature,* XXIX (May 1957), 147-70. My present view of the book, however, differs from the conclusions reached there.

kind of error into which my mode of observation was calculated to lead me" (C, III, 71). As soon as we put a friend
under our microscope we "insulate him from many of his
true relations, magnify his peculiarities, inevitably tear
him into parts, and, of course, patch him very clumsily
together again. What wonder, then, should we be frightened by the aspect of a monster, which, after all—though
we can point to every feature of his deformity in the real
personage—may be said to have been created mainly by
ourselves!" (C, III, 69). This is, to be sure, a familiar Hawthornian paradox, but in *The Blithedale Romance* it
appears to have been carried to a logical extreme. For
Coverdale not only takes poetic liberties with the events he
is narrating; he represents himself as having known how
they would turn out before they occurred. His dreams and
fantasies at Blithedale, if they had been recorded, "would
have anticipated several of the chief incidents of this narrative, including a dim shadow of its catastrophe" (C, III,
38). It is impossible to say whether Coverdale has really
had foreknowledge or has seriously altered the facts in
recounting them; the only certain point is that we are
meant to see some degree of correspondence between his
tale and the secret inclination of his mind. From both
ends of the plot—in apparent foreknowledge and in narrative distortion—Coverdale shows us the condition of a man
in the grip of some private symbolism.

Whatever the basis of Coverdale's obsession, the form
it takes is literary. He imagines that his part has been "that
of the Chorus in a classic play, which seems to be set aloof
from the possibility of personal concernment, and bestows
the whole measure of its hope or fear, its exultation or
sorrow, on the fortunes of others, between whom and itself
this sympathy is the only bond" (C, III, 97). Such aloofness is not to be confused with indifference; Coverdale is
saying that he will allow his hope and fear to be expressed
through his set of "characters." Indeed, that is just what
he calls them—"these three characters ... on my private

theatre" (*C*, III, 70). If in real life he is "but a secondary
or tertiary personage" (*C*, III, 70) with his friends, and
if "these three had absorbed [his] life into themselves"
(*C*, III, 194), he at least has the artistic luxury of contemplating their worthiness for a "sufficiently tragic catastrophe" (*C*, III, 79). "After all was finished," he thinks
with satisfaction, "I would come, as if to gather up the
white ashes of those who had perished at the stake, and
to tell the world—the wrong being now atoned for—how
much had perished there which it had never yet known
how to praise" (*C*, III, 161). Though "real life never
arranges itself exactly like a romance" (*C*, III, 104), this
is precisely what Coverdale has hoped to make of it—a
Blithedale Romance. The abandonment of this hope, after
it has been smashed by a real-life tragedy with no literary
trimming, constitutes the true resolution of Hawthorne's
plot.

To state the case in this manner is perhaps to underrate
the obvious intellectual content of *The Blithedale Romance;* as most critics have chosen to emphasize, the book
is Hawthorne's *apologia* for leaving Brook Farm and scorn-
ing its visionary ideals. I am certainly willing to believe
that this was an important part of his intention when he
began writing, but with Hawthorne self-justification invariably verges into self-criticism. What we in fact find in
The Blithedale Romance is not so much a theoretical
refutation of utopianism as an implied confession that the
Hawthorne-Coverdale temperament is unsuited for real
enterprises of any sort, whether spiritual or practical. One
can abstract Coverdale's negative pronouncements about
Blithedale into a body of social theory only by ignoring
the intemperate sarcasm with which those pronouncements
are delivered and the retractions that speedily follow them.
Coverdale himself is aware, as Hawthorne's critics are
often not, that all his contradictory opinions are dictated
by his excessively self-conscious efforts to achieve a steady
relation to his three "characters."

In order to understand Coverdale's complex situation it is not enough to see that he wants his three friends to act out a ready-made romance. Like other artist-heroes in Hawthorne's work he has a private failure of emotional capacity at the base of his need for aesthetic distance. He is the Hawthornian artist *par excellence:* a poetaster and a retiring bachelor whose emotions can be clearly expressed only within a womblike woodland "hermitage" where the voluptuous entanglement of vines and trees is conducive to spying at secret *rendezvous* and daydreaming about artistic and erotic successes that will never be realized. "Had it ever been my fortune to spend a honey-moon," he explains, "I should have thought seriously of inviting my bride up thither"—namely, into "a hollow chamber, of rare seclusion . . . formed by the decay of some of the pine-branches, which the vine had lovingly strangled with its embrace" (*C,* III, 98f.). And yet the speaker of these lines—eloquent as they are in declaring his oneness with the sexual eccentrics who dominate Hawthorne's tales— tells us, when his "romance" has collapsed, that he was in love with Priscilla all along. Whether or not we are prepared to take the statement at face value, its insertion at the last possible moment is characteristic of the erotic furtiveness which pervades the narrative.

Thus we cannot rest content with the view of Coverdale adopted by Hollingsworth, who accuses him of feigning interest in utopianism only because "it has given you a theme for poetry" (*C,* III, 131), nor with the similar charge brought by Zenobia: "You are turning this whole affair into a ballad" (*C,* III, 223; see also p. 33). These half-truths which exaggerate the definiteness of Coverdale's intention and the steadiness of his aesthetic detachment. The cumulative evidence of Coverdale's own statements suggests that he cannot decide whether to win his companions' affection or to pry coldly into "the secret which was hidden even from themselves" (*C,* III, 160). Generally speaking, what happens in the plot is that Coverdale, harboring this uncertainty of purpose, half-intentionally alienates all three of his potential intimates and is thus driven increasingly into the role of literary snoop. Hollingsworth, Zenobia, and Priscilla become, no longer human companions, but "goblins of flesh and blood" (C, III, 157) from whom he would like to escape—but from whom he simultaneously wants to extort "some nature, some passion, no matter whether right or wrong, provided it were real" (C, III, 159). And correspondingly, his fantasies become at once more destructive and more literary as he is continually rebuffed. Well before the real tragedy of the book occurs, Coverdale

> began to long for a catastrophe. If the noble temper of Hollingsworth's soul were doomed to be utterly corrupted by [his] purpose . . . ; if the rich and generous qualities of Zenobia's womanhood might not save her; if Priscilla must perish by her tenderness and faith . . . ; then be it so! Let it all come! As for me, I would look on, as it seemed my part to do, understandingly . . . The curtain fallen, I would pass onward with my poor individual life, which was now attenuated of much of its proper substance . . . (C, III, 157)

This vengeful daydream recalls the consolations of other embittered artists in Hawthorne's fiction. Having survived his indifferent friends and emptied himself of concern for them (even at the price of losing all further meaning in his life), Coverdale will have the luxury of contemplating their doom "reverently and sadly" (C, III, 157).

Though it is impossible to draw a point-by-point comparison between the actual course of events and Coverdale's fantasies, we can observe that the real calamity of the plot makes Coverdale profoundly ashamed of those fantasies. This may suggest that something more is involved than mere disappointment of the wish to win Priscilla. Like some previous heroes Coverdale is made to feel guilty, or at any rate chastened, about a death he has not caused but has hazily "foreseen" in fantasy. It seems plausible to assume that one component of his feelings toward Zenobia—namely, the anxiety that has made the pale Priscilla a safer object of desire—has found the thought of her removal advantageous. Or we could surmise, with equal likelihood, that it is Hollingsworth, his rival for the affection of both women, against whom Coverdale's aggressive prophecies have been intended. In either case Coverdale has indeed anticipated "a dim shadow of the catastrophe" of his Blithedale Romance, and is jolted by the shocking explicitness of that catastrophe when it occurs.

Coverdale himself has no clear idea of why Hollingsworth, Zenobia, and Priscilla together are more meaningful to him than his relation to any one of them individually. And yet our awareness of the fantasies chronically harbored by Hawthorne's escapists may make us attentive to some revealing clues. Hawthorne and Coverdale have virtually begged us to see the story of Coverdale's friends —not just his attitude toward it, but the bare facts of the story itself—as indicative of the inmost tendency of his mind. That story, we must emphasize, is intricately involved in family matters of a vaguely guilty nature. The sexual rivals, Zenobia and Priscilla, turn out to be half-sisters. Their remorseful benefactor, old Moodie, is revealed to be their common father, who has neglected the child he loved best in order to live vicariously in the other child's splendor (see C, III, 192f.). The devilish mesmerist Westervelt, the touchstone of evil in *The Blithedale Romance,* is said to be Zenobia's former husband. He is thus related, however remotely, to the Priscilla who is perhaps turned over to his mesmeric power through the contrivance of Zenobia herself—a fine example of Hawthornian family co-operation. Priscilla's rescue in turn is effected by the noble Hollingsworth, who, though he has hitherto loved her like "an elder brother" (C, III, 217), promptly marries her.[3]

These facts alone cannot be called proof that the furtiveness and ambivalence of Coverdale's attitudes may be related to a preoccupation with incest. Yet that speculation begins to seem more respectable as we examine the specific feelings his three friends arouse in him. The brash and bosomy feminist Zenobia, Coverdale's first and most deeply engaging figure of challenge, incites anxiety and defensive sarcasm by flaunting her sexuality before him. Her provocative language forces him to picture "that fine, perfectly developed figure, in Eve's earliest garment" (C, III, 47)—a vision not entirely welcome to a nature like Coverdale's. The significant fact, however, is that he can scarcely accept the blatantly obvious fact of her sexual experience, but must dwell on the question with prurient concern: "Pertinaciously the thought—'Zenobia is a wife! Zenobia has lived, and loved! There is no folded petal, no latent dew-drop, in this perfectly developed rose!'— irresistibly that thought drove out all other conclusions, as often as my mind reverted to the subject" (C, III, 47). This dainty pornography is continually rejected as "a masculine grossness—a sin of wicked interpretation, of which man is often guilty towards the other sex" (C, III,

3. Even the nature of Priscilla's affection for Zenobia seems a bit perverse if we follow the implications of Hawthorne's imagery: "Priscilla's love grew, and twined itself perseveringly around this unseen sister; as a grape-vine might strive to clamber out of a gloomy hollow among the rocks, and embrace a young tree, standing in the sunny warmth above" (C, III, 186). The echo of Coverdale's "perfectly inextricable knot of polygamy" (C, III, 98f.) in his tree-vine hermitage casts a metaphorical suspicion of fixated emotion even on the vapid Priscilla—or perhaps merely on Coverdale's interest in her. An article by Allan and Barbara Lefcowitz, soon to be published in Nineteenth-Century Fiction, explores the remarkable sexual innuendoes surrounding Priscilla's role as a mesmeric clairvoyant and a maker of tiny purses.

47). The absurdity of such scrupulous fancies is diminished if we bear in mind that Zenobia is, for Coverdale's mind, less an individual person than "womanliness incarnated" (*C*, III, 44), and that his view of this womanliness is rather that of a scandalized son than a sophisticated bachelor. Like his younger predecessors Goodman Brown and Robin Molineux, Coverdale has not yet forgiven womankind for its deviation from the maternal ideal.

If Zenobia is to this extent eligible for sentiments that should properly attach themselves to a mother, Hollingsworth is more easily recognized as a version of the Hawthornian father. Though Coverdale is forced to respect him and yearn for his affection, the physically imposing, fiercely stern and fanatical Hollingsworth drains life from everyone who must live under his authority, and more particularly usurps all the feminine sympathy that Coverdale himself seeks. In retrospect it seems inevitable that he must eventually appear to Coverdale in the stereotyped role of the Hawthornian father, as "the grim portrait of a Puritan magistrate, holding inquest of life and death in a case of witchcraft" (*C*, III, 214). The transformation has been anticipated since Coverdale's first confession that he feels a need to exaggerate Hollingsworth's awesomeness: "In my recollection of his dark and impressive countenance, the features grew more prominent than the reality, duskier in their depth and shadow, and more lurid in their light; the frown, that had merely flitted across his brow, seemed to have contorted it with an adamantine wrinkle" (*C*, III, 71). Here we are observing Coverdale in the process of creating a bogey-father, a devil; and significantly, the true "devil" of *The Blithedale Romance*, Westervelt, is held responsible for having destroyed Zenobia's much-lamented innocence.

As for Priscilla, she is literally a sister, she looks like a sister, she is loved like a sister by Hollingsworth, and she inspires protective brotherly feelings—mixed with an erotic desire which is confessed later—on Coverdale's part.

The shunting of that desire from Zenobia to her is nothing more than what is demanded by Freudian logic and
Hawthornian precedent. Her integral role in Coverdale's
fantasy-family is indicated by his most revealing dream:
"Hollingsworth and Zenobia, standing on either side of
my bed, had bent across it to exchange a kiss of passion.
Priscilla, beholding this—for she seemed to be peeping in
at the chamber-window—had melted gradually away, and
left only the sadness of her expression in my heart" (C,
III, 153). The reader who doubts that Coverdale has unconsciously cast himself as a son must wonder why this
dream depicts Hollingsworth and Zenobia in the unortho-
dox erotic pose of bending across Coverdale's bed. And
all readers must surely note the moral ambiguity of the
wish expressed in the dream. Priscilla is meant to be dis-
illusioned by the sexual passion which she has discovered
in her elders, yet Coverdale's own intentions toward her,
as we later discern, are those of a lover. As in the unfinished romances, where real brothers and sisters are forever about to become lovers or spouses, the image of
Priscilla-detached-from-Hollingsworth melts away before
its purpose in Coverdale's mental scenario becomes too
plain.

In all this, it may be objected, there is no compelling
evidence that Coverdale's hesitant designs on Priscilla, and
more distantly on Zenobia, are incestuous in quality. I
agree. What we find is, on one side, an extraordinary deviousness in his approach to both women, and on the other
a configuration of attitudes which, if discovered in a real
neurotic, would point to incestuous fixation. A man of
mature years who dwells with awe and titillation on the
possibility that a mature woman may not be virginal, who
must suppose that her experience has been at the hands
of a fiendish seducer, who hopes for the love of a sexless
girl but can do nothing to win her, and who turns his
sexual rival into an imaginary paternal tyrant—such a man
may justly be called a casualty of Oedipal strife. The real

difficulty in applying this reasoning to Coverdale is that the literal reality surrounding him conforms so well to his apparent fixation. We must assume, as so often in the past, that the obsession of *The Blithedale Romance* is jointly owned by the hero and the author. And this assumption is necessary anyway if we are to accept without astonishment the intricacy and secrecy of self-debate in this book. If Hawthorne has blurred all his portraits except Coverdale's, backed away from the simplest explanations of fact, exploited literal scenes for a cabalistic meaning that is lost upon the reader, and included episodes that make virtually no sense apart from such meaning, then we must infer that Hawthorne as well as Coverdale is at the mercy of unconscious logic.

In that logic, *spiritual aspiration, reform of humanity,* and *romantic art* are interchangeable terms; each represents flight from mature sexual challenge. The touchstone of that challenge, and the implicit reproach to all escapism in *The Blithedale Romance,* is Zenobia, whose womanly nature is equally spurned in the poetic fancies of Coverdale and the zealous perfectionism of Hollingsworth. "The presence of Zenobia," Coverdale admits, "caused our heroic enterprise to show like an illusion, a masquerade, a pastoral, a counterfeit Arcadia, in which grown-up men and women were making a play-day of the years that were given us to live in" (*C,* III, 21). In our view it is far from insignificant that the whole Blithedale colony should be accused of regression to childhood. Unconsciously, no doubt, Coverdale is well equipped to grasp the primitive sameness of motive among all attempts to beautify human nature. Nor is it surprising that the event which signals an end to both Coverdale's and Blithedale's picturesque fancies is the death of Zenobia; the *raison d'être* for all such fancies is avoidance of the object of anxiety that has been too violently removed.

If acceptance of Zenobia is the measure of normality in *The Blithedale Romance,* the opposite psychological

extreme is embodied in Westervelt. Cynic, fraud, and unscrupulous possessor of a young girl's will, he partakes of
Ethan Brand, of Rappaccini, of Goodman Brown's devil.
"A part of my own nature," says Coverdale frankly,
"showed itself responsive to him" (*C*, III, 102). Coverdale's
latent sense of mankind's corruption—a sense whose sexual
basis we have tried to suggest—is fully developed in Westervelt. Both men are show-masters of a sort, and both use the
rhetoric of ideality to conceal their aversion to humanity.
Both in fact are trying to present the same "Veiled Lady,"
Priscilla, in a magical and romantic light which they know
to be fakery. Both, too, are snoopers; the real difference
is that Westervelt knows the facts that Coverdale hankers
to learn. If Coverdale is appalled by Westervelt's mockery
of him, he nevertheless finds himself drawn ever closer to
the idea of getting Westervelt's precious information. If
Westervelt is a devil, it is Miles Coverdale who, surrounded
by a band of masqueraders who parody his dissociation
from reality, is accused of being "always ready to dance to
the devil's tune" (*C*, III, 211). When Coverdale actually
attends one of Westervelt's mesmeric sessions and sees the
anti-poet Hollingsworth rush onto the stage to rescue Priscilla from her part in a vulgar and fraudulent art form, the
defeat applies as much to Coverdale as to Westervelt. At
the end of the book both men are unemployed mesmerists,
deprived, by a real marriage, of their "subjects" for the
showmanship of repression.

The structure of *The Blithedale Romance* may be appreciated if we picture two opposite lines of development.
Coverdale, beginning with hopes of establishing human
intimacy with his Blithedale friends, moves more or less
steadily in the direction of Westervelt's alienation, cynicism, and artistic quackery. His real "characters," meanwhile, begin in pastoral attitudes and utopian fancies but
become progressively more eligible for the tragic denoue-
ment which in fact occurs. By the time Coverdale, nearly
maddened by his failure as a man and by the failure of

reality to be adequately romantic, stumbles upon Hollingsworth, Zenobia, and Priscilla in their real scene of parting,
he is so abashed by "the intentness of their feelings" that
he feels "no right to be or breathe there" (C, III, 214).[4]
Just when his literary material has become "all that an
artist could desire" (C, III, 214), Coverdale repents of art.
When Hollingsworth departs with Priscilla, Coverdale is
free at last to give Zenobia some genuine sympathy; for
the two of them have been simultaneously deprived of a
love-object and a romantic dream. It is too late for Coverdale to prevent her suicide, but he can at least answer with
a clear conscience when she bursts out, "Ah, I perceive
what you are about! You are turning this whole affair into
a ballad. Pray let me hear as many stanzas as you happen
to have ready!" "Oh, hush, Zenobia!" he answers, in his
nearest approach to human warmth; "Heaven knows what
an ache is in my soul!" (C, III, 223).

The chapter that follows Zenobia's somewhat histrionic
farewell to Coverdale is generally acknowledged as the
strongest portion of *The Blithedale Romance*. Never again,

4. Coverdale is "left to my own conjectures" (C, III, 215f.) about
the terms of the falling-out between Hollingsworth and Zenobia,
and the diligent reader cannot get much farther than Coverdale does
in divining the omitted truth. It seems that Hollingsworth has accused
Zenobia of some misdeed, perhaps the betrayal of her own sister
into Westervelt's hands. In the scene we witness, however, Zenobia
makes the same accusation against Hollingsworth, who now professes
love for Priscilla. We can, however, surmise why Hollingsworth has
switched his attentions from Zenobia to Priscilla. Their sisterhood
has been revealed, and at the same time Zenobia has learned that
she is not to inherit the fortune she supposed—meaning, I gather,
that Moodie has avenged Priscilla's ill-treatment by making her his
heiress. Thus the logical zealot Hollingsworth has simply continued
his policy of courting the lady who can pay for his philanthropic
project. It seems to me that Coverdale has some notion of this, for
he spends a whole paragraph reflecting on Zenobia's willful incapacity to see the worst side of Hollingsworth's motives.

after this scene of three men grimly probing for Zenobia's corpse in a river pool at midnight, was Hawthorne to write so vividly. Here for once Hawthorne-Coverdale has no need of irony or apology for serving up fantasy as if it were truth; the spectacle is so stark that after twelve years Coverdale can "reproduce it as freshly as if it were still before my eyes" (C, III, 235). The counterpointing of Silas Foster's Yankee banalities against the intrinsic horror of the scene is Shakespearian in effect. All affectation has been dismissed —including the affectation of tragedy. Zenobia, Coverdale finds himself reflecting despite himself, must have seen many a sentimental picture of wronged village maidens who had drowned themselves "in lithe and graceful attitudes" (C, III, 236). Had she been able to anticipate the hideous rigidity of her corpse, "she would no more have committed the dreadful act, than have exhibited herself to a public assembly in a badly-fitting garment" (C, III, 236). This is the end of romance, not only for Zenobia but for Coverdale as well. The frank brutality of the chapter amounts to a devastating commentary on all "spiritual" attitudinizing—Coverdale's, Blithedale's, and, we might add, the future attitudinizing of *The Marble Faun*.

Certainly the power of this chapter has much to do with Hawthorne's memory of a similar episode in his own life. To say this, however, is not to explain why the scene consummates the whole progress of *The Blithedale Romance*. The image of Zenobia in death has been anticipated— literally anticipated by the "nameless presentiment" (C, III, 231) which led Coverdale to the river bank, and anticipated in imagery by all the symbolic rigamarole about the veiling of truth. When blunt Silas Foster states the likelihood that Zenobia has drowned, it is "as if he were removing the napkin from the face of a corpse" (C, III, 230). Surely we are meant to recall, at this moment of supreme reality, "the face of a corpse" (C, III, 110) which the hero of Zenobia's own tale of a Veiled Lady imagined beneath the veil. That hero risked losing a beautiful woman's love rather than kiss the "virgin lips" (*C*, III, 113) beneath the veil; he imagined the unseen visage to be, not only a corpse, but "the grinning cavity of a monster's mouth" (*C*, III, 113) or "a monstrous visage, with snaky locks, like Medusa's, and one great red eye in the centre of the forehead" (*C*, III, 110).[5] Zenobia's body has been the source of all curiosity, all squeamishness, and all regressive flight up to this point. In probing with a hooked pole into the "broad, black, inscrutable depth" of the pool, Hollingsworth makes "precisely such thrusts ... as if he were stabbing at a deady enemy" (*C*, III, 232f.)—the knife-thrusts of Aylmer's dream. Zenobia at the bottom of the black pool is yet another petrified Digby in his overgrown cave. If "reality" has the last word in *The Blithedale Romance*, it is not the humdrum reality that Coverdale has found both irritating and secretly comforting, but the conjunction of a factual event with the worst sadistic fantasy.

So, too, Coverdale's emotions when he studies the corpse remain consistent with his Oedipal preoccupation. Neither he nor Zenobia has hitherto shown a sincere interest in religion,[6] yet her last inflexible pose makes Coverdale wonder about the fate of her soul:

One hope I had; and that, too, was mingled half with fear. She knelt, as if in prayer. With the last, choking

5. For psychoanalytic interpretations of the Medusa figure without Hawthorne's untraditional but appropriate extra detail, see Freud, *Collected Papers*, V, 105f., and Sándor Ferenczi, *Further Contributions to the Theory and Technique of Psycho-Analysis* (London, 1960), p. 360.

6. See, however, the following early reflection of Coverdale's, which is pertinent both to the present scene and to *The Marble Faun:* "I have always envied the Catholics their faith in that sweet, sacred Virgin Mother, who stands between them and the Deity, intercepting somewhat of His awful splendor, but permitting His love to stream upon the worshipper, more intelligibly to human comprehension, through the medium of a woman's tenderness" (*C*, III, 121f.).

consciousness, her soul, bubbling out through her lips, it may be, had given itself up to the Father, reconciled and penitent. But her arms! They were bent before her, as if she struggled against Providence in never-ending hostility. Her hands! They were clenched in immitigable defiance. Away with the hideous thought! The flitting moment, after Zenobia sank into the dark pool—when her breath was gone, and her soul at her lips—was as long, in its capacity of God's infinite forgiveness, as the lifetime of the world. (*C*, III, 235)

Zenobia's imagined defiance of the "Father" makes little sense in terms of anything we have been told about her religion, but it makes perfect sense if we may assume that the thought of reconciliation to a heavenly Father is bound up with feelings toward an earthly father or father-surrogate. This is the case, we recall, in "The Gentle Boy," "Young Goodman Brown," "Rappaccini's Daughter," and "Roger Malvin's Burial." Hollingsworth, the obvious target of Zenobia's spite in committing suicide, is to blame for her death, yet Coverdale—as befits the Hawthornian protagonist who has never emerged from emotional childhood—concerns himself only with whether the father has now been sufficiently appeased. His "faith," like Hawthorne's at his mother's deathbed, is inspired by a hope that the heavenly Father may not be as cruel as he patently appears.[7] Providence has proved sadistic, the impulse to

7. "Oh what a mockery," Hawthorne confided to his notebook, "if what I saw were all ... But God would not have made the close so dark and wretched, if there were nothing beyond; for then it would have been a fiend that created us, and measured out our existence, and not God. It would be something beyond wrong—it would be insult—to be thrust out of life into annihilation in this miserable way. So, out of the very bitterness of death, I gather the sweet assurance of a better state of being" (*American Notebooks*, p. 210). Hawthorne's celebrated faith was never more sincerely cherished, I imagine, than here; yet the passage says in effect that he

defiance persists, and *therefore* he must fearfully hope that all will be well. Hollingsworth in the previous chapter has been sent a final rebellious message by Zenobia—"Tell him he has murdered me! Tell him that I'll haunt him!" (*C,* III, 226)—and in the following chapter Coverdale will goad him in his misery "with a bitter and revengeful emotion" (*C,* III, 243). No wonder, then, that Coverdale finds it so hard (and so urgently necessary) to persuade himself that Zenobia has made her peace with the Father above.

The very sincerity of Coverdale's anguish may explain why his scene of truly effective drama is presented as something beyond the scope of his art. Zenobia's body is in a sense a perfectly mimetic artifact: "She was the marble image of a death-agony" (*C,* III, 235). But neither Coverdale nor Hawthorne can sustain, or indeed tolerate, an art of sordid truthfulness; as Coverdale has earlier complained about a painting of a drunken man on a bench, "The death-in-life was too well portrayed" (*C,* III, 176). Hawthornian art is necessarily an art of ideality, of flight from unacceptable truth. It becomes psychologically penetrating and aesthetically "right" only to the degree that the repressed is allowed to return *within the bounds of characterization,* as in the monomaniacs of the better tales. When, in *The Marble Faun,* characterization stays on the level of sentimental convention while the imagery shrieks of incest, Hawthorne's art is effectively finished. What we see in Zenobia's death is the unmanageable hideousness that Hawthorne will henceforth try to keep wholly out of view.

With this knowledge in mind we may place some importance on an otherwise inconspicuous fact: Coverdale at the end follows his immediate predecessor Holgrave in renouncing art and gaining a measure of mental peace. The

---

must believe in order to stifle his outrage at what he has witnessed. He will be a better Christian by his terror of the atheistic thoughts he cannot silence.

two successive palinodes prepare us for the Hawthorne
who was to complete only one intricately self-defeating
romance in the twelve years that were left to him, and
for the Hawthorne who said of *Mosses from an Old Manse*
in 1854, "Upon my honor, I am not quite sure that I
entirely comprehend my own meaning in some of these
blasted allegories. . . . I am a good deal changed since those
times; and to tell you the truth, my past self is not very
much to my taste, as I see myself in this book." [8] *The
Blithedale Romance* is Hawthorne's cunning farewell to
that "past self" which was responsible for all his greatest
fiction. Half understanding and wholly disapproving of
the nature of Coverdale's artistic purposes, Hawthorne
was able to rise for the last time to the level of sustained
self-criticism. The aftermath will be sheer evasion.

8. Letter to Fields, quoted by Stewart, *American Notebooks*,
p. 332n.

XII

Subterranean Reminiscences

" 'My secret is not a pearl,' said she; 'yet a man might drown
himself in plunging after it.' "
—Miriam to Kenyon in *The Marble Faun.*

Hawthorne's moral interpreters have been very sure of
what his last complete romance, *The Marble Faun* (1860),
is really about. The theme is man's lapse from primal
innocence and his possible regeneration. "Did Adam fall,"
asks the sculptor Kenyon, "that we might ultimately rise
to a far loftier paradise than his?" (VI, 519). It is scarcely
noticed that Kenyon shrinks from the implications of
his question and decides to drop the whole matter; the
theologically oriented critic can give an answer without
Kenyon's help. The "crucial problem" of *felix culpa* is
resolved (but in divergent ways) by reference to a mixture
of genuine evidence and "the background of Christian
thinking on the subject" or "the central meaning of Christianity." [1] Though the critics when taken together leave
us bewildered, they do concur in feeling indulgent toward
the book's artistic defects. "For on the thematic level it is,
for the most part, such *good* Hawthorne." "For *The
Marble Faun* is concerned with the way in which nature
and spirit, innocence and evil, time and eternity may be
conquered and reconciled in a moment of incarnation." [2]
Such an emphasis misrepresents Hawthorne, not only

1. The quotations are from Fogle, *Hawthorne's Fiction*, p. 190;
Wagenknecht, *Hawthorne,* p. 194; and Waggoner (1955 ed.), p. 220.
2. Waggoner (1963 ed.), p. 225; Male, *Hawthorne's Tragic Vision,*
p. 163.

because it credits him with more conviction than he has, but because it treats only a tiny fraction of his book. Instead of saying that he has affirmed or refuted a certain religious doctrine, it would be more appropriate to say that he found it hard to sustain his interest in such niceties. The theological speculations that his characters timidly raise and abandon are placed amid authorial comments that approach nihilism. The rude fact of death keeps reappearing to erase distinctions between good and evil, truth and falsehood; and all life is seen in a backward glance from the brink of nothingness. "For it is thus, that with only an inconsiderable change, the gladdest objects and existences become the saddest; hope fading into disappointment; joy darkening into grief, and festal splendor into funereal duskiness; and all evolving, as their moral, a grim identity between gay things and sorrowful ones. Only give them a little time, and they turn out to be just alike!" (VI, 261) It would seem that in the years since his departure from America in 1852 Hawthorne had visited, not only the depressing slums of Liverpool and Rome, but E. M. Forster's Marabar Caves as well.

Weariness and despair are the real keynotes of *The Marble Faun,* beginning with Hawthorne's confession in his Preface that he no longer believes in the Gentle Reader's existence and continuing until the pathetic apologies and evasions in the subsequently appended Conclusion. His dark mood is reflected in countless little remarks about the "demon of weariness" (VI, 383) that haunts gallery-goers, the loneliness and heartsickness of expatriates, and the remorse of old age, "when the accumulated sins are many and the remaining temptations few" (VI, 183). The absurdity of much of his plot—the heaping-up of useful coincidences and the cheap mystification that is never justified or explained—appears as a further confession of despair, oblique but unmistakable. "When we find ourselves fading into shadows and unrealities, it seems hardly worth while to be sad, but rather to laugh as gayly as we may, and ask little reason wherefore" (VI, 21). The fictional equivalent of forced gaiety is a book which no longer tries to capture human character with honest fullness, as in *The Scarlet Letter*, but slides off into patent allegory on one side and chatty circumstantiality on the other.

We must also question whether *The Marble Faun* is "such *good* Hawthorne" on the thematic level. It is true that all his former concerns are present, but they are handled with timid ambiguity. This is most obviously true of the *felix culpa* theme, but it applies to every other as well. Depending on the passages he cares to stress, the reader can see *The Marble Faun* as a Rousseauistic tract about man's decline from a golden age or an Emersonian tract about man's ascent to the ideal; as an attack on Roman Catholicism or a prelude to conversion; as a work of homage to Western history or a declaration of independence from it; as a hymn to America or a satire on its moral fastidiousness; as an allegory of artistic truth or yet another indictment of the creative imagination; as a tribute to feminine purity or a muted plea against sexual hypocrisy. Each irresolute theme is eventually submerged in gloomy ambivalence.

As we might almost be able to predict, the chief focus of this ambivalence is a choice between an overblown, oversexed, aggressive woman and a fragile, childlike, impregnable and impenetrable maiden. In Hawthorne's conscious view all merit belongs to the virgin Hilda. There is a general assumption in the romance, shared even by the characters who supposedly represent "experience," that femininity and absolute purity of imagination are synonymous—in other words, that Hilda *must* prevail over Miriam. As an embodiment of Mr. Podsnap's idea of chastity Hilda could easily be a comic figure. Her characteristic response to reality is the following: " 'It perplexes me,' said Hilda, thoughtfully, and shrinking a little; 'neither do I quite like to think about it' " (VI, 27). And yet her "elastic faculty of throwing off such recollections as would be too painful for endurance" (VI, 435) is precisely what Hawthorne feels increasingly necessary for himself. In creating Hilda and insisting, against his plain misgivings, that her vaccination against bodily thoughts is a moral virtue, he has provided himself with a (very inadequate) refuge from those same thoughts.

It is true, of course, that Hilda is to some extent an allegorical character, standing for Purity or the Ideal or Heaven or the American Girl or the Muse of Art or the Virgin Mary; all these identities can be justified through explication of the symbolic props that attend her. Insofar as she is allegorical, it is idle to criticize Hawthorne for having made her one-dimensional. Yet beyond all her allegorical roles Hilda is a human character within the romance's human plot, and Hawthorne is asking us to believe that her behavior toward her friends is above criticism. To do this he must, in effect, convince himself that misfortune and entrapment in the world's evil deserve no sympathy, for this is Hilda's own position. Her friend Miriam has been gratuitously tormented beyond endurance and has involved herself in a crime—the murder of the "model" or "monk" who has pursued her—through a moment of acquiescence in the deed. Miriam is considerably more sinned against than sinning, and in her remorse and anguish she needs Hilda's pity. When Hilda turns her back on Miriam, Hawthorne does his best to condone her —and so do all the other characters. Even Hilda's relenting, long after it might have been useful, is taken not as evidence that she was formerly wrong but as a proof of virtually divine magnanimity.[3]

3. When Hilda herself entertains the thought that she has been cruel to Miriam, Hawthorne half-heartedly opposes the idea. Hilda contemplates "the delinquencies of which she fancied (we say 'fancied,' because we do not unhesitatingly adopt Hilda's present view, but rather suppose her misled by her feelings)—of which she fancied herself guilty towards her friend . . ." (VI, 439).

It should go without saying, by now, that when Hawthorne (or indeed, any writer) takes extraordinary pains to
emphasize the asexuality of a girl, he is preoccupied with
the general sexuality of women. In Hilda's case, as is appropriate to the most insistent exaggeration of purity in all
his fiction, sexual symbolism and sexual innuendo follow
the heroine wherever she goes. I do not mean that her
lofty tower, like the Man of Adamant's cave, represents
what she cannot face; that may be true, but Hawthorne
does not employ his characteristic *doubles entendres* in
describing the tower. He does, however, create an intricately detailed analogy between sexuality and crime, so
that the murder which Hilda witnesses becomes a kind of
vicarious sexual initiation. Though she is pure, Hilda is
susceptible to what she repeatedly calls "stain"; she does
not wear "garments that never could be spotted" (VI, 243).
God, she says, wants her to return the robe He gave her
"as white as when [I] put it on" (VI, 243). The ambiguous
stain is significantly associated with the stain of Beatrice
Cenci, who happened to have been raped by her father
before she had him murdered; and while this lurid fact is
never mentioned directly, Hawthorne's readers certainly
knew it. When Hilda, contemplating Guido Reni's portrait of Beatrice, asks, "Am I, too, stained with guilt?"
(VI, 239), the double reference is maintained; and inter-
estingly enough, the portrait does resemble Hilda's own
face. Later, a young Italian artist paints Hilda as "gazing
with sad and earnest horror at a blood-spot which she
seemed just then to have discovered on her white robe"
(VI, 377). The picture, which connoisseurs take to be
inspired by Guido's Beatrice, is called by others, "Innocence, dying of a blood-stain!" (VI, 378).

Such language does not, of course, suggest that Hilda
really is "guilty" of having been deflowered, any more than
it proves her a criminal. At most it reveals a sexual fascination on Hawthorne's own part when he ponders the "dark
pitfall" (VI, 469) and "fathomless abyss" (VI, 520) separat-

ing Hilda from Miriam. On the whole it is futile to try
to match Hilda's rendered character against the prurient
imagery that surrounds it; the latter serves almost as a
Mercutio voice to sneer at the unreal perfection of the
former.

This, I fear, is a comment that holds for characterization in *The Marble Faun* generally. Any attempt to discuss Hawthorne's people in literal terms, or even according
to their apparent allegorical values, must falsify the prevailing air of self-contradiction. The virgin Hilda resembles
Beatrice Cenci and therefore is associated with the Bea-
trice-like Miriam, her supposed opposite; Miriam occasionally acts with Hilda-like altruism, and can find "none
but pure motives" (VI, 327) in her heart; Donatello is
simultaneously as voluptuous as Miriam and as easily
shocked as Hilda; and the sculptor Kenyon—at once a
prude and a freethinker—mediates among his three friends
with an ease that proves their estrangement to be only
provisional, however "abysmal" it may appear. The only
clear point is that some private discomfort has made all
Hawthorne's portraits insincere.

In order to arrive at the significance of this peculiarity
we must follow the direction of Hawthorne's images. His
Rome is an incessant reminder of the unconscious pit
beneath his characters' surface banalities. We are asked to
think of ruined pagan temples under the "evanescent and
visionary" (VI, 21) Christian world; catacombs which suggest "the possibility of going astray into this labyrinth of
darkness" (VI, 41) or the re-emergence of some "fiendish
malignity" (VI, 49) of ancient days; chasms which are
among "the orifices of that pit of blackness that lies beneath us, everywhere" (VI, 191); and dungeons, into one
of which Donatello will be committed at his own request
after failing to carry his burden of guilt unacknowledged
in the upper world. And these heavily symbolic locales of
action are scarcely distinguishable from other, sheerly
figurative, representations of the human mind. The model's

past relation to Miriam emerges from "subterranean rem-
iniscences" (VI, 35); Donatello learns how to master his
emotions and thrust them once again "down into the
prison-cells where he usually kept them confined" (VI,
289); Hilda's glimpse of evil has "allowed a throng of
torturing recollections to escape from their dungeons into
the pure air and white radiance of her soul" (VI, 438);
she has been helplessly "straying farther into the intricate
passages of our nature" (VI, 377); and Donatello "had
already had glimpses of strange and subtle matters in those
dark caverns, into which all men must descend, if they
would know anything beneath the surface and illusive
pleasures of existence" (VI, 302). Is it fortuitous that all
these figures for the terrible unknown are hidden cavities,
and that female sexuality is the taboo of the surface Hawthornian world? In a backhanded way Hawthorne enjoins
us not to be satisfied with his own and his characters' dis-
infectant ideals, but rather to mark their emergence from
and protection against an all-consuming sexual obsession.

In one sense we can agree with those critics who have
found *The Marble Faun* to be a book about man's fall,
about initiation into evil and the consequences of that
initiation. If we formulate that theme in strictly literal
terms, however, we must confine the central plot to
Miriam and Donatello. It is more comprehensive to say
that the book deals with initiation into a *sense* of evil,
whether real or only vicarious, and that this sense is ultimately a euphemism for knowledge of sexuality. For *The
Marble Faun*—like *The Blithedale Romance* but without
its irony toward an obsessed protagonist—dwells on the
very existence of sexual passion as if this were the most
hideous of the world's evils. All Hawthorne's major characters, even the latest counterpart of Zenobia, share the
author's distaste for the idea which somehow insinuates
itself into all their doings. The single committed crime
which has to bear the weight of four characters' brooding
about guilt is powerfully sexual in itself, not only in its

traumatizing effect on its virgin witness, Hilda, but in its essential circumstances and emotional atmosphere. The victim is in some way perceived as a sexual rival, and in killing him Donatello does make a tie of erotic guilt between Miriam and himself. The murder is an act of mutual consent, of guilty impulse which should not have been gratified, of "passion," and it produces both "horror" and "ecstasy" (VI, 203) in the woman who has consented. Like Milton's Adam and Eve after a similarly ambiguous misdeed, the offending couple at first feel an intimacy "closer than a marriage-bond" (VI, 205):

> She turned to him,—the guilty, blood-stained, lonely woman,—she turned to her fellow-criminal, the youth, so lately innocent, whom she had drawn into her doom. She pressed him close, close to her bosom, with a clinging embrace that brought their two hearts together, till the horror and agony of each was combined into one emotion, and that a kind of rapture. (VI, 204f.)

When second thoughts begin to urge the folly of the act, Miriam and Donatello still have the consolation of knowing "how close, and ever closer, did the breadth of the immeasurable waste, that lay between them and all brotherhood or sisterhood, now press them one within the other!" (VI, 206). And finally this suggestive coupling is seen with disgust: Donatello begins to envision "the ever-increasing loathsomeness of a union that consists in guilt. Cemented with blood, which would corrupt and grow more noisome forever and forever, but bind them none the less strictly for that" (VI, 207). When Miriam argues, "Surely, it is no crime that we have committed" (VI, 206), she has assumed Hester Prynne's role before Arthur Dimmesdale. The chief point of difference is that Hawthorne's sum of frankness has now dwindled to the point where even the Hester-figure, though surrounded with hints of a long sexual history, remains technically chaste and shares in the general hypersensitivity and reticence.[4]

The sexual connotations of the murder scene alone might not be strong enough to support the reading we have given, but they are the culmination of multiple innuendoes about Miriam's symbolic nature. Without ever saying directly that she is sexually stained, Hawthorne has labored ingeniously to ensure that we get that impression. He uses the fact that "nobody knew anything about Miriam, either for good or evil" (VI, 35) to speculate whether her "freedom of intercourse" might mean that one could easily "develop a casual acquaintance into intimacy" (VI, 36) with her. If, as Hawthorne goes on to suggest, this supposition is false, it is not because of Miriam's chastity but because "by some subtle quality, she kept people at a distance" (VI, 36). That is to say, people recognize something fearful in her—the "abyss" from whose brink they timidly withdraw. The lack of rapport between Miriam and the others is thus a factor of their inexperience, not her coldness; and throughout the romance she is the victim of Hawthorne's paradox that intense passion places one beyond the community of respectable lovers. Like Hester and Zenobia, Miriam is not an outcast *and* oversexed but an outcast *because* she is oversexed. And like them, she is driven by her enforced isolation into occasional questionings of man-made law (see, e.g., VI, 246).

The mystery over her family background and personal troubles is well calculated to reinforce Miriam's aura of sexuality. Hawthorne manages to draw upon racial fears which in our own time have led to genocide: Miriam is not only part English and part Italian, but part Jewish as well, and it is rumored that she also has "one burning

4. At a much later stage Miriam and Donatello are constant companions, but even then Hawthorne avoids the question of whether they are sexual partners. Miriam's motive for seeking a union with Donatello is alleged to be merely a wish "to instruct, to elevate, to enrich his mind"; she wants to "guide him to a higher innocence than that from which he fell" (VI, 326).

drop of African blood in her veins" (VI, 38). The equation
of obscure, esoteric origins with promiscuity is already
familiar to us from the metaphorically "Oriental" character of Hester and Zenobia, and Miriam too, in addition
to her literal ancestry, has "a certain rich Oriental character in her face" (VI, 38). As for her Jewishness, Hawthorne reveals what he thinks of that when he describes
Hilda's trip through the Jewish ghetto—"the foulest and
ugliest part of Rome . . . where thousands of Jews are
crowded within a narrow compass, and lead a close, unclean, and multitudinous life, resembling that of maggots
when they over-populate a decaying cheese" (VI, 441).
Such prose, which reminds us more of *Mein Kampf* than
of the theological works that are usually adduced to explain Hawthorne's ideas, vividly demonstrates that Jewishness, earthliness, filth, and sexuality are symbolically interchangeable in his imagination. Miriam's fate in the plot
of the romance is to be the scapegoat for a sexual nausea
that Hawthorne, along with his other characters, prefers
to vent upon the foreign temptress and her sensual race.[5]

The chief character for whom Miriam's sexuality is
oppressive is Kenyon, who occupies approximately the
same place in this romance that Holgrave and Coverdale
did in previous ones. That is to say, he is the artist-figure
who is closest to Hawthorne himself, and who escapes from
dangerous fantasies and radical opinions by giving himself
over to a Sophia-figure: Hilda is the new Phoebe or Priscilla. Kenyon's rebellious leanings are, of course, considerably milder than his predecessors', as is appropriate to the
generally greater repression in *The Marble Faun*. He is so
prudish that "he almost reproached himself when sometimes his imagination pictured in detail the sweet years

5. Like her self-portrait, Miriam "seemed to get into your consciousness and memory, and could never afterwards be shut out,
but haunted your dreams, for pleasure or for pain; holding your
inner realm as a conquered territory, though without deigning to
make herself at home there" (VI, 65).

that [he and Hilda] might spend together" (VI, 318). But the fact that he does have such an imagination, capable of picturing marriage "in detail," leaves him subject to intimidation by the idea of Miriam and consequently very much in need of antiseptic Hilda. He must respond to Miriam's proffered confidences with "a certain reserve and alarm" (VI, 155), and later must declare that Hilda was right to spurn her. "The white shining purity of Hilda's nature," he explains to Miriam with pitiless pomposity, "is a thing apart; and she is bound, by the undefiled material of which God moulded her, to keep that severity which I, as well as you, have recognized" (VI, 331).

In any previous work a figure like Kenyon would be subject to the incisive irony which Hawthorne reserves for the characters who most closely resemble himself. There is, indeed, more than a hint of satire behind Kenyon's extravagant and unsubstantiated fear of "that mass of unspeakable corruption, the Roman Church" (VI, 416; see also VI, 467), and toward the end of the book his unconscious misogyny gets mocked by the "gay persecutors" (VI, 503) of the Roman Carnival.[6] Yet Hawthorne is too involved in Kenyon's uneasiness to sustain an ironic distance from it; the Carnival must be set aside as "a feverish dream" (VI, 505) from which one awakens to Hilda and the fireside. For Hawthorne fully shares the spirit that has gone into Kenyon's sculptural masterpiece, a Cleopatra who is sensed to be

> the fossil woman of an age that produced statelier, stronger, and more passionate creatures than our own. You already felt her compressed heat, and were aware of a tiger-like character even in her repose. If Octavius should make his appearance, though the marble still held

6. See VI, 503f., where Kenyon is subjected to a remarkable series of symbolic torments, including the unwelcome erotic attentions of a seven-foot "Titaness" who subsequently covers him with lime-dust from a toy pistol.

her within its embrace, it was evident that she would tear
herself forth in a twinkling, either to spring enraged at
his throat, or, sinking into his arms, to make one more
proof of her rich blandishments, or, falling lowly at his
feet, to try the efficacy of a woman's tears. (VI, 430)

This statue speaks, mutely but emphatically, of everything that Octavius-Kenyon-Hawthorne is secretly attracted
to and wary of. Female tenderness and female aggression
are utterly intertwined—passion is tiger-like—and consequently one must have recourse to passionless Hilda in
order to calm one's terror.

The other important male character, Donatello, has a
closer yet more shifting relation to Miriam than Kenyon
does. Loving her in a doggy way at first, then shrinking
from her with "shuddering repugnance" (VI, 324) after
the murder, and finally joining her in a brief fellowship
of guilt, he exemplifies the whole range of attitudes that
might be appropriate to her sexual meaning—from ignorant devotion through the terror of discovery to a mature
reconciliation with reality. Beneath the obvious metamor-
phosis of "the sylvan Faun" into "the man of feeling and
intelligence" (VI, 367) lies an implied mastery of the
"fear" and "disgust" (VI, 61) which first assault him, significantly, not at the time of the murder but when he sees
Miriam's self-revealing sketches depicting the beheading
of men by vengeful females. In terms of the symbolism
we have been following, Donatello may be said to survive
the crisis of adolescence that Kenyon, with Hawthorne's
encouragement, refuses to undergo.

Needless to say, however, this development on Donatello's part takes place *only* in symbolism, and is further
compromised by the uncertainty of Hawthorne's attitude
toward him. Is natural impulse inherently corrupt or not?
Hawthorne cannot decide, and so he teases us desperately
with innuendoes about Donatello's ears, his supposed tail,
his gross ancestors, his resemblance to a voluptuous statue

—and yet insists that his innocence prior to the murder is total. The net result is a smutty equivocation.

It may now be appreciated that our critical task is not to find moral or religious consistency in *The Marble Faun*, but to grasp the connection between its pervasive anxiety and its overt story and themes. If Hawthorne's religious musings are at once inconclusive and pathetically sincere, it must be because he has tacitly supplied a real basis for his characters' seemingly exaggerated guilt-feelings, and one which no expiation will suffice to remove. It is clearly not enough to say that those characters have been made uneasy about sexuality; mere uneasiness does not call up Hawthorne's grim vision of "the crown of thorns, the hammer and nails, the pincers, the spear, the sponge" (VI, 341). There is in *The Marble Faun* a remarkable savagery of self-punishment and, accompanying it, a perverse and persistent sense of renewed criminality.[7] Our expectation, drawn from comparable instances elsewhere in Hawthorne's career, is that the nature of this criminality will be indicated both by a symbolic configuration of the main group of characters and by the nature of the central action they perform.

7. Note, for example, the case of the model, whose "acts of depravity" are followed by "severe and self-inflicted penance" and then "fresh impulses to crime" (VI, 488f.). Donatello contemplates becoming a monk *because* it is "a horrible idea" (VI, 308), and Miriam is exhorted to "a severe and painful life" (VI, 370), not just a holy one. Kenyon, who is not to be numbered among Hawthorne's more fiendish characters, likes to think of Roman ghosts "striving to repent of the savage pleasures which they once enjoyed, but still longing to enjoy them over again" (VI, 185); and he later entertains the Poe-like notion of wedded bliss within the sepulchre of Pope Gregory (see VI, 420). Such is the unwholesome atmosphere of Hawthorne's book about Christian expiation. When Christ's words bear repeating in *The Marble Faun* they are not the counsel of faith but "the saddest utterance man ever made, 'Why hast thou forsaken me?' " (VI, 387).

Let us first note that in a certain sense Hawthorne's four main characters share the same predicament. Hilda and Donatello are repeatedly described as children, and the four together make a troupe of siblings: Miriam sees Hilda as a "younger sister" (VI, 242), Kenyon offers Miriam "brotherly counsel" (VI, 138), and so on. All four, furthermore, are isolated from parents. Hilda is an orphan with no near relatives; Kenyon has no discernible family ties; Donatello is the only surviving member of the Monte Beni line; and Miriam, having "lost her English mother" (VI, 486) at an early age, seems to have been victimized by the dictates of a father who is conspicuously omitted from direct mention.

By now every reader will know what to expect when he comes across a Hawthornian orphan—to say nothing of a quartet of them. The absence of literal parents will entail, not a sense of playful freedom, but a dual obsession, a feeling of vague parental tyranny and a longing for an ideal parent-figure to restore security and forgive offenses. The removal of the literal parent makes way for the dichotomized fantasy-parents, the creatures of disjoined accusation and remorse.

In *The Marble Faun* there is an excellent candidate for the role of ogre-father in the bearded, ageless specter who emerges simultaneously from Miriam's past and from her hidden thoughts (see VI, 46). His reappearance to remind her that "our fates cross and are entangled" (VI, 117) may be correlated with the mystery of silence about her family in general and her father in particular. Indeed, at two moments Hawthorne unaccountably refers to him as "Father" when the context calls for "Brother" (see VI, 218, 228). His bizarre double role as satyr-like villain and penitent monk is appropriate to the child's idea of sexual excess and remorse in the offending parent. None of these facts, of course, proves that the model *is* Miriam's father; the point is that Hawthorne, having symbolically regarded his other characters as siblings, appears to have endowed the model with traits that would justify filial resentment.

The model's haunting effect, as we might anticipate after such relationships as those between Major Molineux and Robin, Jaffrey Pyncheon and Holgrave, applies not only to Miriam (who *may* be his daughter) but also to a male character who is distinctly not his literal son: Donatello. The "instinctive, unreasoning" (VI, 52) antipathy that Donatello feels for the model when the latter first interferes with his childlike frolicking with Miriam may be regarded as Oedipal if we take Hawthorne's family symbolism seriously. And there is every encouragement to do so. For the principal deed of *The Marble Faun* is the joint murder of this same villain by Miriam and Donatello—a murder which separates them from "all brotherhood and sisterhood" (VI, 206), clearing the way for a later ambiguous union but at the same time demanding an eventual repentance. Surely it is no coincidence that this obscure figure from Miriam's earlier days is thought to be the one obstacle between Donatello and Miriam's love, and that the very act of his murder is rendered in the sexual imagery we have examined. The consummation which appears to be made possible by the model's death, but which cannot be forthrightly mentioned, is an act of incest in Hawthorne's mind if not in the minds of his characters.

Thus we gather that Hawthorne has taken the Cenci case, which figures so prominently in the allusive symbolism of *The Marble Faun,* and in his scarcely perceptible way has given it a twist that his predecessor Shelley would have appreciated. In both versions the paternal figure is evidently guilty of sexual misconduct toward the daughter-figure; the bond between the model and Miriam "must have been forged in some such unhallowed furnace as is only kindled by evil passions and fed by evil deeds" (VI, 115), and Miriam confesses that "with one word he could have blasted me in the belief of all the world" (VI, 489). In both cases, too, the "Beatrice" is joined in the murder by a "brother" who is equally anxious that the "father"

die. The novelty comes in Hawthorne's implication of a
sexual advantage in this death; the removal of an incestuous tyrant only provides the circumstances for still further
hints of wicked love.[8]

Let me repeat, lest I be misunderstood, that these are
conclusions not about Hawthorne's characters but about
their meaning within a pattern of authorial obsession.
Like *The House of the Seven Gables* and *The Blithedale
Romance, The Marble Faun* does not treat a literal instance of incest, or even of incest-temptation; it exploits
a rather slender story for its vague and bizarre incestuous
overtones. As in the former romances, Hawthorne's characters are neither consciously aware of this fantasy-meaning nor free from its distorting effects; they display an
outlandish prudery and guilt whose source in incest-fear
can only be located in Hawthorne himself. And so, too,
they must make amends proportionate to the imagined
misdeed. The greater part of *The Marble Faun* may be
said to explore various avenues of possible escape, not
from the guilt that has been objectively incurred in the
plot, but from the incestuous theme behind that plot. Even
where, as in Donatello's case, there are adequate literal
reasons for oppressive guilt, the precise form taken by
that guilt is dictated by Hawthorne's concern with incest.

Thus, in turning our attention to the much-applauded
Christianity of this romance, we must observe how the
issue of repentance is informed and twisted by an intimidated filial imagination. As befits his crime against a
father-surrogate, Donatello lives in constant terror of the
avenger above, who "glows with Divine wrath" (VI, 351)

8. We must also recognize in the "happy ending" of *The Marble
Faun* a subtle perpetuation of the morbid idea it was evidently meant
to allay. Kenyon and Hilda, who are enabled to marry after the symbolic patricide has been expiated, are even more sibling-like than
Miriam and Donatello. In the same way, the marriages that conclude *The House of the Seven Gables* and *The Blithedale Romance*
are vaguely tainted by the symbolic family relationships among the
participants.

in his fantasy. This terror, coupled with resentment over the spiritual bondage it creates, pervades the romance after the murder-scene. God is "the dread eye-witness" (VI, 327) who may demand the "sacrificing [of] every earthly hope as a peace-offering towards Heaven" (VI, 308). Swift and horrible vengeance against those who try to overthrow authority is a general preoccupation of the book, from Miriam's initial disquiet, to the haunting effect of the slain Francesco Cenci and the model, to reflections about the way the Roman state dealt with miscreants on the Tarpeian Rock: "Just in the moment of their triumph, a hand, as of an avenging giant, clutched them, and dashed the wretches down this precipice" (VI, 201).

Balanced against such oppression is a pathetic homage to the idea of the benevolent parent, who is as much a product of psychological need as the avenger is. All four of the major characters long for a restoration of childish dependence on the all-wise, all-solicitous provider. Significantly, the figure of the mother enters prominently here; as always among Hawthorne's symbolic couples, the mother is the less guilty and more easily idealized partner. And as we would expect, the handling of what Hilda calls "the idea of divine Womanhood" (VI, 71) embraces every level, from childhood reminiscence of an actual mother to an intense worship of the Virgin Mary to a kind of secular incarnation of the Virgin in Hilda herself. "Oh, my mother!—my mother!" laments Hilda; "Were she yet living, I would travel over land and sea to tell her this dark secret, as I told all the little troubles of my infancy" (VI, 245). When she prays before an image of the Virgin, "It was not a Catholic kneeling at an idolatrous shrine, but a child lifting its tear-stained face to seek comfort from a mother" (VI, 379). "Ah," she thinks a little later, "why should not there be a woman to listen to the prayers of women? a mother in heaven for all motherless girls like me?" (VI, 396)—a religious idea, incidentally, that occurred to Mary Baker Eddy as well as Hilda. And when she is finally drawn into St. Peter's for confession, Hilda "felt

as if her mother's spirit, somewhere within the dome, were
looking down upon her child" (VI, 400). Parallel to this
informal Mariolatry is the more orthodox behavior of
Donatello, who prays at every roadside shrine "because the
mild face of the Madonna promised him to intercede as
a tender mother betwixt the poor culprit and the awful-
ness of judgment" (VI, 342). Here, perhaps, we get closest
to the chief role of the mother figure in Hawthorne's
imagination. Between the guilty son and the implacably
offended father steps the one party who combines power
and love, insight and mercy, and who thus holds out the
one slim possibility of forgiveness.

There is also, however, a strong appeal to the benev-
olent-father image in *The Marble Faun*—an image con-
jured up by fear of its opposite rather than by faith. The
sculptor of the Capitoline Marcus Aurelius, Kenyon remarks, "knew . . . the heart of mankind, and how it craves
a true ruler, under whatever title, as a child its father"
(VI, 196). Miriam, who has good reason to doubt that
fathers are true rulers, cries out in reply: "Oh, if there
were but one such man as this! . . . One such man in an
age, and one in all the world; then how speedily would
the strife, wickedness, and sorrow of us poor creatures be
relieved. We would come to him with our griefs, whatever
they might be,—even a poor, frail woman burdened with
her heavy heart,—and lay them at his feet, and never need
to take them up again. The rightful king would see to
all" (VI, 196f.).

There are two scenes in *The Marble Faun* in which the
"good" father, summoned by an overpowering desire for
him, makes his influence felt. The more arresting of the
two is the meeting of Miriam and Donatello, with Kenyon
a very involved third party, beneath the "paternal aspect"
(VI, 329) of Pope Julius's statue in the main square of
Perugia. Donatello's arrival at this rendezvous occurs only
after innumerable prayers to the Virgin for intercession,
and Miriam, too, has undergone a period of self-abnegation and penitence. Hawthorne devotes nearly two full

chapters to arranging for the moment of "benediction" (VI, 360, 362, 371) by the "kindly yet authoritative" (VI, 360) figure of "patriarchal majesty" (VI, 360). The desolate heart, he says, "recognizes in that image the likeness of a father" (VI, 363), and Miriam looks up to it "as if she had come hither for his pardon and paternal affection" (VI, 365). From the moment the blessing is felt to descend, Miriam and Donatello behave with the serenity of ex-prodigals who have found a *modus vivendi* with the benevolent despotism they no longer challenge or question.

The only major character excluded from this benediction is Hilda, but she is paternally blessed in Saint Peter's and continually thereafter. Having been drawn toward confession by thoughts of her mother, she finds herself "a girl again" (VI, 407) in the presence of "a venerable figure with hair as white as snow, and a face strikingly characterized by benevolence" (VI, 408). Addressing each other as "Father" and "daughter," Hilda and the priest establish a confessional intimacy that is essentially unaltered by the priest's discovery that Hilda is not a Catholic and was therefore technically disqualified from the sacrament. When Hilda subsequently disappears after having entered the Cenci Palace—"a spot of ill-omen for young maidens" (VI, 443)—she is really quite safe, for this father still has her under his solicitous eye.

If the blessing in Perugia seems, coming from a bronze statue, to be little more than a wish-projection, the one in Saint Peter's makes us wonder if Hawthorne may not be meaningfully asserting a faith in Providence. Hilda's inviolability, suggestively threatened yet maintained by a mysterious religious power, reminds us of the inviolability of the Lady in *Comus,* and certainly Hawthorne is no less careful than Milton to suggest a theological rationale for his plot. In *The Marble Faun,* however, this rationale remains a subject of debate and even of confusion. There may well be "a Providence purposely for Hilda" (VI, 485), as Miriam asserts, but this may also mean that Providence discriminates against non-Hildas. Hilda herself cannot answer this suspicion. When Miriam tells her, "I would give all I have or hope—my life, oh how freely—for one instant of your trust in God! . . . You really think, then, that He sees and cares for us?", Hilda replies with her customary penetration: "Miriam, you frighten me" (VI, 197). We could say, of course, that the incident in Perugia tips the scales in favor of Providence; but that too appears to be an exception to Providence's rule. For outside the charmed circle of Hawthorne's major characters there are countless others who are conspicuously less fortunate, as Kenyon and Donatello are reminded:

> From village to village, ragged boys and girls kept almost under the horses' feet; hoary grandsires and grandames caught glimpses of their approach, and hobbled to intercept them at some point of vantage; blind men stared them out of countenance with their sightless orbs; women held up their unwashed babies; cripples displayed their wooden legs, their grievous scars, their dangling, boneless arms, their broken backs, their burden of a hump, or whatever infirmity or deformity *Providence had assigned them for an inheritance.* (VI, 352; my italics)

What Satanic irony! And in Rome, too, the grace afforded Hilda is noted to be something apart: "Yet the ways of Providence are utterly inscrutable; and many a murder has been done, and many an innocent virgin has lifted her white arms, beseeching its aid in her extremity, and all in vain . . ." (VI, 469). To say that such a Providence is inscrutable is not much different from saying that it is simply inoperative, or even sadistic.[9]

9. If we regard Providence as a paternal agent, its favoritism toward Hilda becomes understandable; Hilda is the most obedient, the most unquestioning, of the four "children." She is therefore entitled to expect that "A miracle would be wrought on her behalf, as naturally as a father would stretch out his hand to save a best-beloved child" (VI, 469).

Thus it is understandable that Hawthorne, along with his earnest gestures in the direction of Christianity, casts about for quite opposite remedies for guilt. Neither the mediating function of Catholicism nor Protestantism's direct appeal to God can suffice if there is continued reason for doubting the Father's benevolence, and this reason is implied in all the allusions to incest. In such a predicament Hawthorne can dwell wistfully on the worldly hedonism of Rome and on Miriam's bold faith in a passion "mighty enough to make its own law" (VI, 232)—but neither attitude is a serious possibility for a temperament like his own.

The one remaining alternative, and one which has been pondered many times previously in Hawthorne's fiction, is a regressive pastoralism. *The Marble Faun* sustains an elaborate analogy between the childhood of an individual man and the prehistory of mankind. The diffuse joyousness of Donatello's Etruscan ancestors, "while Italy was yet guiltless of Rome" (VI, 268), becomes an implied ideal in the neurotic modern world, and Hawthorne occasionally preaches that ideal directly. Men, he says, "are getting so far beyond the childhood of their race that they scorn to be happy any longer" (VI, 276), and he summarizes his lament for "the careless and happy soul": "We go all wrong, by too strenuous a resolution to go all right" (VI, 276). Perhaps Hawthorne recognized the anti-Christian implications of this very modern theory of mental health, and resorted to his patently literary sylvan myth in order to lend picturesque distance to an idea that was all too immediate in its significance to him. Under the cloak of an acceptable pastoral nostalgia he argues for an age "before sin, sorrow *or morality* itself had ever been thought of" (VI, 27; my italics)—that is, for mankind's "innocent childhood" (VI, 27).

Of course, the whole point about Etruria and Rome is that the old innocence is irrecoverable; the lurid adult vices of Rome are everyday reality in the world surround-

ing Hawthorne's modern characters, and the Roman landscape is a depressing witness to death and vengeance
through the centuries.[10] When those characters experience
pastoral delight in the countryside, furthermore, Hawthorne's imagery compromises that delight with furtiveness. There is something beyond naïve innocence in his
concentration on "the patches of moss, the tufts of grass,
the trailing maiden-hair, and all sorts of verdant weeds
that thrive in the cracks and crevices of moist marble . . ."
(VI, 54).[11] And there is something beyond "a remote,
dream-like, Arcadian charm" (VI, 335) in such images as

10. That landscape is strewn not only with skulls, bones, and
sarcophagi, but with images of the castration which is hinted in
Miriam and Kenyon's art. The Flaminian obelisk, Trajan's Column
and the pillars of Trajan's Forum, the Column of Phocas with its
attendant "shattered blocks and shafts" (VI, 194), and numerous
mutilated statues whose most prominent aspect is a missing nose
(see, e.g., VI, 144, 229), all become conspicuous—like the innumerable
images of fallen trees in Hawthorne's American notebooks—when
we grasp the extent to which he is absorbed in the idea of punishment for sexual presumption.

11. The reader who doubts that his own mental image of "maiden-
hair" could be pertinent here is invited to examine another "certain
little dell" visited by Kenyon and Donatello:

> It was hollowed in among the hills, and open to a glimpse of
> the broad, fertile valley. A fountain had its birth here, and fell
> into a marble basin, which was all covered with moss and shaggy
> with water-weeds. Over the gush of the small stream, with an
> urn in her arms, stood a marble nymph, whose nakedness the
> moss had kindly clothed as with a garment; and the long trails
> and tresses of the maidenhair had done what they could in the
> poor thing's behalf, by hanging themselves about her waist.
> (VI, 281)

The passage goes on to say that because the urn now has a great
crack in it, "the discontented nymph was compelled to see the basin
fill itself through a channel which she could not control" (VI, 281).

that of a "fig-tree that had run wild and taken to wife the
vine, which had likewise gone rampant out of all human
control," or of a grape vine which, clinging to a tree,
"imprisoned within its strong embrace the friend that had
supported its tender infancy; and . . . (as seemingly flexible
natures are prone to do) . . . converted the sturdier tree
entirely to its own selfish ends . . ." (VI, 280, 336). Here as
everywhere in Hawthorne's fiction, the recourse to pastoralism ends by exposing the very fixations which make that
recourse seem attractive and necessary.

The Marble Faun, then, infects all its efforts at thematic
consistency and resolution with a desperate anxiety. The
attentive reader cannot be amazed when he finds half-
hearted mystification at the end and silence thereafter.
Though Hawthorne was to try frantically to complete another romance—indeed, four of them—the reason for his
failure to do so is already discernible in the oddities of
The Marble Faun. It is characteristic of Hawthorne's compulsive self-revelation that this last finished romance
should contain, among its numerous buried patterns of
meaning, an elaborate rationale for his subsequent incapacity as a writer.[12]

In artistic matters as in sexual ones Hawthorne is now
committed to a "purity" which he obliquely recognizes to
be sterile and repressive. His conscious choice of "ideal"

12. Which is not to deny Paul Brodtkorb, Jr.'s conclusion that
The Marble Faun can be read as a more optimistic art-allegory in
which Hilda, by keeping intact her aesthetic ideals as well as her
chastity, rescues the spirit of the Old Masters from an unworthy
modern Europe. On the contrary, this pattern of intention testifies
to Hawthorne's need to refute his suspicions of art. As Brodtkorb
acknowledges, "ambivalence seems to have defeated parable" in the
final effect of the book. See "Art Allegory in *The Marble Faun,*"
PMLA, LXXVII (June 1962), 254-67; the quoted phrase is from
p. 266.

over "emotional" art is invalidated by the fact that both
Miriam and Kenyon, the true creators, do their best work
in moments of penetration into the hidden ugliness of
human character. Hawthorne cannot succeed in convincing himself that such art is inferior to "Loulie's hand with
its baby-dimples" or "Harriet Hosmer's clasped hands of
Browning and his wife, symbolizing the individuality and
heroic union of two high, poetic lives!" (VI, 146). And the
equation of moral purity with artistic power—the indis-
pensable part of any vindication of the copyist Hilda—is
utterly refuted by Miriam. Even Kenyon must agree that
Miriam's idea for improving Guido's picture of the
Archangel Michael triumphing effortlessly over Satan—
Miriam prefers to make the contest more equal and thus
add some fierce dramatic tension—would produce a "masterpiece" (VI, 217) if faithfully executed. Such a masterpiece would give the lie not only to Guido and Fra
Angelico, but to Hilda and Sophia as well. Yet only a
Satanic consciousness could create it, and once the devil
had been given his due, perhaps "the victory would fall
on the wrong side" (VI, 217). Here and in numerous other
passages Hawthorne shows that we must choose between
artistic profundity and Hilda-ism; they are incompatible.

Art theory in *The Marble Faun* is not really separable
from Hawthorne's omnipresent brooding about sex. As its
title implies, the book deals in an oxymoronic marriage of
marble and faun, of cold artistic stasis and the raw passion
which it imprisons. Thus in Kenyon's sensitive reaction to
the Laocoön, form and passion are in perfect equilibrium.
The Laocoön

> impressed Kenyon as a type of the long, fierce struggle
> of man, involved in the knotted entanglements of Error
> and Evil, those two snakes, which, if no divine help inter-
> vene, will be sure to strangle him and his children in the
> end. What he most admired was the strange calmness dif-

fused through this bitter strife; so that it resembled the
rage of the sea made calm by its immensity, or the tumult
of Niagara which ceases to be tumult because it lasts
forever. (VI, 445)

The symbolism of family entanglement here, with its suggestion of an unrelenting sexual threat, can hardly be seen
as fortuitous after all we have found in *The Marble Faun;*
and it is evident that in Hawthorne's view artistic form is
cast into the struggle on the side of control. Art is a way
of managing too-powerful feelings. And thus Miriam, the
oversexed one, can say enviously to Kenyon, "You turn
feverish men into cool, quiet marble. What a blessed
change for them! Would you could do as much for me!"
(VI, 145).

At the same time, however, art is a means of registering
anxiety. Miriam's expressionistic works, which are "ugly
phantoms that stole out of my mind ... things that haunt
me" (VI, 62), plainly serve this purpose, and when she tries
instead to produce trite scenes from common life she is
invariably compelled to portray a likeness of herself spying at lovers through a window or "between the branches
of a shrubbery" (VI, 63). This accusation of vicarious
sexuality helps to explain Hawthorne's emphasis on artistic
shame, and particularly on the hypocrisy of sensualists who
revel in female nudity with the pretext of creating worship-
ful Madonnas (see, e.g., VI, 149, 162, 384). But more important for Hawthorne's future troubles is the implication,
fostered by both Miriam and Kenyon, that the artist cannot contain himself. If he has no choice but to reveal his
sexual fears in his art, then the only way to prevent such
revelation is to give up art altogether. And if Kenyon is
permitted to escape this logic and continue his pursuit of
banal ideality, I suggest that Hawthorne himself was not.
The unfinished romances that follow *The Marble Faun*
consist of innumerable false starts in which formerly serv-

iceable clichés of plotting get contaminated by sexual fantasy and are therefore abandoned.

Hilda's arrival to rescue the bewildered sculptor in *The
Marble Faun* powerfully reinforces the whole erotic meaning of Hawthornian art. I refer not so much to the scene
in the Corso [13] as to the earlier one where her safety is first
announced to Kenyon. There, out on the Campagna,
Kenyon makes one last descent into the caverns of the unconscious whose antithesis is Hilda. A "cellar-like cavity"
(VI, 479) within "old subterranean walls" is the setting,
which "might have been the ruins of a bath-room, or
some other apartment that was required to be wholly or
partly under ground" (VI, 478). The ruins of a bath-room!
—indeed a spot where one is likely to hit upon "some discovery which would attract all eyes" (VI, 478). What
Kenyon finds are the parts of a lovely antique Venus who,
when her limbs are reassembled, "showed that she retained
her modest instincts to the last. She had perished with
[her arms], and snatched them back at the moment of
revival. For these long-buried hands immediately disposed
themselves in the manner that nature prompts, as the
antique artist knew, and as all the world has seen, in the
Venus de' Medici" (VI, 479). With this graceful gesture
the statue calls attention to the genital obsession of the
entire scene, an obsession bearing an obvious relevance to
the fears for Hilda, who was last seen heading for the Cenci
Palace.

To find Hilda intact, in other words, one must get this
Venus, with its "lovely crevice of the lips" (VI, 480), out
of one's mind. The figure is not only a woman, however,
but a masterful work of sculpture as well; it ought to
appeal to Kenyon, who is alleged to be a sculptor himself.
Yet having created a work of art which charmingly em-

13. Where, by the way, Hilda stands conspicuously above "faces
that would have been human, but for their enormous noses" (VI,
504).

bodies both normal erotic feeling and normal modesty, Hawthorne dismantles it in loyalty to the amply demonstrated need· for Hilda. After a first show of interest Kenyon lapses into apathy; he

> strove to feel at least a portion of the interest which this event would have inspired in him a little while before. But, in reality, he found it difficult to fix his mind upon the subject. He could hardly, we fear, be reckoned a consummate artist, because there was something dearer to him than his art; and, by the greater strength of a human affection, the divine statue seemed to fall asunder again, and become only a heap of worthless fragments. (VI, 481)

Hawthorne remains duplicitous to the end. He seems to be saying that Kenyon's human love is supplanting his cold aesthetic taste—an economy that further implies a vicarious erotic function for art, since direct love makes art seem empty. Yet when we reflect that vapid Hilda is here dethroning a supple and lovely Venus, the surface meaning becomes exactly reversed. The remainder of the scene shows that in his clandestine way Hawthorne has not abandoned his awareness that commitment to Hilda is simply a form of panic. Only after forswearing any interest in the Venus is Kenyon entitled to hear the good news that Hilda will be safely returned to him. And though Hawthorne is bound, for reasons that are at once conventional and personal, to make the dreary exchange of Venus for Hilda, he cannot resist the honest impulse to count his loss, and Kenyon's. "Does it not frighten you a little," teases Miriam, alluding to the statue—"like the apparition of a lovely woman that lived of old, and has long lain in the grave?" "Ah, Miriam! I cannot respond to you," says Kenyon. "Imagination and the love of art have both died out of me" (VI, 483).

XIII

Falling in Love at Cross-Purposes

"Split lives never 'get well.' "
—EMILY DICKINSON

It is time to spell out the biographical implications of Hawthorne's art. In doing so we shall inevitably incur the
blame that attaches to all efforts at "psychoanalyzing the
dead"—a task generally regarded as preposterous.[1] Let me
say, however, that I do not pretend to have located specific
infantile traumas at the base of Hawthorne's neurotic
fears, nor do I wish to suggest any flagrant abnormality in
his behavior as a man. From all accounts that behavior was
notably guarded and distant; I do claim that we are prepared to say what Hawthorne felt guarded *about*. His coldness, his shyness, his taste for anonymity are surely signs of
the tyrannical superego that polices his fiction. There is an
inescapable connection to be drawn between the Oedipal
obsession of that fiction and the facts that Hawthorne never
once alluded directly to his father in print and that he said
of his dying mother, "I love my mother; but there has
been, ever since my boyhood, a sort of coldness of intercourse between us, such as is apt to come between persons
of strong feelings, if they are not managed rightly" (*American Notebooks*, p. 209).[2] Psychoanalysis shows us that such

1. I have replied to this view in an essay on psychological criti-
cism, shortly to be published in an MLA pamphlet, *Relations of
Literary Study; Essays on Interdisciplinary Contributions,* ed. James
Thorpe.

2. It may be of interest that Sophia Hawthorne reported that her
husband suffered a "brain fever" after his mother's death; we can

coldness is the opposite of indifference; it is a defense against fixation.

Thus, though I have no desire to rewrite Hawthorne's biography, I would remind future biographers of certain circumstances in his life that match the conclusions we have drawn from his art. Psychoanalysis invariably shows that an obsession with incest and its prevention, and indeed a general concern with sin and guilt such as Hawthorne displays, stem from an incomplete resolution of early Oedipal feelings. This failure of development, furthermore, is commonest in men who, like Hawthorne and Melville, lose their fathers at a young age and are raised by "well-bred" women.[3] Unresolved fantasies of filial hatred, and of punishment for that hatred, thrive in isolation from the real parent, and the very death of that parent becomes a matter of personal guilt. Can anyone doubt that Hawthorne's fiction provides an inadvertent record of precisely this guilt? As Louis B. Salomon has maintained in a brief but highly perceptive article, such stories as "Alice Doane's Appeal" and "Roger Malvin's Burial," along with the remarkable sketch of Dr. Johnson in "Biographical Stories," "constitute a sort of expiatory ritual whereby Hawthorne strove to say *Rest, rest, perturbed spirit* to the ghost of his sailor-father."[4]

The very first things that are known about Hawthorne's life already suggest the possible makings of neurosis. Take, for example, his father's death; his peculiar and probably

---

only guess at the nature of this affliction. See Stewart, *Nathaniel Hawthorne,* p. 91.

3. See Freud, *Leonardo da Vinci: A Study in Psychosexuality,* tr. A. A. Brill (New York, 1947), p. 61; and Sándor Ferenczi, *Further Contributions to the Theory and Technique of Psycho-Analysis* (London, 1950), pp. 76f.

4. "Hawthorne and His Father: A Conjecture," *Literature and Psychology,* XIII, No. 1 (Winter 1963), 12-16; the quotation is from p. 16. See also Mark Kanzer, "Writers and the Early Loss of Parents," *Journal of the Hillside Hospital,* II (July 1953), 148-51.

psychosomatic lameness, which set him apart from his contemporaries; the fact that, as his sister Elizabeth recalled,
he was "particularly petted, the more because his health
was then delicate and he had frequent illnesses"; [5] his intense dislike of his maternal uncle, on whom he was finan-
cially dependent; and his early resort to secrecy, and
notably secrecy about his writing. We have seen that this
writing is charged with a guilty self-revelation, and we
have already argued that this must have some bearing on
his twelve-years' insulation from "the world" and his lifelong coyness about displaying his inner self.

It is equally difficult to ignore the link between the circumstances of Hawthorne's marriage and his evident terror
of female sexuality—a terror that psychoanalysis traces to
thoughts of incest. We know that in marrying at the age of
thirty-eight the "spiritual" and semi-invalid Miss Peabody,
he regarded himself as having been "rescued" from his
own fantasies. That he was not merely cold-blooded is
proven by his intensely erotic letters to Sophia [6] and by
the occasional prurience of his notebooks. Those notebooks, which have never been properly examined for the
light they cast on Hawthorne's personality, sustain at a
lower intensity all the ambivalences of his art, and reinforce our view of him as a man who felt required to be
constantly on guard against the tendency of his own imagination.[7] The natural images that point to sexual anxiety

5. Quoted by Stewart, *Nathaniel Hawthorne,* p. 4.

6. See *Love Letters of Nathaniel Hawthorne,* 2 vols. (Chicago,
[1907]).

7. On the latter point we might mention Ernest Jones's remark
that men who feel intimidated by their superego are typically
obsessed with self-control, and are particularly afraid of hypnotism
because of its relaxing effect on repression (*Essays in Applied Psycho-Analysis,* II, 185). I find this helpful in explaining not only
Hawthorne's fear of mesmerism but also his general concern over
"violations" and "invasions" of the human spirit. Throughout his
fiction there is an implicit assumption that the repressed must stay
repressed; man's mind is a Pandora's box.

in his fiction can be shown to have the same meaning in his nonfiction; I would call attention particularly to his dwelling on powerful and "ancestral" *tree-trunks; uprooted* or *blighted* or *chopped* trees, and *decaying branches; caves, ravines,* and *gorges,* with water characteristically rushing through them; and *tangled vines* which are choking off some sturdier growth. The recurrence in Hawthorne's fiction of these literally observed phenomena has been taken merely as a "working up" of notebook material, a way of sketching scenic background; but the critics who see Hawthorne in these thrifty terms invariably miss the obsessiveness of his fiction and the symbolic aptness of his landscapes to his inmost themes. In point of fact, sexual anxiety is the dominant tendency of the entire imaginative record he has left us.

The strongest evidence of this anxiety has not yet been examined; it resides in the unfinished romances that are so little discussed by Hawthorne's moral critics. It is easy to understand why this stage of Hawthorne's career is omitted from consideration or explained away with hasty tautologies. For the last romances display a literary mind not simply in ruins, but in embarrassingly recognizable ruins. The fragments of plotting and imagery that no longer cohere are the permanent stock-in-trade of Hawthorne's imagination, the raw ingredients of his finest works. His reversals of intent, slips of the pen, and outbursts of exasperation while trying to recombine these ingredients have evidential value for an understanding of his art in general. But such an understanding is amoral and iconoclastic. It is not possible to look clearly at Hawthorne's last phase and continue to maintain that he was fundamentally a didactic writer, a serene allegorist who consciously chose his themes for their uplifting effect.[8]

8. Any discussion of this period must be indebted to the editorial work of Edward H. Davidson. See his *Hawthorne's Last Phase* (New Haven, 1949), his edition of *Doctor Grimshawe's Secret* (Cambridge, Mass., 1954), and his essay, "The Unfinished Romances," in *Haw-*

Hawthorne's four projects, grievously and intermittently labored over between 1858 and his death in 1864, really amount to two. *The Ancestral Footstep* and *Doctor Grimshawe's Secret,* his "Romances of England," were versions of the same plot, while *Septimius Felton* and *The Dolliver Romance* were efforts to complete a single "Romance of Immortality." Even this distinction breaks down: again and again we find the same themes, the same ideas, the same legends and anecdotes cropping up in both pairs. The two abiding themes are a desire for an elixir of immortality and a search for an ancestral birthright among English nobility. The prevailing atmosphere is one of intimacy, of mystery, of half-intended violence, and of what Edward H. Davidson calls moral incompetence: the characters show no interest in exploring their own motives or moral status. In Hawthorne's own words about *The Ancestral Footstep,* there are legal contests followed by "blows and blood; and the devil knows what other devilish consequences . . . Besides this, there was much falling in love at cross-purposes, and a general animosity of everybody against everybody else, in proportion to the closeness of the natural ties and their obligation to love one another" (XI, 488).

The first thing to be said about such a mechanically eventful world is that it expresses a further step backward from psychological truth. In *The Marble Faun* we could at least read between the lines and see that with one part of his mind Hawthorne remained contemptuous of the

---

thorne Centenary Essays, pp. 141-63. Davidson's textual work is invaluable. His account of the reasons for Hawthorne's decline, however, is superficial; he speaks of Hawthorne's failure "to fuse image and moral in a symbol" (*Hawthorne's Last Phase,* p. 152) as if this were a cause rather than a symptom of trouble, and when he gets closer to the biographical heart of the question he contents himself with saying that Hawthorne was prematurely aged and overworked—as if the bizarre twists of plotting in the late romances could somehow be a product of fatigue.

one-dimensional Hilda; a standard of criticism based on an awareness of universal corruptibility was latent if not directly expressed. Now, however, Hawthorne appears to bend his attention solely to matters of outward fact: will the young man in one plot discover that he is the long-lost heir? Will another succeed in manufacturing the elixir to which he has sacrificed every other interest? It is as if the thread connecting Hawthorne's plot-devices to their meaning had been put under such strain that it finally snapped, leaving the author with his assembled contrivances and a dim, maddening recollection that they used to have some significance.

This is to say that in his last romances Hawthorne wanted to produce agreeable plots without suffering the emotional strain that is increasingly apparent in the three preceding romances; he wanted to be an artist but not a *Hawthornian* artist. This is attested by numerous passages of commentary in which he shows that he no longer understands his previous method and no longer cares to revive it. In a letter to his publisher Fields he says of *The Dolliver Romance:* "There is something preternatural in my reluctance to begin. I linger at the threshold, and have a perception of very disagreeable phantasms to be encountered if I enter. I wish God had given me the faculty of writing a sunshiny book" (quoted by Lathrop, XI, 10). He repeatedly scorns the Gothic paraphernalia of his former works, and in one exceptionally revealing aside he admonishes himself: "The story must not be founded at all on remorse and secret guilt—all that Poe wore out." [9] There is little doubt that this seemingly obtuse remark reflects a fear of "disagreeable phantasms," for elsewhere Hawthorne positively begs us—and himself—not to pursue self-knowledge. The moral he explicitly draws from his hero's vicissitudes in *The Ancestral Footstep* is: "Let the past

9. *Hawthorne's Doctor Grimshawe's Secret,* ed. Davidson, p. 105. Further references to this romance will imply Davidson's edition.

alone: do not seek to renew it; press on to higher and
better things,—at all events, to other things; and be assured
that the right way can never be that which leads you back
to the identical shapes that you long ago left behind.
Onward, onward, onward!" (XI, 488f.). In any previous
work this neurotic advice would have been offered with
at least a modicum of irony, but here there is none. Hawthorne can express his old feeling for hidden truth only
when he plainly calls it error—as when, to take one example, Septimius Felton is roundly rebuked both by a
minister-adviser and by Hawthorne himself for making
this radical speech:

> "It has seemed to me," observed Septimius, "that it is not
> the prevailing mood, the most common one, that is to
> be trusted. This is habit, formality, the shallow covering
> which we close over what is real, and seldom suffer to be
> blown aside. But it is the snakelike doubt that thrusts
> out its head, which gives us a glimpse of reality. Surely,
> such moments are a hundred times as real as the dull,
> quiet moments of faith or what you call such." (XI, 237)

Hawthorne's career as a serious writer is based on this
premise, but now it scandalizes him.

Common sense might suggest that Hawthorne's heightened determination not to probe his fantasies would be
completely successful, and that the last romances would be
works of vacant conventionalism. Psychoanalytical expectations, on the other hand, would follow the principle that
intensified repression signifies an intensified "return of the
repressed"; and this is what we find here. The one psycho-
analytically trained observer who has gone into the last
romances in detail demonstrates the presence of a trans-
parently Oedipal theme in all four plots and is able to
follow Hawthorne's uneasy battle against this meaning as
he casts about for images and commits significant mistakes
of the pen. John H. Lamont shows that both the search

for an ancestral birthright and the search for an elixir of life represent an investigation into one's own past—the very investigation that Hawthorne pronounces fruitless and wrong.[10] Lamont finds in Hawthorne's imagery a relentless obsession with the figure of the long-sought father, and he demonstrates how the "falling in love at cross-purposes" and the "general animosity of everybody against everybody else" express the twin Oedipal themes of incest and parricide. He connects Hawthorne's failure to complete any of his plots with the parallel difficulties of his heroes, whose researches into their identity and history are broken off or confuted just as the truth seems within grasp. The cast of characters we met in Hawthorne's earliest fiction— the benevolent father-figure and the evil one, the young man and his rival, the beautiful lady who may turn out to be either sister or sexual object but who is really both— are once again engaged in their old business of murder, of crossed identities, of tangled lust and hatred; and as before, neither the author nor the hero can follow the plot's Oedipal logic through to its conclusion.

The only essential difference, I would say, between Hawthorne's first phase and his last one is that he has now insulated his characters more thickly against the erupting of repressed emotion. Murders take place by accident, and elaborate explanations are provided to exonerate the culprit from guilt for a deed that removes the one barrier between him and his "birthright"—possession of the paternal estate and the disputed lady. The very faculty for registering a sense of guilt has disappeared—a subtraction which may remind us of Erik Erikson's statement that an incapacity to feel "is the final predicament of the compul-

10. See "Hawthorne's Unfinished Works," *Harvard Medical Alumni Bulletin*, XXXVI, No. 5 (Summer 1962), 13-20. Since Dr. Lamont's conclusions are so welcome, it may be of interest that his article came to my attention only after all the foregoing chapters were written.

sive character." [11] These figures, along with Hawthorne himself, are morally imperceptive *because* the guilty meaning of their interrelationships is so close to being obvious. As always, Hawthorne's personages are twisted and inhibited by thoughts that never literally occur to them, but which menace the author's private mental economy. And that economy is now so bankrupt that every transaction must be broken off before the cost is counted.[12]

Thus the last romances embody in extreme form the principle of psychological allegory that rules Hawthorne's previous fiction. We have seen that in his world things often happen, not because of overt motives and intentions, but because of symbolic values that the characters must represent for the author. In these final works the pretense of literal motivation is almost abandoned: the characters mechanically and unquestioningly obey Hawthorne's own

11. Erik H. Erikson, *Young Man Luther: A Study in Psychoanalysis and History* (New York, 1962), p. 164. I might add that Luther's later career as Erikson expounds it—powerful identification with a father after a titanic rebellion—may cast some light on Hawthorne's ancestral researches in England and the last romances. The difference would seem to be that Hawthorne's more timid and covert rebellion had to persist, despite his earnest gestures of family piety, because the Oedipal antagonism behind it remained unresolved. Luther in contrast became the tyrant he had so boldly opposed. See Erikson, pp. 231-8.

12. Occasionally Hawthorne does take up the question of blame, but only in the most ambiguous way. One recurring situation, for example, is that of three brothers who fall into deadly enmity over the love of "a young lady, their cousin" (*Grimshawe,* p. 101). The youngest brother, whom the lady really loves, is banished or kidnapped—Hawthorne cannot decide which—for "some disgraceful cause" (p. 107)—Hawthorne cannot decide what—and is perhaps innocent, perhaps guilty. The bloody footstep that appears in all four romances may turn out "to be the track, not of guilt, but of persecution" (p. 108)—but again the author is not quite sure. The only certainty is that Hawthorne himself is experiencing the greatest difficulty in evading the plain import of his incest fantasy.

obsessions. The father-figures in particular become objects of unreasoning hatred, without even being put to the trouble of misbehaving. In *Doctor Grimshawe's Secret,* for example, a kindly old pensioner who has Hawthorne's complete moral approval suddenly appears as a personification of "conscience, morbid, sick, a despot in trifles, looking so closely into life that it permitted nothing to be done" (*Grimshawe,* p. 111). Before the young hero is through with his fit of silent rage against this innocent old fellow, he has come to understand "how a brutal nature, if capable of receiving his influence at all, might find it so intolerable that it must needs be rid of him by violence —by taking his blood if necessary" (p. 113). Symbolic patricide has been contemplated, not because the figure of authority is evil, but simply because he *is* a figure of authority; literal character steps aside to make room for imago.

In its most radical instance this tendency gives us the legend of the ageless Indian sachem in *Septimius Felton*— a wise and good man whose tribe nevertheless decides that he must die. Hawthorne's description of the ritual murder and his ensuing statement of intention provide the clearest and most gruesome proof of his unresolved filial aggression:

> So he cheerfully consented, and told them to kill him if they could; and first they tried the stone hatchet, which was broken against his skull; and then they shot arrows at him, which could not pierce the toughness of his skin; and finally they plastered up his nose and mouth (which kept uttering wisdom to the last) with clay, and set him to bake in the sun; so at last his life burnt out of his breast, tearing his body to pieces, and he died.
>
> [*Make this legend grotesque, and express the weariness of the tribe at the intolerable control the undying one had of them; his always bringing up precepts from his own experience, never consenting to anything new, and so impeding progress; his habits hardening into him, his as-*

*cribing to himself all wisdom, and depriving everybody
of his right to successive command; his endless talk, and
dwelling on the past, so that the world could not bear
him. Describe his ascetic and severe habits, his rigid calm-
ness, etc.*] (XI, 318f.)

It may not be irrelevant to add that this sachem is alleged
to be a direct ancestor of Septimius Felton, who is looking
for the elixir that made his forebear nearly immortal.

The last romances also bring into sharp focus a startling
characteristic that occasionally forced itself on our attention in prior works. This is Hawthorne's use of vivid
sexual images that make the goal of a supposedly spiritual
quest equivalent to a moment of voyeuristic perception.
Like Swift, though without Swift's conscious satire, Hawthorne reduces intellectual zeal to the unsublimated prurience from which it presumably sprang. The search for a
birthright leads, not to legal clarity, but to birth-fantasies:
Etherege in *Doctor Grimshawe's Secret* feels "a paltry confusion and embarrassment" when he contemplates his
"coming out of the squalid darkness as if he were a thing
that had had a spontaneous [origin] birth out of poverty,
meanness, petty crime . . ." (*Grimshawe*, p. 71). To find an
aristocratic ancestry is to be rescued from physical squalor
—that is, to overcome the disgust produced by graphic
thoughts of how one entered the world. But unconscious
preoccupation ensures that the genital, not the coat-of-
arms, will lie at the end of the search. And thus in *The
Ancestral Footstep*, after the young hero has once again
accidentally murdered his rival claimant and is encouraged by the sisterly lady to "enter the old house, the
hereditary house, where—now, at least—you alone have a
right to tread" (XI, 456), the seemingly imminent consummation of knowledge and power dissolves in an absurd
and highly symbolic disappointment. Middleton and Alice
pass through chamber after chamber, arriving finally at a
further chamber—a miniature palace-cabinet which, when

opened with Middleton's key, reveals still another "secret and precious chamber" (XI, 461), within which—incredibly —is yet another "receptacle," quite empty:

> It brought Middleton up with such a sudden revulsion that he grew dizzy, and the room swam round him and the cabinet dazzled before his eyes. It had been magnified to a palace; it had dwindled down to Lilliputian size; and yet, up till now, it had seemed to contain in its diminutiveness all the riches which he had attributed to its magnitude. This last moment had utterly subverted it; the whole great structure seemed to vanish. (XI, 462)

Naturally, however, in a dreamland where slain enemies reappear unslain on the next page, where fiancées are abruptly transmuted into sisters, and where purpose and inadvertence are constantly replacing each other, even this letdown must be revoked. Not many pages later the once-enlightened Middleton is again brooding about the "dark and sinister" events of his family history, which have been "thrown into the deep pit, and buried under the accumulated débris, the fallen leaves, . . . [so] that it seemed not worth while to dig it up; for perhaps the deadly influences, which it had taken so much time to hide, might still be lurking there, and become potent if he now uncovered them" (XI, 475). As in "The Man of Adamant," the buried pit takes its power to terrify from the genital obsession of the mind that contemplates it.

It seems to me, then, that in the last romances Hawthorne was not merely "tired" or "overworked" or—a favorite theory in our time—bewildered by a mysterious decline in his religious faith. These accounts posit a simple absence of direction, whereas Hawthorne's images show him to be in the grip of a titanic obsession which is all too purposeful. Rather than being without energy he is fully engaged at every moment in a death-struggle against the conscious emergence of patricidal and incestuous thoughts. The obscurity and hesitancy and garbled causality of his literal plots register the inhibiting effect of this struggle, while its energies are locked in rash emotions and lurid images.

These symptoms—for that is what they are—can be followed in even greater detail than Lamont's essay suggests. While recognizing all the familiar appurtenances of Oedipal conflict in the late works, Lamont finally says that Hawthorne and his heroes are questing for "a source of strength and success linked with the distant past, whether seen as a patrimony or an elixir." [13] This, I would say, is a handsome concession to a more "literary" approach to the romances, but it is more literary than the evidence warrants. We must realize that Hawthorne's imagination is not looking for sexual metaphors to convey a quest for generalized "strength," but rather is steadily reliving the primary Oedipal strife itself.

Let us test this assertion by investigating the meaning of the key term, "elixir," in *Septimius Felton,* the most complete of the four plots. The question is whether elixir stands for "power and grandeur" [14] in general or for a more specific referent. The man who would like to make use of it is in a thoroughly familiar predicament; though he has a fiancée, he conceives it his "doom to be only a spectator of life" (XI, 250), and he wants to become immortal as a recompense for "sharing none of [life's] pleasures and happiness" (XI, 250f.). Needless to say, he is a prospective artist (see XI, 412)—we might say that he is *the* Hawthornian artist. For the pattern of his career is the anticipated one of stepping gradually aside from heterosexual love, leaving his fiancée to a "wholesome young man" (XI, 273) who better deserves her, and devoting himself increasingly to a monomaniac project of self-perpetuation that is a direct substitute for love. Thus the logic of compensation might suggest a masturbatory significance

13. Lamont, p. 19.
14. *Ibid.,* p. 19.

for the elixir; detached, vicarious, imaginative, and "immortal" experience is preferable to direct love because it circumvents the object of fear and provides an outlet for the fantasies whose strength and grotesqueness made the object fearful.

Why should Septimius Felton be victimized by these hypothetical fantasies? The answer is contained in the fundamental terms of the plot. Like the other late heroes, Septimius kills "the only person who could have contested his rights" (XI, 396)—a soldier who not only shares in the customary tangle of ancestry but also has taken a free and flirtatious manner with Septimius's fiancée. At a certain moment in the plot this fiancée is significantly demoted to be Septimius's half-sister, but she is replaced by another girl who tells him, "We have an intimate relation to one another" (XI, 386). This ambiguous taunt is eventually revealed to mean that the second girl was engaged to the slain soldier, so that once again Septimius has inadvertently cleared away his sexual rival; but the sentence also hints at a continuation of the pervasive theme of blood kinship. All this is hard to follow, but its import is clear: for Septimius the love of woman is inevitably a version of incest. What he escapes by leaving one girl to his neighbor and by spurning the other is not simply sex, but the combined disgust and appeal of incest.

At this point I want to introduce an independent discussion of the meaning of elixirs. Ernest Jones argues that an obsession with death always signifies an unconscious dread of impotence, and that the corresponding yen for an elixir of immortality is in effect a desire to overcome this dread.[15] The dread, furthermore, "always comes from the fear of being castrated as a punishment for . . . incestuous wishes." [16] Finding youth equated with virility, Jones claims that the magical fluid has the exact unconscious

15. *Essays in Applied Psycho-Analysis,* II, 141f.
16. *Ibid.,* p. 142.

meaning of semen. Is this dogmatic series of equivalences applicable to *Septimius Felton,* where a desire to obtain immortality through a magic brew is held by a man who has resolved not to accept the pseudo-incestuous love that he has twice earned through killing a rival and possible relation? Hawthorne's imagery pertaining to *elixir* should provide an answer.

Hawthorne tells us that the manuscript giving the recipe for the elixir is better left untranscribed, since it promulgates the dreadful error of "yielding the spiritual to a keen sagacity of lower things," and since it seems to prove "that earthly life was good, and all that the development of our nature demanded" (XI, 339). Elixir, then, promotes an unabashed, "lower" bodily vigor that seems opposed to the restraints of religion. This vigor has a precise and peculiar connection with women. The regimen of life accompanying the recipe demands that he who would be immortal "shun woman, for she is apt to be a disturbing influence" (XI, 340). On the other hand, he is urged to "drink . . . the breath of buxom maids, if [he may] without undue disturbance of the flesh" (XI, 341). I submit that this apparent contradiction makes sense if, and only if, the elixir is a remedy against impotence. Women contain a sexual power that must be extracted and stored up by men, yet direct contact with women saps that power again.

The chief ingredient in Septimius's elixir is a flower that is said to grow only on the grave of a "pure young boy or girl" (XI, 329), and in the legends surrounding the elixir it is clear that the boy or girl ought to be a close relation. One old man is said to have murdered his daughter in order to produce the flower—"the most gorgeous and beautiful, surely, that ever grew; so rich it looked, *so full of potent juice*" (XI, 333; my italics). In Septimius's case the flower grows from the grave of the kin-and-rival he has murdered, whose sexual aura is apparent from his first entrance into the story. The elixir can be manufactured from this and other ingredients if one follows the recipe and regimen faithfully, and these latter have emanated, in Hawthorne's metaphor, "from a mind very full of books, and grinding and pressing down the great accumulation of grapes that it had gathered from so many vineyards, and *squeezing out rich viscid juices,—potent wine,*—with which the reader might get drunk" (XI, 279; my italics). If we are to put any trust in imagery, *Septimius Felton* would seem to provide striking corroboration of the symbolic values proposed by Jones.[17]

The irrational logic surrounding elixir in this romance is extremely complex. The elixir-flower makes its "resurrection" (XI, 345) after the murder of an Oedipal rival, and thus may be said to spring from thoughts of incest.[18] Yet the elixir itself is a remedy against the impotence that follows from those same thoughts—which is not to say that it restores normal love. Everything in Hawthorne's emphasis suggests that one's precious bodily fluids must be hoarded from their chief enemy, womankind. Note, for

17. Note, too, the association of elixir with unnatural sexual ambition elsewhere in Hawthorne's fiction. When an elixir of immortality is taken in "Dr. Heidegger's Experiment" it produces the grotesque spectacle of "three old, gray, withered grandsires, ridiculously contending for the skinny ugliness of a shrivelled grandam" (I, 269); and Aylmer, whose perverse revulsion from his wife has been discussed, resembles Rappaccini in hoarding "the most precious poison that ever was concocted in this world" (II, 59). His description of its properties scarcely gibes with his calling it "the elixir of immortality" (II, 59), but it does possess a "virtuous potency" (II, 59) as well as a harmful one. It is an elixir, significantly, that finally erases Georgiana's "birthmark of mortality" (II, 66) by killing her.

18. This is metaphorically confirmed in Septimius's early withdrawal from his unhealthy feelings toward the first-contested girl, "in relation to whom, there was perhaps a plant that had its root in the grave, that would entwine itself around his whole life, overshadowing it with dark, rich foliage and fruit that he alone could feast upon" (XI, 273).

example, the extraordinary image of squeezing out viscid juice; [19] the detached and imaginative life that is promised to the imbiber of the fluid; the bookish nature of both Septimius and the author of the recipe; the injunction against direct contact with women; and most obviously, Septimius's own withdrawal from offers of love into an ever more absorbed devotion to his little specialty. Fear of woman has reached such an intensity in Hawthorne's fiction that Septimius's element of savage ancestry—"the wild, natural blood of the Indian, the instinctive, the animal nature" (XI, 424)—is what warns him *against* dealing with the second girl, "whispering me of harm, as if I sat near some mischief" (XI, 424). Nature itself has been made neurasthenic. If "elixir" appears at first to serve Oedipal ambitions, for that very reason it must be shifted to an auto-erotic function, since those ambitions lead to intolerable fears of punishment. [20]

Not many readers will have agreed with our analysis of "elixir" in every detail, and certainly we have incurred the risk of being amateurish in a problematic field. But this example, along with the total atmosphere of the late romances, may pose for us once again the fundamental choice of methodology that any critic of Hawthorne ought to face. In the late works Hawthorne has conspicuously failed to

19. And note how that passage illuminates the parallel case of Miles Coverdale, another spectator who would rather press out his swelling grapes than declare his love. We may also recall at this point the anxiety of Hawthorne's autobiographical Oberon, who pictures himself in middle age "still telling love-tales, loftily ambitious of a maiden's tears, and squeezing out, as it were, with his brawny strength, the essence of roses" (XII, 28).

20. This logic may account for the case of the old man who murdered his beautiful daughter for the magic flower that would grow from her grave. In this instance the shortest path to incest-prevention has been taken, whereas Septimius first kills his rival and only later realizes that he must choose absolutely between "immortality" and possession of the girl.

add the stucco of ideas and moralizations to his structure
of obsession. No "meaning" in a rational sense attaches to
these fragments, yet they follow the psychoanalytical pattern of symptom-formation with astonishing exactitude;
they offer an unceasing flow of repressed fantasy which is
counteracted by unceasing denial and distortion. There
can really be little honest dispute over the level on which
Hawthorne's mind is creating characters and incidents
here. But exactly the same Oedipal situations, the same
images, the same fears, the same dynamics of repression
and expression are discernible in Hawthorne's most polished and powerful work. Must we not conclude that he
is an obsessed writer throughout his career, and that the
differences from one phase to another are finally differences in self-control rather than in energy or ideas?

XIV

Hawthorne, Freud, and Literary Value

"It has to do with drawing a reality out of the unconscious in such a way as to make it enter into the realm of the intellect, while trying to preserve its life, not to garble it, to subject it to the least possible shrinkage . . ."
—MARCEL PROUST on the writing of an introspective novel.

The psychological emphasis of this book, and the untraditional account of Hawthorne's career that results from such an emphasis, must pose some questions about our aesthetic criteria. If some of our early chapters create an impression that Hawthorne is good insofar as he is Freudian, some later ones may support the opposite fallacy: Hawthorne is obsessed and therefore artistically handicapped. I would be as sorry to leave the reader with one of these crude formulas as the other. Plainly, I am convinced that some correlation exists between Hawthorne's psychological themes and the enduring appeal of his works; the question is whether that correlation is simple and direct. In this final chapter I propose to review the evidence that justifies our calling Hawthorne Freudian; to measure, as best I can, the part played by psychological insight in the effect of his plots; and finally to define the limitations of the Freudian aesthetic on which so much of Hawthorne's claim to greatness must rest.

I hope, after all that has gone before, that I need not insist at length on the propriety of using psychoanalytic terms to describe authors and works that antedate Freud. Revolutionary as his influence has been, Freud did not alter human nature; either we are entitled to use Freudianism retroactively or we must say that it is false. The point seems obvious enough, yet in the academic world—and conspicuously in Hawthorne studies—there persists a quixotic attempt to say that an author's psychological portraiture can be nothing other than a conscious illustration of the theories current in his day. Thus in Hawthorne's instance we have not only the venerable claim that his deliberate antitheses of head and heart adequately account for his characters' behavior, but a more recent and bolder effort to bind him to the "mental philosophy" of his college professor, Thomas Upham. Hawthorne, it seems, loyally followed Upham's schematization of the mind into intellect, sensibilities, and will, and used his fictional characters as personifications of one or another of these functions.[1]

Such a proposal seems scarcely worth pausing over. Though Upham was the best-known psychological theorist of his day,[2] Hawthorne never mentions his teachings and is not known to have read his books. The mixed motives, hidden scruples, and maniacal projects of Hawthorne's

1. For the head-heart dualism see Austin Warren, *Nathaniel Hawthorne: Representative Selections,* pp. xlv-xlvi; F. O. Matthiessen, *American Renaissance,* pp. 337-51; and Donald A. Ringe, "Hawthorne's Psychology of the Head and Heart," *PMLA,* LXV (March 1950), 120-32. The Uphamite position is defended by Leon Howard, "Hawthorne's Fiction," *Nineteenth-Century Fiction,* VII (March 1953), 237-50; Marvin Laser, " 'Head,' 'Heart,' and 'Will' in Hawthorne's Psychology," *Nineteenth-Century Fiction,* X (September 1955), 130-40; and John T. McKiernan, "The Psychology of Nathaniel Hawthorne," *Dissertation Abstracts,* XVII (1957), 3019.

2. See Jay Wharton Fay, *American Psychology Before William James* (New Brunswick, 1939), passim. Upham's chief works were *Elements of Intellectual Philosophy* (1827); *A Philosophical and Practical Treatise on the Will* (1834); *Outlines of Imperfect and Disordered Mental Action* (1840); and most influentially, *Elements of Mental Philosophy* (1831; 2-volume edition, 1840 *et seq.*).

heroes would have appalled Upham, whose system was
frankly designed as a justification for Christian moral im-
peratives. The verdict of consciousness, says Upham, "is
in the highest degree authoritative and decisive," and "No
man has it in his power to refuse obedience to the deci-
sions of reasoning . . ." [3] He ridicules the very possibility—
on which most of Hawthorne's plots are based—that a
man's mind might be subject to hidden forces; he even
argues tautologically that muscular habits must be perfectly
voluntary, for otherwise men would be "machines, mere au-
tomatons." [4] As for sexuality, without which a description
of motives among Hawthorne's characters is rather incomplete, Upham refuses to discuss it. Sex has no place in his
exhaustive list of human desires, instincts, appetites, and
propensities.[5] To confine Hawthorne's terrible insights
within Upham's tediously subdivided and inert categories
is too high a price to pay for the illusion of fidelity to the
history of ideas.

We are left, then, with Hawthorne the self-examining
neurotic—a role highly comparable to that of Freud himself at the start of his career. Given the mechanistic science
of his time, Freud's discovery of psychoanalytic principles
appears almost as "anachronistic" as Hawthorne's; in both
cases we are dealing not with the orderly transmission and
refinement of knowledge but with a struggle to univer-
salize the results of introspection. Not surprisingly, it is
impossible to draw a clear line between Hawthorne's
rational statements anticipating Freud and his inadvertent

3. *Elements of Mental Philosophy* (New York, 2 vols., 1840), I,
42, 47.

4. *Ibid.,* I, 158.

5. Only once in Upham's voluminous works is sex mentioned—it
is reluctantly included in a quotation from Dugald Stewart—and
even there Upham hastens to assure us that "on this subject, as this
Treatise is designed for general reading, we do not propose to
dwell." (*Outlines of Imperfect and Disordered Mental Action* [New
York, 1840], p. 287.)

illustration of Freudian principles in his losing war against obsession. If we may suppose that his "psychoanalytic" generalizations represent efforts at self-understanding, we may appreciate why the dwindling frequency of such generalizations is paralleled by a heightening of the signs of obsession. In every phase, whether through a power of reasoning or through unwitting self-revelation, Hawthorne provides an intricate chart of the ways of the unconscious. And this fact must inevitably have some bearing on our estimation of his achievement.

Thus, to begin with concrete examples, Hawthorne appears less arbitrary, more "true to life," in some of his fantastic plots if we happen to be familiar with modern case-histories. Reuben Bourne, who murders his son out of a sense of his own prior guilt, may outrage our sense of justice but he cannot really surprise us; "criminals from a sense of guilt" [6] are a well-defined and common type. Reuben's guilt for a crime he never committed, his ability to find a path he had consciously forgotten, even his killing of Cyrus on the exact anniversary of his deserting Roger Malvin, all are the stuff of commonplace realism in case-histories.[7] Again, Arthur Dimmesdale's impulse to blaspheme after leaving the forest—an impulse which strikes some readers as out of character and others as displaying a state of moral error—is in fact brilliantly appropriate to Dimmesdale's rigidly pious nature once repression has been suddenly relaxed. Dimmesdale's whole psychology of self-punishment and renewed indulgence in forbidden thoughts—or, to be exact, of self-punishment which *makes possible* continued indulgence—is offensive to moral logic but perfectly observes the logic of psychoanalysis.[8] And

6. Freud, *Collected Papers*, IV, 342.

7. On the question of anniversaries see Karl Menninger, *Man Against Himself* (New York, 1938), p. 59n.

8. *Ibid.*, p. 238: "The punishment actually permits the continuance of guilty indulgences and in this way becomes in itself a kind of indulgence."

we can say that Hawthorne's ascetics generally are viewed
in a Freudian light. That is, Hawthorne never rests content with the avowed spiritual motive for asceticism, but
rather provides us with clues to obsessive flight from sexuality. In donning a veil which effectively shields him from
an impending marriage, the Reverend Hooper illustrates
a classic pattern of phobia,[9] and in retreating to a cave
which turns out to be a refuge from the same threat,
Richard Digby in "The Man of Adamant" likewise reveals
a sub-religious motive that psychoanalysis assumes to un-
derlie gestures of aggressive saintliness.[10] In no case does
Hawthorne absolutely compel us to accept the lower and
less conscious motive, and it is doubtful whether he himself would have explained his plots as we do. What matters,
however, is that his insistent distinction between surface
appearances and buried reality encourages us to recon-
struct the causes of sublimation and monomania, and that
these causes are nearly always apparent when we look for
them.

This, I think, is Hawthorne's distinction as a psychologist—not simply that his characters' seemingly freakish
behavior can be matched by real-life examples, but that
the total fabric of his plots manages to display fundamental
yet elusive processes of the mind. Most importantly, those
plots depict with incredible fidelity the results of unresolved Oedipal conflict. After establishing, as I trust we
have established, that this conflict is re-enacted everywhere
in Hawthorne's fiction, we can appreciate the intense
malice behind his treatment of literal and symbolic fathers
—a malice which often meets with no justification on moral
grounds. We can likewise appreciate why his handling of
women invariably leads either to sexless idealization or to
innuendoes of uncleanness, and we can grasp the adolescent

9. See, for example, the parallel case of a woman who wore a
veil and goggles in order to make herself sexually forbidding to her
husband. Karl Abraham, *Selected Papers* (London, 1954), p. 205.

10. See Menninger, *Man Against Himself*, pp. 111-43.

dilemma of a Giovanni Guasconti or a Young Goodman Brown. All these considerations have the effect of rescuing Hawthorne's works from the charge of resting on frivolous fantasy; they do rest on fantasy, but on the shared fantasy of mankind, and this makes for a more penetrating fiction than would any illusionistic slice of life.

What shall we say, asks Hawthorne with mock concern, when a man like Arthur Dimmesdale finds divine revelations addressed to himself alone? "In such a case, it could only be the symptom of a highly disordered mental state, when a man, rendered morbidly self-contemplative by long, intense, and secret pain, had extended his egotism over the whole expanse of nature, until the firmament itself should appear no more than a fitting page for his soul's history and fate" (*C*, I, 155). Morbid or not, this is the operative principle of some of Hawthorne's greatest plots. The ambiguity between literal outward fact and an "extension of egotism over the whole expanse of nature" not only applies to such individual protagonists as Dimmesdale, Brown, Hooper, and Brand; it is practised by Hawthorne himself when he makes psychological metaphors out of history and ancestry, God and Satan. What appears at first to be religious meaning in such works as "The Gentle Boy" and "Rappaccini's Daughter," and what appears at first as an objective theory of history in the Puritan and Revolutionary tales and in *The House of the Seven Gables,* can be shown to be Oedipal dramatization on a magnified scale. And this psychological aptness, in my judgment, is precisely what saves Hawthorne from antiquarian pedantry and affable pietism. "The fiend in his own shape," as we learn in "Young Goodman Brown," "is less hideous than when he rages in the breast of man" (II, 100). Less hideous, and less compelling for the reader.

Hawthorne's art acquires much of its power from the displacement of logic and fact by autonomous fantasy. His plots typically record some clash between fantasy and

fact, and their customary outcome is a rash deed resulting
from a confusion of the two. Thus Aylmer, Giovanni,
Digby, and Brown become cruel after mistaking the impurity of their thoughts about womankind for impurity in
the women who love them, and thus Reuben Bourne
exacts punishment for a murder which took place only in
his imagination. In certain rare cases, such as "The Prophetic Pictures" and *The Blithedale Romance,* Hawthorne
even toys with the possibility that his heroes may acquire
a measure of fantasy-power over other lives.

If Hawthorne's compulsive egotists are determined to
test the omnipotence of wishes, the usual pattern of his
plots is to block, to distort, and finally to allow perverse
and partial expression to those wishes. The sick "luxuriance" of imagery surrounding the unspoken thoughts is
a sign of their isolation from consciousness.[11] The "lurid
intermixture" of emotions that colors Hawthorne's most
intense fiction comes not from a blending of wish and
reality but from a regressive withdrawal of feeling from
normal objects, a surrender to fantasies of sexual accusation and terror. Hence the curious development of a

11. Freud himself describes this phenomenon in Hawthornian
language. Instinct-presentation, he says, "develops in a more unchecked and luxuriant fashion if it is withdrawn by repression from
conscious influence. It ramifies like a fungus, so to speak, in the
dark and takes on extreme forms of expression..." (*Collected
Papers,* IV, 87). A comparable image of Karl Menninger's, character-
izing the effects of a smothering narcissism, is even more strikingly
Hawthornian: "It is as if the personality were like a growing tree...
But were such a tree to be so injured near the base that the sap
flowed out in large quantities to promote the healing and the protection of this stem injury, an insufficient supply would be left for the
development of the foliage of the branches. These, then, would
remain bare, stark, aggressive—and dying, while the sap fed and
overfed the basal wound." (*Man Against Himself,* p. 436.) See pages
93f. above for a closely related image with an identical psychological
meaning.

Goodman Brown, who flees from his nuptial bed to a satanic rendezvous with Gothic sexuality; and hence the sadism of the "investigators" Brand and Aylmer. Such characters can perform loathsomely aggressive acts without ever holding themselves to moral account, for the acts are aimed against fantasy-enemies and are made possible by emancipation from the surface world to which moral standards might apply. The "morals" frequently tacked onto such actions either by Hawthorne or by his critics thus have an air of irrelevance; indeed, one might almost say that the emotional sense emanating from a deed like Aylmer's is one of satanic triumph, of momentary victory over inhibition. The truth is out at last, and it is murderous.

Yet Hawthorne *can* be said, at least occasionally, to have a moral ideal—or rather an ideal of normality. It is simply the psychoanalytic ideal of being free from feelings of guilt. In *The House of the Seven Gables,* for example, the general task is not to exact justice or to act charitably, but to lift the oppressive weight of the past as it is applied by the figure of Judge Pyncheon.[12] The Judge's removal produces not moral insight but a vengeful euphoria—one which itself must be checked by reactionary behavior. Mental peace, in other words, consists in weakening or pacifying the superego whose symbolic agent may be a real father but is more likely to be a surrogate figure like Jaffrey, a watchful Deity, a line of stern ancestors, or even the collective past itself. It was Freud who defined neurosis as "abnormal attachment to the past" and who urged what Philip Rieff calls an "ideal contemporaneity" as the measure of health,[13] but it was Hawthorne who complained

12. One of Abraham's patients, incidentally, had an obsessive fear of bright sunlight (Jaffrey Pyncheon's chief symbolic attribute) and "complained about his failure in life, and said that his father literally weighed him down" (Abraham, *Selected Papers,* pp. 174f.).

13. See *Freud: The Mind of the Moralist* (New York, 1959), pp. 44, 38.

that Aylmer had "failed to look beyond the shadowy scope of time, and, living once for all in eternity, to find the perfect future in the present" (II, 69). Allowing for a difference in rhetoric, I see no difference in meaning between the two goals. And in the same light we may understand the contradiction in Hawthorne's treatment of "earthly" and "spiritual" values, of the ideal and the material. He cannot unambiguously recommend either extreme because he senses that the separation of the two is itself a sign of neurosis; his healthiest characters are invariably those to whom antitheses of body and soul never occur at all. Here again we might remind ourselves of Freud's statement that the very act of calling into question the meaning of life is a sign of sickness. The reader may find this an intellectually cramping idea, but he can hardly deny that Hawthorne's monomaniac heroes illustrate it.

Where Hawthorne truly and significantly differs from Freud is in the therapeutic application of the non-repressive ideal. The Freudian process of normal development might be called a series of adaptations to inevitable traumas. In the case of Robin Molineux one could find a similar idea; Robin appears ready for adulthood only when he has resolved, or seen symbolically resolved, his mixed feelings of awe and contempt of parental authority. More usually, however, the Hawthornian hero is doomed to abnormality from the moment he entertains any rebellious thoughts. He is rarely "cured" after obsession has taken hold of him, and when a cure is offered it is an obvious nostrum, the aspirin of submission to a Phoebe or a Hilda. Hawthorne grasps the causes of neurosis but cannot face its remedy; his normality is merely the negative ideal of escape. This is only to say, after all, that Hawthorne sees neurosis from the perspective of a neurotic, not a physician. In a negative way, by remaining obsessed despite all efforts to dismiss obsession from view, he illustrates Freud's hard edict: "whoever is to be really free and happy in love must have overcome his deference for women and come to terms with the idea of incest with mother or sister." [14] Hawthorne is finally a prisoner of the repression whose devastating effects he so faithfully portrays.

At the end of his life this imprisonment is clearly artistic as well as emotional; no one has yet put forward the thesis that the unfinished romances are Hawthorne's major phase. Yet at what point can we say that Hawthorne went wrong as an artist? The incest obsession which riddles the last works was present from the beginning. If, however, we turn to the fiction that is generally agreed to be his best, we invariably find a dramatic tension that is lacking not only in his slight sketches and works of popular sentiment, but also in the tales and romances where obsession has become *too* intense. Tales like "Young Goodman Brown" and "My Kinsman, Major Molineux" sustain a highly energized struggle between inadmissible fantasies and the punishment and denial of those fantasies; they reach a point of catharsis after giving simultaneous and balanced voice to outrage and confession. In the serious works that are generally thought to fail, inhibition dominates the surface effect.

Thus it seems possible to correlate Hawthorne's decline, not with the presence or absence of his obsessive theme, but with the degree of deviousness he finds necessary to avoid bringing that theme into consciousness. In *The Scarlet Letter* obsession is an overt and steady subject; in *The House of the Seven Gables* it begins to be abstracted into a whimsical theory of history and a toying with magical causality; in *The Blithedale Romance* it remains cryptically hidden in the narrator's attitude toward the story he is telling; and in *The Marble Faun* Hawthorne's inconsistent characters no longer have any conception of why they still feel a vague sense of trouble. By this point, if we have not given up the pursuit of his intention, we find ourselves decoding it from images whose meaning almost

14. *Collected Papers*, IV, 211.

certainly remained unknown to Hawthorne himself. For-
feiting our interest in literal characterization, he calls
upon an astonishing but ultimately fatiguing knack for de-
vising innuendoes—and the innuendoes are aimed against
his own fervent, and by now desperate, wish to take a
sunny view of things. Ambiguity and surface hypocrisy
become total as Hawthorne's warring feelings increasingly
elude his once-powerful will to put on view the essential
truth of the heart.

Without pretending to offer a simple psychological yard-
stick of value, perhaps we may suggest that fiction profits
both from contact with unconscious material and from the
participation of consciousness in that contact. Hawthorne
is truly himself only within a certain range of half-percep-
tion in which curiosity and anxiety can strike an equilibrium. And though the components may be antithetical,
the effect produced must be unitary. Here, perhaps, is
where a psychological aesthetic may join hands with an
aesthetic of plausibility. All readers can agree that Hawthorne fails when, for whatever reason, he is forced into
inconsistent characterization, embarrassed apology and
digression, and incomplete plotting. What happens to his
fiction after 1850 is, in the simplest terms, a lapse of illusion. In our view the immediate cause of this lapse is a
dissociation of unconscious conflict from its never sturdy
tie to outward reality. When heightened obsession calls
forth heightened efforts at repression, no room remains
for created characters to exist freely. In the words of the
storyteller Zenobia, "Our own features, and our own
figures and airs, show a little too intrusively through all
the characters we assume" (*C*, III, 107).

In this light I find it significant that Hawthorne's acknowledged masterpiece, *The Scarlet Letter*, not only
treats unconscious compulsion more directly than his other
romances, but also keeps his specific filial obsession better
concealed from view. How many readers have been aware
of the allusions to incest which Leslie Fiedler has made

so prominent in his reading? [15] The same theme is (or ought to be) inescapable in any reading of Hawthorne's subsequent works. Who has noticed, as well, that for both Pearl and Dimmesdale the plot eventually fulfills a need for the benevolent father who remains absent until Dimmesdale's confession—and that Dimmesdale earns his mental peace by eradicating the part of his nature that would be offensive to the parent-rival? [16] To put discussion of *The Scarlet Letter* on this level seems an impertinence; the hell-fired story is perfectly dramatic and coherent in its overt terms, as all Hawthorne's subsequent fiction is not.

And yet I think we are finally obliged to take a broader aesthetic view than one that places *The Scarlet Letter* at the summit of fictional greatness. Brilliant as he is within his province, Hawthorne must be recognized as a peculiarly narrow writer—narrow not only in the underlying sameness of his themes from work to work, but in the more obvious sense of a paucity of represented life. The traditional complaints that his lights and shades are too monotonous, his characters too alike, his dialogues too formal, his manner too uniformly distant, seem to me justified. The danger in our own age, once the extent of Hawthorne's anticipation of psychoanalysis is understood, is not that he will be neglected but that he will be overrated. For we place a high value on the dramatization of psychic strife, even to the extent of feeling impatient with literalism; as Lionel Trilling has said, "in the degree that the world can be thought of as thinly composed, the autonomy of spirit is the more easily imagined." [17] Trilling himself goes so far as to regret the degree to which "for

15. See *Love and Death in the American Novel,* pp. 497-500.

16. "This man," as Chillingworth thinks to himself, "hath inherited a strong animal nature from his father or his mother" (*C,* I, 130). Only when this animal nature is wholly renounced can Dimmesdale make peace with his heavenly Father and himself become a worthy father to Pearl.

17. "Our Hawthorne," *Hawthorne Centenary Essays,* p. 448.

Hawthorne the [outer] world is always and ineluctably
there ...," [18] undermining and ridiculing the truth of
fantasy. Yet surely this is not Hawthorne's true limitation.
The problem is not that literal reality interrupts Hawthorne's psychological drama, but that it has been too
wholly assimilated to that drama. "Reality" for Hawthorne
merely plays the role of censor in an unconscious dialogue
between rebellion and repentance; the thread of a single
obsession is too easily traced through all his efforts at
rendering things as they are.

This latter point may remind us how risky it is to use
our descriptive terms evaluatively. Some of Hawthorne's
least satisfying works—"Alice Doane's Appeal" and the unfinished romances—lend themselves most readily to the
archaeology of motives we have been practicing. Where
Hawthorne's "case" is most apparent his fictional world
seems least whole, his moral vision most captive to emotions of aggression and fear that lack public content. Without some degree of self-revelation, I suppose, art loses its
urgency; but when self-revelation usurps every other aspect
of meaning the work dwindles to a recital of symptoms.
And Hawthorne at his best remains incapable of ventur-
ing much beyond the gates of his neurosis. In a unique
burst of fervor he can extend ambiguous sympathy to a
Hester Prynne, yet Hester's very existence as a figure of
sexual reproach seems in retrospect to have been too inevitable. All Hawthorne's serious fiction amounts to versions
of the same unconscious challenge; not one of his characters stands apart from the endless and finally suffocating
debate about the gratification of forbidden wishes.

Ultimately, however, we cannot wish away Hawthorne's
narrowness without also losing his peculiar value. Good
Romantic that he was, he located reality squarely in the
buried life of the mind. Before the sadly gifted eye of the
seer, we recall, the whole structure of an outward char-

18. *Ibid.,* p. 449.

acter like Jaffrey Pyncheon's "melts into thin air, leaving only the hidden nook, the bolted closet, . . . or the deadly hole under the pavement, and the decaying corpse within" (III, 274). Without such radical simplifications Hawthorne would not be Hawthorne. Like Sade, Baudelaire, and Swinburne; like Melville and Poe; and like the "Romantic conservative" [19] Freud, Hawthorne rested his whole achievement on the premise that the only important truth is that which has been repressed. We may doubt the premise and yet recognize that the achievement is something formidable.

Our Hawthorne, of course, ends by seeming more pathetic than the Christ-like figure depicted in recent monographs. At his best, it appears, he clung to everyday banalities as to a life raft, and at his nadir he surrendered to a neurotic despair whose origins he did not quite dare to understand. The exemplary nature of his outward life —his conspicuous dutifulness as a father, a public official, a friend—does not erase this sense of melancholy isolation, any more than his professed love of Dutch painting, of Trollope, of factual journalism can erase the fact that his own art was based on fantasy. Only an indifference to mental suffering can make us grateful for the emotional starvation that perversely nourished Hawthorne's art; we must admire the art and separately regret the life. And yet it is a fact that the two are inextricable. As Freud himself remarked in a moment of self-dramatization—and here Freud becomes one with Ethan Brand, with Aylmer, and with the Hawthorne we have met in this study: "No one who, like me, conjures up the most evil of those half-tamed demons that inhabit the human breast, can expect to come through the struggle unscathed." [20] Let that be our epitaph for a writer whose anguished brooding has given us an urgent, a subtle, and an emotionally profound fiction.

19. Rieff, *Freud: The Mind of the Moralist,* p. 217.
20. *Collected Papers,* III, 131f.

Index

273